48625

CANADIAN WONDER TALES

CANADIAN WONDER TALES

being the two collections

Canadian Wonder Tales & Canadian Fairy Tales

collected from oral sources by

CYRUS MACMILLAN

Illustrated by

ELIZABETH CLEAVER

THE BODLEY HEAD
LONDON SYDNEY
TORONTO

PUBLISHER'S NOTE

The stories in this volume originally appeared in two books: *Canadian Wonder Tales*, illustrated by George Sheringham and published by John Lane The Bodley Head, London, John Lane Company, New York and S. B. Gundy, Toronto in 1918; and *Canadian Fairy Tales*, illustrated by Marcia Lane Foster and published by John Lane The Bodley Head, London in 1922. Some degree of mystery surrounds their compilation. It is not known, for instance, from which particular areas of Canada Professor Macmillan gathered his stories, although some of the legends are peculiar to certain tribes or groups of Indians. A few stories are clearly European imports, remembered and retold by French-Canadian settlers; while others are basically Indian but show signs of assimilation, with an admixture of European fairy tale *motifs*, witch, wand, ogre and giant. Again, it is not clear how much of this assimilation is attributable to Professor Macmillan's adapting his material for publication, or whether it was because the storytellers were whites rather than Indians. It does seem evident, however, as Sheila Egoff remarks in *The Republic of Childhood* (Oxford University Press, Toronto, 1967) that he 'saw the Indian legends as an extension of the European folk- and fairy-tale tradition and, although he had actually heard the tales . . . and had studied the originals, he clothed them in the lighter form of fairy tale.'

Whatever the details of their provenance, these collections were long one of the best sources of Canadian tradition in an easily accessible form: 'Those who knew these books as children still feel a nostalgic reverence for them,' says Sheila Egoff. But they have long been unavailable in a complete edition and are now reissued in their entirety for the first time.

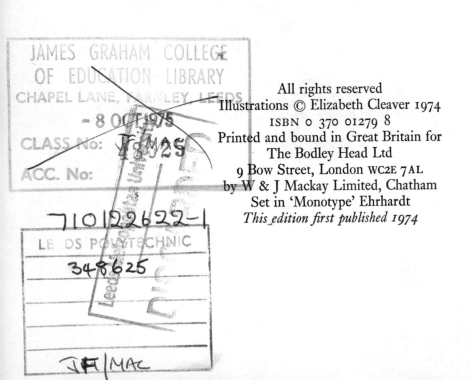
Illustrations © Elizabeth Cleaver 1974
ISBN 0 370 01279 8
Printed and bound in Great Britain for
The Bodley Head Ltd
9 Bow Street, London WC2E 7AL
by W & J Mackay Limited, Chatham
Set in 'Monotype' Ehrhardt
This edition first published 1974

Contents

CANADIAN WONDER TALES

Foreword by WILLIAM PETERSON, ix
Preface by CYRUS MACMILLAN, xi

1. The Baker's Magic Wand, 1
2. Star-Boy and the Sun Dance, 7
3. Jack and His Magic Aids, 12
4. The Bad Indian's Ashes, 17
5. The Mermaid of the Magdalenes, 20
6. The Boy and the Dancing Fairy, 24
7. The Mouse and the Sun, 30
8. Glooskap's Country, 34
9. How Rabbit Lost His Tail, 40
10. The Partridge and His Drum, 44
11. How Summer Came to Canada, 50
12. How Turtle Came, 55
13. The First Mosquito, 59
14. The Moon and His Frog-Wife, 64
15. Glooskap and the Fairy, 67
16. The Passing of Glooskap, 69
17. The Indian Cinderella, 76
18. The Boy and His Three Helpers, 79
19. The Duck with Red Feet, 82
20. The Northern Lights, 85
21. The Boy and the Robbers' Magical Booty, 91
22. The Coming of the Corn, 97
23. The Dance of Death, 100
24. The First Pig and Porcupine, 103
25. The Shrove Tuesday Visitor, 108
26. The Boy of Great Strength and the Giants, 112
27. The Strange Tale of Caribou and Moose, 115
28. Jack and His Wonderful Hen, 119
29. The Sad Tale of Woodpecker and Bluejay, 123
30. The Stupid Boy and the Wand, 126
31. The Blackfoot and the Bear, 130
32. The Boys and the Giant, 134

CANADIAN FAIRY TALES

Introduction by JOHN GRIER HIBBEN, 139
Preface by CYRUS MACMILLAN, 140

33. How Glooskap Made the Birds, 141
34. Rabbit and the Grain Buyers, 147
35. Saint Nicholas and the Children, 153
36. The Fall of the Spider Man, 160
37. The Boy who was Called Thick-head, 166
38. Rabbit and the Indian Chief, 171 ———
39. Great Heart and the Three Tests, 178
40. The Boy of the Red Twilight Sky, 184
41. How Raven Brought Fire to the Indians, 188
42. The Girl who Always Cried, 194
43. Ermine and the Hunter, 199
44. How Rabbit Deceived Fox, 203
45. The Boy and the Dragon, 209
46. Owl with the Great Head and Eyes, 214
47. The Tobacco Fairy from the Blue Hills, 220
48. Rainbow and the Autumn Leaves, 224
49. Rabbit and the Moon-Man, 229
50. The Children with One Eye, 233
51. The Giant with the Grey Feathers, 237
52. The Cruel Stepmother, 242
53. The Boy who was Saved by Thoughts, 246
54. The Song-Bird and the Healing Waters, 250
55. The Boy who Overcame the Giants, 253
56. The Youth and the Dog-Dance, 258
57. Sparrow's Search for the Rain, 263
58. The Boy in the Land of Shadows, 268

Index of Stories, 275

CANADIAN WONDER TALES

To my mother
who first taught me to see the fairy world
and to hear the horns of elf-land blowing

Foreword

CANADIAN WONDER TALES

THIS is the book of a soldier-student. Captain Macmillan interrupted his teaching work in Montreal to go overseas with one of our McGill Batteries, and from 'Somewhere in France' he has asked me to stand sponsor for his volume.

The author's method resembles that followed by the brothers Grimm a century ago. He has taken down from the lips of living people, pretty much as they were given to him, a series of stories which obviously contain many elements that have been handed down by oral tradition from some far-off past. They are mostly animal stories, with all the usual features of magic and transformation, articulate speech on the part of the animals, and interchange of more or less kindly offices between man and beast.

The result is a collection of fables which—especially as illustrated by an eminent artist*—will prove a very acceptable Christmas book for children, and will give their elders also some food for reflection. Not that there is, so far as I have been able to discover, any moral about some at least of the tales. They are not 'stories with a purpose'. But they suggest to the adult reader the essential identity of many of the methods by which in a more or less remote antiquity the human race expressed itself in various parts of the world.

That has now become a matter of scientific study. The floating material of popular tradition at different times and in different places has been spread out, as it were, on a dissecting-table by our Folk-lore Societies, and the thoughts and beliefs, customs and superstitions therein preserved have been studied from the comparative point of view for the light they throw on the primitive development of the human mind. Those of us who read the Journal of American Folk-lore, or the papers on Indian mythology recently contributed by C. M. Barbeau to the anthropological series issued by the Geological Survey of Canada, have many sources at hand with which Mr Macmillan's folk-tales may

---

* This of course refers to the original illustrations by George Sheringham for the 1918 edition.

be profitably compared. Some of the stories—those, for instance, that refer to Shrove Tuesday on the one hand, and packed sardines on the other—are obviously of no earlier date than 'the days when Canada was owned by the French.' But many of them go back to 'long before the white men came to Canada'. That these are folk-tales of the universal type is evidenced by the primitive traditions which they embody. In all such stories striking resemblances occur, whether they are the records of Algonquins or Zulus, Hottentots or Australian Bushmen. To say nothing of charms and incantations, magic coats and magic wands, ogres and giants, mermen and mermaidens, supernatural creatures and speaking beasts, evil spirits in disguise, there are the standing-dishes of all such folk-tales—the strong man and his adventures, the bride carried off by the youthful hero and pursued by her father, the promise that the bride shall be given to anyone who shall accomplish some difficult task, with death as the penalty of failure. These and such-like features are all examples of primitive methods of self-expression, and represent, in the case before us, the Indian's elemental ideas of the universe around him and his relation to it.

Thus Mr Macmillan's 'Wonder Tales', while serving for the pleasure and delight of children, have their points of contact with what we must take to be the background of prehistoric culture on the continent of America. But the children will read and enjoy them for their own sake, and unhampered by any such applications of the comparative method. They will learn in this book the answers to such conundrums as the following—Why Frog croaks, Why Bear eats fish, Why Bunny has a short tail and long hind-legs and a split upper-lip, Why Partridge makes a drumming noise, Why Mosquitoes sting, Why Aspen leaves tremble, What Woodpecker and Bluejay were before they were changed into birds, Why the Moon usually travels alone in the forest. And, if they find anything unsatisfactory about the answers herein recorded, they will have the opportunity of exercising their imaginations to better purpose than was done by those who gave these answers in the days when the world was young!

WILLIAM PETERSON
OCTOBER, 1917

Preface

CANADIAN WONDER TALES

THE tales in this collection have been gathered in various parts of Canada. They have been selected from a larger collection of folk-tales and folk-songs made by the writer for more academic and scientific purposes. They are not the product of the writer's imagination; they are the common possession of the 'folk'. Many of them are still reverently believed by the Canadian Indians, and all are still told with seriousness around camp fires in forests and on plains, upon the sea and by cottage hearths. The dress in which they now appear may be new, but the skeleton of each story has been left unchanged.

Canada is a country with a romantic past. The atmosphere in which our ancestors lived in the early days of exploration and colonization, if not one of enchantment, was at least one of mystery. The traditions and tales of our country's past are rapidly disappearing in its practical present, and the poetry of its former times is rarely heard above the hum of its modern life. Its 'old unhappy far-off things and battles long ago' are fading memories, for comparatively little has been done to save its old tales from oblivion. That the children of the land may know something of the traditions of the mysterious past in which their forefathers dwelt and laboured is the writer's only excuse for the publication of this volume.

The writer's deepest thanks are here expressed to the nameless Indians and 'habitants', the fishermen and sailors, 'the spinners and the knitters in the sun', from whose lips he heard these stories.

It is perhaps but fair to explain that the proofs were corrected by the writer in the intervals between other duties on Vimy Ridge, France, and that to this fact and the consequent haste any minor errors may in part at least be attributed.

CYRUS MACMILLAN

1. The Baker's Magic Wand

ONCE very long ago in the days when Canada was owned by the French there lived on the banks of a great river a wicked lawyer who was in love with a baker's wife. He tried in various ways to get rid of the baker, but without success. They lived not far from the Seigneur who owned all the land around and was very powerful. Now, in front of the Seigneur's palace there was a great lake of more than twelve thousand acres. One morning the lawyer went to the palace and knocked at the door. When the Seigneur came out, he said to him, 'Sire, there is a man not far from here who boasts that in less than twice twenty-four hours he can change this lake into a beautiful meadow covered with grass that would give hay enough for all your horses and would be to the great advantage of the colony.' Then the Seigneur said, 'Who is this man?' The lawyer answered, 'He is no less than the baker who furnishes your household with bread.' So the Seigneur said, 'I will send for him.'

The lawyer went away, and the Seigneur sent a letter to the baker saying that he wanted to see him. The poor baker thought he was to get his pay for the bread he had provided for the Seigneur and all his servants and soldiers. So he was very glad, and went quickly to the palace and knocked at the door. When the Seigneur came out, he asked what was wanted of him. The Seigneur answered that he had heard of his boast that in less than twice twenty-four hours he could change all the lake into a beautiful meadow covered with grass and clover that would feed all the Seigneur's horses and would be a great advantage to the colony. Now, unless within twice twenty-four hours the lake was changed into a meadow, the baker should be hanged before the door of the palace.

Then the Seigneur turned away and the baker went out discouraged, for he did not know what to do. He walked off into the woods and sat down on a log to weep. After a long time an old woman came along and asked what was the matter. He said he was very miserable; he was going to be hanged in twice twenty-four hours; for the Seigneur had commanded him to change all the lake into a meadow, covered with grass and clover, and he was not able to do it. Now, this old woman was a good fairy in disguise and when the baker had done speaking she told him not to be troubled but to go to sleep. She gave him a wand just like a broken stick, which she told him to wave before he slept; it had great power, she said, and while he slept it would bring to pass whatever he desired. So he waved the wand and went to sleep. When he had slept an hour, he was awakened by the smell of hay, and when he looked about him, he saw that the lake was all gone and that there was only a small river that ran through the middle of a beautiful meadow down to the great river not far away. The good fairy was still by his side. She told him to go to the Seigneur and show him what he had done. He went to the palace, and when he came near, he saw the Seigneur looking out of the window at the meadow, and all the men and horses at work making hay. He knocked at the door, and when the Seigneur came downstairs, he asked him if he was satisfied. The Seigneur said he was not satisfied, because the river had been left running through the middle of the meadow. The baker told the Seigneur that the river had been left to provide water for the animals and to help in making hay, because there was so much hay that all the horses in the land could not draw it and it would have to be brought in boats. Then the Seigneur was satisfied and sent the baker away.

Soon the wicked lawyer came again, and the Seigneur showed him the meadow and the men and women and horses making hay. The lawyer was much surprised to see all this, but he did not say so. Instead, he told the Seigneur that he had no doubt the baker could do a great deal more than that; the baker, he said, had boasted that he could make a 'tiens-bon-la' for the Seigneur that would be worth a great deal more than the meadow and would be a great advantage to the colony. 'What is a "tiens-bon-la"?' asked the Seigneur. 'I do not know,' answered the lawyer; 'but the baker said he could make one.' 'I will send for him,' said the Seigneur. So he sent for the baker, who was just making his bread. When he had put the bread into the oven, he went to the palace and knocked again, and the Seigneur came to the door. The Seigneur said: 'I have heard that you boasted that you can make a "tiens-bon-la" that would be worth more than the meadow and a great advantage to the colony. Now you shall go home and make it, and unless you bring

it to me in twice twenty-four hours, you shall be hanged before the palace gate.' The baker asked, 'What is a "tiens-bon-la"?' The Seigneur said, 'I do not know, but I must have one within twice twenty-four hours.' Then he went into his palace again.

The poor baker went away more sorrowful than before. He had no idea of what a 'tiens-bon-la' was; but yet he knew he should be hanged unless he made one within twice twenty-four hours. He went out into the forest again and sat down on the same log as he had sat on before, and wept as hard as he could. When he had cried himself to sleep, the good old fairy came again and waked him up and asked him what was the matter. He told her that he should certainly be hanged this time, for he had been ordered to make a 'tiens-bon-la' for the Seigneur, and he did not know what it was. Then the fairy said, 'It is only that wicked lawyer who is in love with your wife and wants to get rid of you. You must do what I tell you and the lawyer will be punished, for we shall make a "tiens-bon-la" that will satisfy the Seigneur. Go to your home and tell your wife that you are commanded to make a "tiens-bon-la" for the Seigneur and that you have nothing to make it of. Tell her to put two days' provisions in a bag for you, and when she has them all ready, go to your room and take the latch off the window. Then say good-bye to your wife, and walk about the country until it is dark. As soon as you are gone your wife will send for the lawyer and invite him to supper. Before he comes, and after it is dark, you must come back to your house

3

and get in at the window and hide yourself under the bed. Now, the lawyer will not eat without first washing his hands. When he comes, your wife will send him into the room where you are hiding to wash, and when he takes hold of the wash-basin you must cry out "tiens-bon-la." Take this wand that I will give you and anything you wave it at when you cry "tiens-bon-la" will hold fast to whatever it is touching.' Then she gave him another wand and went her way.

The baker did as the fairy had told him, and his wife was very glad to learn that he was going away; and she packed up a large bag of provisions and sent him off. As soon as he was out of the house she sent a note to the lawyer telling him that her husband was gone away for two days and that she would like to have him come to supper. The baker walked around the country until it was dark, and then came back and hid himself under the bed. His wife told the servant to set the table and prepare a nice supper, and then she went to get ready to receive the lawyer. Soon the lawyer arrived. The servant showed him into a room where he might wash his hands after his day's work before he sat down to his meal. The baker was under the bed in the room. There was some water that was not very clean in the wash-basin, and when the lawyer took hold of the basin to throw the water out, the baker, who was under the bed, waved his wand and cried out 'tiens-bon-la,' and the lawyer's hands stuck to the basin so that he could not let go and the basin stuck to the wash-stand. He called out to the servant to come and help him, but she was busy about the supper and did not hear him. So then he cried out as loud as he could, 'Madame, Madame.' When the baker's wife heard him, she was dreadfully frightened and ran in to see what was the matter. When she found the lawyer stuck to the wash-stand, which was very large and heavy, she took hold of him with both hands to pull him away. Then her husband cried out from under the bed 'tiens-bon-la,' and the wife could not let go the lawyer. Then the baker went out and called in some of his friends, and they ate the supper and drank the wine that had been prepared for the lawyer who was stuck to the wash-stand, and the wife who could not let go the lawyer.

When morning came, the baker took the wand that the fairy had given him and told his wife and the lawyer that if they wanted to get loose they must do as he told them. With his wand he loosened the basin from the wash-stand. Then he made them go out into the street, and he started them towards the Seigneur's palace.

As soon as they all came out into the light, the baker saw that there

4

was a hole in his wife's dress, so he pulled some grass and twisted it into a wisp and filled up the hole. Presently they came to a cow that was feeding by the side of the road. There was not much grass there and the cow was hungry, so when she saw the wisp of grass sticking from the woman's dress she began to eat it; but the baker waved his wand and cried 'tiens-bon-la' and the cow's teeth stuck in the grass and the grass stuck to the dress. They all went along until they came to a house where there was a large dog on the doorstep. When the dog saw the people, he jumped over the fence to see where they were going. The cow gave him a switch with her tail across the nose, the baker cried 'tiens-bon-la,' and the dog stuck to the cow's tail and went along with the rest. When the old woman who owned the dog saw him going off in this manner, she was very angry; she called him but he would not come; then she ran out with the broom that she was using to sweep the floor, and began to beat the dog to drive him home. But the baker cried out 'tiens-bon-la' again and so the broom stuck to the dog and the old woman could not let go the broom. The old woman's husband was quite lame; he ran after his wife, limping along with a stick. He could not go very fast, but he went as well as he could to see what his old woman was beating the dog for. When he came up, he took hold of the woman's dress to pull her away, but the baker cried out 'tiens-bon-la' again and the lame farmer had to go limping along with the others.

So they all went to the Seigneur's palace—the lawyer with the heavy wash-basin, the woman holding on to the lawyer, the cow trying to eat the wisp of hay, the dog barking at the cow and sticking to her tail, the old woman with her broom, and the lame farmer limping along with his stick. The baker knocked at the door and when the Seigneur opened it he said: 'Oh, my Seigneur, you ordered a "tiens-bon-la" and I have brought you one, the best that was ever made. If you will be pleased to try it, I hope you will be content.' The Seigneur took hold of the basin to take it away from the lawyer, the baker cried 'tiens-bon-la' again, and the Seigneur was held to the basin as fast as the others. He tried hard to get away but the 'tiens-bon-la' was good and would not let go.

Then the Seigneur asked the baker what he would take to let him off. After a long time the baker said he would let him go if the Seigneur would give a great sum of money every year to himself and to each of his fifteen children. The Seigneur consented, but the baker said he must have a deed made by a notary. So they sent for the notary and the deed was made, and the Seigneur signed it on the wash-basin. The baker waved his wand backwards, the 'tiens-bon-la' was broken, and they all went away happy again, and the baker's wife never again deceived her husband.

2. Star-Boy and the Sun Dance

ONCE long ago when the Blackfeet Indians dwelt on the Canadian prairies, it happened that a band of the people were camped near the mountains. It was spring-time, and the warm winds blew over the prairies laden with the scent of wild flowers. One hot cloudless night two girls slept in the long prairie grass beside their tents with no covering but the sky. The elder awoke before dawn and saw the Morning Star just rising. Very beautiful and bright he looked in the clear morning air, with no smoke or dust to hide him. The girl looked long at the Star, and she had strange fancies, and imagined that he was her lover. At last she called her sister and said, 'Look at the Morning Star. He is bright and wise. I love only the Morning Star for he is more beautiful than man.'

One day in the autumn when the flowers were faded and the grass was yellow with age and the cool winds blew over the prairie and the birds were flying south, as the girl was returning home from a long walk she met a young man on the trail. In his hair was a yellow plume, and in his hand a small shrub with a big spider-web hanging to it. He was very beautiful, and he wore fine clothes of soft skins, and the odour of his dress was that of the sweet-grass and the pine. As the girl drew aside from the trail to pass, he put forth his hand and stopped her. 'Stand aside,' she said, 'and let me pass.' But he answered, 'I am the Morning Star. One night in spring when the flowers were blooming, I saw you sleeping in the long grass outside your tent, and I loved you. I heard you say you loved only me, and now I have come to ask you to come with me to the sky to the home of my father, the Sun, where we shall live together and you will have no more troubles nor cares. It is the Land of Little People, the Land of the Ever-Young, where all are happy like children, and no one ever grows old.' Then the girl remembered the hot cloudless night in the spring-time when she slept in the tall grass, and

7

she knew now that Morning Star was to be her husband.

And she said, 'I must first say good-bye to my father and mother.' But Morning Star said, 'There must be no leave-taking,' and he would not let her go home. He fastened his yellow plume in her hair, and gave her the shrub to hold. He told her to place her feet upon the lowest strand of the spider's web and to hold the uppermost strand in her hands. Then he told her to shut her eyes. After a brief time when he asked her to open her eyes, they were in the sky. They passed on to a large tent. Morning Star said, 'This is the home of my father and mother, the Sun and the Moon,' and he asked her to enter. As it was day, the Sun was away on his long journey, but the Moon was at home and she welcomed the girl as her son's bride. And the girl lived happy in the Star country with her husband, and she learned many wonderful things. Not far from her home, near the tent of the Spider Man who weaved webs, a large turnip was growing about which she wondered greatly. But the Moon seeing her wonder said, 'You may dig any roots that grow in the sky, but I warn you not to dig up the large turnip. If you do, unhappiness will follow you.'

After a time a son was born to the girl, and everywhere the girl went she carried the child. She called him Star-Boy. She often saw the large turnip near the tent of the Spider Man who weaved webs, but mindful of the Moon's warning, she was afraid to touch it. One day, however, her wonder overcame her, and she decided to see what was underneath the turnip. She tried to pull it up but it stuck fast, and she was unable to move it. Then two large cranes, flying from the east, came to her aid, and catching the turnip with their long bills they moved it from side to side, loosened it, and pulled it up. The girl looked through the hole, and saw the earth far beneath her. It was the same hole through which Morning Star had brought her to the sky. She looked long through the hole, and she saw the camps of her people, the Blackfeet, on the plains far below. What she saw was well known to her. It was summer on the prairies. The men were playing games; the women were tanning skins or gathering berries on the rolling hills. She grew very lonely as she watched, for she wanted to be back on the green prairies with her own people, and when she turned away to go home she was crying bitterly.

When she reached home, Morning Star and his mother the Moon were waiting for her. Morning Star at once knew from her face what had happened, and he said, 'You have pulled up the sacred turnip.' When she did not answer, the Moon said, 'I warned you not to dig it up, because I love Star-Boy and I do not wish to part with him.' It was day, and the Sun was away on his long journey. When he came home in the evening, he asked what was the matter with his daughter for she looked sad and troubled. And the girl answered that she was lonely because she had looked down that day upon her people on the plains. Then the Sun was very angry, and said to Morning Star, 'If she has disobeyed, she must go back to her people. She cannot live here.' Morning Star and the Moon pleaded with the Sun to let her remain, but the Sun said that it was better that she should go back to the prairies, for she would no longer be happy in the sky.

Then Morning Star led the girl to the house of the Spider Man who had weaved the web that had drawn her up to the sky. He placed Star-Boy on her breast, and wrapped around them both a bright robe. Then he bade them farewell, saying, 'We will let you down where your people on the plains can see you as you fall.' Then the Spider Man with his web let her down as she had come, through the hole in the sky.

It was a hot still evening in midsummer when the girl returned to her people. Many of the people were outside their tents, and they saw a bright light in the northern sky. They watched it slowly drop until it reached the ground. They thought it was a shooting star. They ran to the place where the bright light fell, and there they found a strange bundle, inside of which were the woman and her child. Her parents knew her, and she returned with them to their home and lived with them. But she was never happy. Often she took Star-Boy to the top of a high hill in the west, where she sat and mourned for her home in the sky. And daily she watched Morning Star rise from the plains. Once she begged him to take her back to the country of the stars, but he answered, 'You disobeyed, and therefore I cannot take you back. Your sin is the cause of your sorrow, and it has brought great trouble to you and your people.'

So the Star-Woman lived alone and unhappy upon the earth because she had disobeyed. After a time she died, and her son, Star-Boy, was left alone. Although born in the home of the Sun, he was very poor. He had little of the world's goods, and but few clothes to wear. He was so timid that he never played with other children, and he lived much by himself. On his face was a strange scar which became more marked as he grew older. Because of this and his shy and timid ways, he was laughed at by everybody; other boys stoned him and abused him and called him Scarface.

9

When Star-Boy became a man he loved a girl of his own people. She was very beautiful, and many young men wanted to marry her, but she refused them all. She told Star-Boy that she would not marry him until he removed the strange scar from his face. He was much troubled by this answer and he talked about it to an old medicine-woman who knew many things. The medicine-woman told him that the scar had been placed on his face by the Sun and that only the Sun himself could take it off. So he decided to go to the home of the Sun.

He went across the prairies and over the mountains for many days, meeting many dangers and suffering great hardships. At last he came to the Great Water in the West—the Pacific Ocean. For three days and nights he lay on the sand fasting and praying to the Sun God. On the evening of the fourth day he saw a bright trail leading across the water to the west. He ran along this path across the water until he came at last to the home of the Sun, where he hid himself and waited. Early next morning the Sun came out of his tent, ready for his day's journey. He saw Star-Boy, but he did not know him, for Star-Boy had grown since he left the country of the stars. The Sun was angry when he saw a creature from earth, and calling his wife, the Moon, he said, 'We will kill him, for he comes from a good-for-nothing race.' But the Moon, being kind, prevented it and saved the boy's life. Then Morning Star, the boy's father, handsome and bright, came from his tent. He recognized his child. And, after the usual fashion in the sky, he brought dried sweet-grass and burned it so that the smoke curled around the boy and cleansed him from the dust of the earth. Then he brought him to his father and mother, the Sun and the Moon, and told them who the boy was. And Star-Boy told his story of his long journey, and of the marriage refusal of the girl he loved because of the scar on his face. And they took pity on him, and promised to help him.

Star-Boy lived in the home of the Sun and Moon with Morning Star. Once he went hunting and killed seven large birds which had threatened the life of his father. He gave four of the dead birds to the Sun and three to the Moon. And the Sun, glad to be rid of these pests, resolved to pay him well for his work. As a reward, he took the scar from his face, as the medicine-woman had said. And he made him his messenger to the Blackfeet people on the Canadian plains, and promised that if they would give a festival in his honour once a year, he would heal their sick. The festival was to be known as the Sun Dance. He taught Star-Boy the secrets of the dance and the songs to be used in it, so that he could tell his people. And he gave him two raven feathers to wear, as a sign that he came from the Sun, and a very wonderful robe. And he gave him a magic flute and a wonderful song, with which he could charm the heart of the girl he loved.

So Star-Boy returned to his people, the Blackfeet of the plains, running along by the Milky Way, the short, bright path to the earth. When he had taught them the secret of the Sun Dance, he married the girl he loved, and the Sun took them back to live with him in the sky. And he made him bright and beautiful, just like his father Morning Star, and gave him work to do. Sometimes the father and son can be seen together in the sky; the people of earth sometimes call the father Venus, and the son Jupiter, but Indians call them Morning Star and Little Morning Star. And since that time, once a year, the Blackfeet of the plains hold the Sun Dance that their sick may all be healed, as it was promised to Star-Boy by the Sun God in the old days.

3. Jack and His Magic Aids

THERE was once a poor widow who had but one child, a son, Jack by name. Her husband had left her money when he died, but in a few years it was all used up. Jack was a silly fellow; he was always doing stupid things and was of no help to his mother, although his father had said that some day he would do great deeds. Soon the widow became very poor. She lived on a large farm rented from a greedy landlord who lived in the town near by. The rent had to be paid once a year, and when pay day was drawing near, she found she had no money to give the landlord. She had several fine cows, so she thought she would sell one and get money to pay her rent.

One morning she sent Jack off to market with the finest cow she had. As Jack drove the cow along, he passed a house standing in the forest near the road. A man sitting on the steps called to him. 'Where are you going with the cow?' he asked. 'I am driving her to market to sell her,' answered Jack. The man asked him to come in and rest a while, and Jack tied the cow to a tree and went in. Then the man said, 'You must give the cow to me.' But Jack answered, 'I cannot give her to you; I will sell her to you, for my mother needs the money.' The man asked Jack to have something to eat, and placed before him on the table a plateful of food. Jack ate heartily, but the food did not grow less. He ate and ate and could not stop. Soon he became so full that he was almost bursting, but the food had grown no smaller, and he could not stop eating, although he tried very hard. He called to the man to take away the food. But the man answered, 'If you will give me your cow, I will take away the plate; if not, you may eat away.' So Jack agreed to give him the cow, for he was afraid he would burst from overeating, and in return for the cow the man gave him the dish of magical food. Then he went back home.

When he reached home, his mother asked him for the money from the sale of the cow. But he told her he had been robbed of the cow by the man in the forest. She scolded him, and called him many harsh names, and took the broom to beat him. But when she took hold of him, he placed a little of the magical food in her mouth, and his mother, charmed with the taste, at once asked for more. He gave her the dish, and just as he had done at the man's house, she ate and ate until she too was almost bursting, but she could not stop. When she pleaded with him to take the food away, he said, 'I will take it away if you will not beat me,' and she agreed.

The next morning his mother sent Jack off to market with another cow. He passed the same house as on the previous day, and the same man was again sitting on the steps. The man asked him for the cow, but Jack, remembering what had happened the day before, hurried on without reply. Then the man took off the belt he was wearing and threw it down in the middle of the road. At once the belt leaped around both Jack and the cow, tying both tightly together. The man said he would let them free if Jack would give him the cow. But Jack refused. Then the belt began to tighten slowly; it got tighter and tighter, pressing Jack to the cow until he could hardly draw his breath. At last, when he could stand it no longer, he agreed to give up the cow, and the man set him free. In return Jack received the magic belt. When he reached home, his mother again asked him for the money from the sale of the cow. When he told her that he had again been robbed, she was more angry than before; she called him harsh names again, and rushed at him saying she would kill him. But Jack unclasped his magic belt, threw it on the floor, and at once it leaped around his mother, tying her hand

13

and foot. As the belt became tighter and tighter, his mother began to gasp for breath, and cried out to be set free. But Jack said, 'I will untie you, if you promise not to beat me.' So his mother, almost smothered, agreed. Then he untied her, and she kept her promise.

As the rent-day was near at hand, his mother resolved to try once more to sell a cow, and the next morning Jack was again sent to market driving the third cow. As he passed the same house by the side of the forest road, the man who had already taken two cows from him sat on the steps. He asked Jack to give him the cow he was driving, just as he had done before. But in answer, Jack picked up a large stone and threw it in anger at the man's head. The man dodged the stone, and took from his pocket a small flute and began to play it. In spite of his efforts to keep still, Jack began to dance. The cow joined in the jig, and both danced and danced up and down the road and could not stop. They danced until Jack was tired out, but he could not stop, although he tried hard. He pleaded with the man to stop playing the flute. The man said, 'I will stop if you will give me your cow.' But Jack had already lost two cows and he refused. 'Then dance away,' said the man, and Jack danced until he was almost dropping. Finally he agreed to give up the cow. The dance was stopped, and in return for the cow, Jack received the magic flute.

When he reached home and told his mother that he had been robbed a third time, her rage knew no bounds. She said she would surely kill him this time, but as she sprang upon him, he began to play his flute. His mother began to dance, and when she ordered him to stop playing, he said, 'I will stop if you promise not to beat me.' At first she refused, but as she danced until she was very tired, she finally agreed, and Jack escaped punishment. He found too that by playing another tune, he could call with his flute a great swarm of wasps which could not be seen by anyone but himself and which would obey all his commands.

The next day was the rent-day, and there was no money to pay the landlord. The widow was troubled, but Jack said, 'I will pay him; be not troubled.' Soon the landlord and his servant drove up to the widow's house. When they entered the house, the widow hid herself, for she did not want to meet the cruel landlord without her rent. But Jack met them and politely gave them seats. Then he offered them food after their long drive, and placed before them the dish of magical meat. And they ate and ate, just as Jack and his mother had done, and could not stop. At last they were almost bursting with the food, which grew no less on the dish, and they pleaded with Jack to take the dish away. Jack replied, 'I will take it away if you will give up the farm to my mother, for we have paid you more rent than the farm is worth.' Finally the landlord, fearing he would burst, agreed. Jack removed the food, and the landlord returned to the town, leaving the farm to Jack and his mother.

Jack soon left the farm and all upon it to his mother, and started out to make his own fortune, taking with him his magic dish, belt and flute. He travelled far, and came at last to a town where a great man lived who had one beautiful daughter. She had many suitors, but she said that she would marry the man who could make her laugh three times. Jack resolved to make the trial, and went to the man's house. He was an awkward, ugly fellow, and the girl looked on him with great disgust, but she consented to let him make the trial. First Jack produced his magical dish, and offered it to the girl. She tasted the food and liked it so well that she ate more. She ate and ate as all who had eaten from it had done before her, until she cried out to have it taken away. But Jack would take it away on one condition—she must first laugh. Finally, when she too was almost bursting, she agreed, but she said to herself, 'He will not make me laugh a second time.'

As soon as Jack had taken away the dish, the girl and her servants rushed upon him to punish him. But he threw down his magic belt, and at once they were all bound together in a heap, tied from head to foot. They begged to be untied. 'I will untie you,' said Jack to the girl, 'if you will laugh.' At first the girl refused, but as the belt slowly tightened, and she could stand it no longer, she agreed, and laughed feebly. Then Jack let them go.

No sooner were they set free than they rushed at Jack again to punish him. But he began to play on his flute, and at once the whole company began to dance. When they grew tired, they tried to stop, but they could not. They begged him to stop playing, but he replied, 'I will stop when the girl laughs.' For a long time she refused, but when she became so weary of the dance that she could scarcely stand up she agreed, and laughed the third time.

Before Jack could claim her, her father heard what had happened, and he ordered Jack to be brought before him. When he saw such an ugly fellow, he too was disgusted, and said that Jack must be secretly put to death. So poor Jack was seized unexpectedly before he could use his magic aids and thrown into a cage of wild beasts. But when the

15

beasts rushed upon him to eat him up he threw down his magic belt, and they were all tied up in a heap, while Jack escaped from the cage.

Meanwhile a very rich man had won the hand of the man's daughter. On the day of the wedding Jack went again to the man's house and waited. Just as the wedding ceremony was to begin, Jack went in; he sat behind a door in the corner and played a soft tune on his magic flute and called up a great swarm of wasps. The wasps could not be seen by any eyes but Jack's, but they swarmed into the room. Jack told them to sting the rich man waiting at the altar to be the girl's husband. At once the man, feeling them stinging, but unable to see anything, began to jump and scream like a madman. The people looked on in terror, believing that he had become suddenly crazy. The man jumped and yelled and slapped himself, until the girl declared that she would not marry a madman, and her father led her away and the people went out in great disorder. As the girl's father went out, he saw Jack sitting behind the door. He was surprised to see that he had escaped from the wild beasts' cage, for he believed that the beasts had eaten him up. He knew too that in some mysterious way Jack had been the cause of the uproar. Then the servants brought him word that the beasts in the cage were all tied up, and could not be set free. The man then knew that Jack had great power, so he sent for him and said, 'You are a very wonderful man; you have won my daughter.' So with great joy and splendour the wedding took place. Jack built a great house, and when the girl's father died, he received all his lands, and he lived happy ever afterwards with his bride, because of the magic dish and belt and flute he had taken in exchange for his cows.

4. The Bad Indian's Ashes

IN THE old days when giants roamed along the North Pacific Coast, there lived on the banks of a great river a poor Indian woman. She was the daughter of a dead chief—a great man—but she had fallen on evil days. Against her parents' wishes, she had married a worthless fellow; he was lazy and useless, and she was very poor and unhappy. One night a son was born to her. It was a wild stormy night; the winds roared, the thunder crashed, and terrible lightnings forked the sky. The boy was born with strange marks upon him, and on his head were horns like sharp arrow-points. The wise men of the place shook their heads and said, 'No good can come from him; he will come to a bad end.'

As the boy grew up, it was seen that the prophecy of the wise men would surely come true. He was very wicked, and he soon became known for his bad deeds. He was the terror of all the country on the Pacific Coast. But his mother loved him well, for he was her only child, and she petted him like a baby, even after he was a big boy. He did not take kindly to his mother's caresses, and when she petted him he always grew angry and said, 'Don't pet me, I am not a baby.' One day as she petted him, he became very cross as was his habit, and in his rage he ran the arrow-points of his head into her breast and killed her. Then he took to the woods, and lived as an outlaw in the forest. He robbed all who came his way, until he had a great store of goods hidden in a secret place. His hand was against everybody's, and everybody's was against his.

Soon the tale of his crimes spread all over the North Pacific Coast, and he was held in great fear. The Chief of the people called a meeting of his wise council to decide what should be done. They resolved that he must be killed and the land rid of his terrors. So they drew lots to see who should seek him in the forest. The lot fell to his uncle—the brother of his mother—a very brave man. And the uncle set out into the woods to seek his wicked nephew, who was known as 'the arrow-headed-one.'

The outlaw had found a cave in the forest, and there he lived in security. He killed everybody who came near it, and he marked on his spear a notch for each one he killed. In a very short time the notches on his spear numbered fifty. He heard of the council of the wise men and of their effort to capture him, and that his uncle had drawn the lot for the task. He resolved to defend himself against an attack, and he made his cave as strong as he could. He thought that his uncle would come to the cave in search of him.

But his uncle was a very wise old Indian. He knew better than to attack his nephew's stronghold. Instead, he too selected a cave and turned it into a fort. He took bundles of dry grass and leaves, and shaped them like men, and stood them up around his cave like soldiers always on guard. And he told all the people of the village to stay in hiding until 'the arrow-headed-one' was killed. Then he waited alone in his cave.

For several nights 'the arrow-headed-one' stayed in his cave waiting for his uncle's attack. But no attack was made. Then he grew tired of waiting, and in a spirit of recklessness and daring he resolved to attack his uncle, for he knew that he was in the cave hardby. He took his spear and bow and arrows, and went to his uncle's cave to kill him. He took with him his helping evil spirit in the form of a small bird about the size of a robin. When he came to the cave, he thought that one of the dummy

18

grass men was his uncle and he hurled his spear at it. And while he was about it, his uncle, hidden behind a rock, shot a poisoned arrow at him and wounded him so badly that he fled back to his own cave. The small bird sucked the poison from his wound, but the wound left him very weak. His uncle had followed in his tracks, and soon came upon him. But 'the arrow-headed-one,' tired out because of his wound, had little stomach for a fight, and when his uncle entered the cave, he pleaded with him not to kill him. 'Do not kill me,' he said, 'I have a great store of goods hidden in the cave. If you spare me, I will give you all and make you rich. And I will never kill another person.'

But his uncle resolved to put him to death because he had killed his mother and had so many notches on his spear. So he killed him and dragged his body outside and burned it. Then he went home. 'Fear no longer,' he said to the villagers, ' "the arrow-headed-one" is dead.' But the evil that the bad Indian had done lived after him. The four winds drove his ashes from the spot where his body was burned. The ashes blew everywhere, and were changed into the little black flies whose descendants to-day torment people in the summer in the northern woods of Canada. And the bad Indian's wickedness still lives in the black flies that came from his ashes.

5. The Mermaid of the Magdalenes

F AR off the north-east coast of Canada is a group of rugged islands called the Magdalenes. They are a lonely, barren group, where grass and flowers and trees grow scantily. There, the northern storms rage with their wildest fury, and the sea breaks with its greatest force upon the bleak rocks. Numberless birds of strange cries and colours fly constantly about. On days when the storm dashes the sea white and angry against the coast, even the thunder of the surf is almost shut out by the screaming of countless gulls; and on clear days the sun is hidden when the birds rise in clouds from their nests. The 'Isle of Birds,' the Jesuits called one of the islands when they first visited the group hundreds of years ago, and it is an 'Isle of Birds' still. It is a wild and rock-bound desolate land.

But although the islands are barren of grass and flowers and trees, the waters around and between them are rich in fish. 'The Kingdom of Fish,' men call the place, for adventurous traders grow wealthy there reaping the harvest of the sea. The greatest product of the waters is the lobster. He always inhabited these northern seas, and about his power in olden times strange tales are told. Away off the coast of one of the islands, you can still see on fine moonlight nights in May, and also during the day once a year, a maiden holding a glass in her hand, combing her long hair, and looking wistfully to the land. Sometimes, too, on calm nights you can still hear her strange song above the murmur of the waves. She is the phantom lady of the Island over whom the Lobster in far away days used his power. She is now a prisoner in the deep, held there as a punishment for her deeds.

Now, it happened that long ago when fish were first canned for food there was a great slaughter of sardines—the tiny fish of the sea—by

cruel money-greedy traders who caught them, packed them in small boxes, and shipped them to far countries, just as they do to-day. These traders received large money rewards for their labour, for people all over the world liked the little fish and paid a high price for them. The sardines saw their number slowly growing smaller, for, being little, they were helpless against their captors, and among all their family there was great sorrow. In despair they asked the big fish of the sea to help them. At last, in answer to their appeal, a meeting of all the fish in the sea was called. Here the big fish took an oath to help their small cousins in their struggle with man, and to punish when they could all who ate or fished the sardine family. And the little fish rejoiced greatly.

One May day a large ship loaded with packed fish was wrecked on the sunken rocks of the Magdalene Islands. Soon the ship was broken up by the heavy surf on the sharp reef, and her cargo was strewn along the shore. It happened that in the cargo were many boxes of sardines, and they too were washed up on the beach by the tide. In the evening, after the sea had calmed, a fair maiden who lived on the Island with her father, a fish trader, walked along the shore alone to view the wreckage of the broken ship. She found, to her delight, one of the boxes in which the sardines were packed. She resolved at once to eat the contents, for she too, like all the world at that time, liked the little fish. But although she tried as hard as she could, she was unable to open the box. She sat by the side of the sea and sang a song of lament, calling on anyone who could to open the box for her. She sang:

> 'I love sardines when they're boiled with beans,
> And mixed with the sands of the sea.'

Away out from the beach a skate-fish was resting on a sand-bar. Hearing the song of the maiden, he quickly swam towards the shore. When he came close enough to hear the words of the song and to know what the box contained, he swam away in great disgust, for he was cousin to the sardines in the box, and came from the same family tree as they. But he was too timid to try to punish the maiden. Then a bold merman heard the song. He had long looked for a land wife to live with him in his home under the sea; now he said, 'Here at last is a shore maiden for me,' for the voice of the singer was beautiful to him. So he went to his looking-glass to dress himself in the most genteel fashion. From bright clean sea-weeds and sea-leaves he quickly made himself a new suit, all green and yellow; and he covered his feet with bright-coloured shells, and his neck with pearls which the oyster gave him; and dressing himself carefully, he hastened in the direction of the song. But when he came close enough to hear the words and to know what the box contained, he remembered his oath at the great gathering of the fish, and although he loved the singer he swam hurriedly away. For, like the skate-fish, he too feared to try to punish the maiden.

The maiden was now sore distressed, for it was growing late and the moon was already far up in the sky. The box was still unopened, and the girl was hungry for the fish. Going to the edge of the sea, she knocked the box hard against a large rock that lay in the water, hoping thereby to break it open. But the box would not break. Now, it chanced that under the rock a large black lobster lay sleeping quietly after a long battle with an enemy in the sea. The tapping on the roof of his sleeping-place awoke him, and he rubbed his eyes and listened. The maiden was again singing her song:—

> 'Oh I love sardines when they're boiled with beans,
> And mixed with the sands of the sea.
> I am dying for some. Will nobody come
> And open this box for me?'

Then the Lobster remembered his oath at the great gathering of the fish. Unlike the skate-fish and the merman, he had no fear of the maiden, for he knew his power. He determined to punish her, and he resolved at once upon a crafty trick. He came out of his hiding place, and waving his claw politely he said, 'Fair lady, I can open the box for you; give it to me and let me try.' But when, in answer, she held the box out towards him in her hand, he grasped her by the wrist with his strong claw, and, holding her fast, he swam with her far out to sea. Where he went and what he did with her, no man knows. It is believed that he sold her to the merman who had long sought a shore-wife, and that she is still being slowly changed into a fish. One thing is certain—she never came back to land. But on the first day of May she always appears on the water away off the coast of the Island; and if that day is fine and clear you can still always see her there. She holds in her hand a looking-glass in which in the sunlight she looks at herself to see if she is nearer to a fish than she was on May Day the year before when she last appeared in the sun; and she is combing her long hair which is now covered with pearls; and she looks with longing eyes to the shore and her old home. And sometimes on moonlight nights in May, when the wind is still and the sea is calm, the fishermen hear her strange sad song across the waters. They know then that she is lonely, and that she is singing her song to lure land-comrades for company to her side. And on these nights they stay on shore, for they know that if they venture out to sea she will seize them and carry them off for playmates to her home of bright shells far under the sea.

6. The Boy and the Dancing Fairy

LONG ago two Indian boys lived in the Canadian forest with their parents. One boy was much older and larger and stronger than the other. He forced his little brother to do all the hard work about the place. He stole from him all the good things his parents gave him and often he beat him until he cried with pain. If the little boy told his parents of his brother's cruelty, his brother beat him all the harder, and the little boy found that it was more to his comfort not to complain. But at last he could stand the cruelty no longer, and he decided to run away from home. So one morning he took his bow and arrows and an extra pair of moccasins, and set out alone to seek his fortune and to find a kinder world.

Although the boy was small and young, he could run very fast. He could run so fast that when he shot an arrow from his bow, he could outstrip the arrow in its flight. So he ran along very quickly, and when night came on he was very far from home. He was lonely too, for he thought of the bright warm camp fires in the twilight at home, and of his father and mother, and he wished he was back again in his own soft bed. He was frightened too by the strange noises, and every sound startled him. At last when he was about to cry in his loneliness, an old man came along. The man was very old but he had a kindly face, all wrinkled and weather-beaten, and twinkling eyes that told of a merry heart. 'Hello,' he said to the boy, 'where are you from, and where are you going?' 'I have come a long way,' said the boy, 'and I am very tired and lonesome and far from home, and I don't know where I am going. I am looking for a pleasant land.' 'You look like a good boy,' said the old man; 'you say you have come a long way, but I have come much farther than you, and from a very pleasant place. When I began my journey I was young

like you. I have never stopped, and now you see that I am very old and
bent and wrinkled, while there is not a line in your face. I have travelled
a very long road, the road of Long Life.' Then the boy said, 'I want to
go to the place you came from since it is pleasant.' But the old man
answered, 'You can never reach it; it is the Land of Youth; the Childhood Land, men call it, and those who leave it never go back. It is a land
of wonderful sights and sounds and dreams. It can be reached only from
the road on the other side; you have passed that road and it is too late
for you now to go back to it.' Then they were silent for a long time, and
the boy looked at the old man and wondered. He saw that the old man's
shoes were worn out from his long journey and that his feet were sore
and weary. So he gave him the extra pair of moccasins he carried. The
old man was very thankful. He gave the boy a little box he had in his
pocket and he said, 'Take this box; you will find it will help you in
times of need, and it will be useful to you in your travels. I am near the
end of my journey, and I shall need it no more. You have a long journey
before you.' The boy put the box in his pocket and lay down to sleep.
Then the old man went on his way, and the boy never saw him again.

The next morning, before the boy began his day's journey, he wondered what was in the box the old man had given him. He took it out and opened it. Inside was a little man no bigger than his own thumb, dancing as hard as he could. As soon as the cover was opened and light entered the box, the little man stopped dancing and called to the boy, 'What do you want?' The boy knew then that the old man had given him a little fairy to help him in his need. He closed the box and answered, 'I wish to be carried far away to a beautiful land where I can get a lovely girl for a comrade, for I am very lonely.' At once darkness came upon him and he slept. When he awoke he found he had been asleep but a few seconds, but he was now in a large village in a beautiful land. It was a land of trees and flowers and wonderful streams, where many birds were singing. He came to a house on the border of the village and entered it. Inside was a very old woman; she was the only person in the house. When she saw the boy, she began to cry. He asked her why she was weeping. She answered, 'I know why you have come here. I knew from a dream that you were coming. You have come to seek a very lovely girl as your wife and comrade. She lives in the village. Her father is very rich. He is a great Chief. He asks that each man who seeks to win his daughter must do very hard and dangerous and impossible tasks. If they fail they are put to death. The girl has had many suitors, but all have failed to do her father's tasks and all have been killed. You too will fail and you will surely die.' Then the old woman cried louder than before. But the boy said, 'I can do any task he sets for me. He cannot kill me.' For the boy knew that the dancing fairy would save him.

Soon the boy went to the Chief's house to ask him for his lovely daughter. The Chief told him the conditions on which she could be won. He said that all her suitors had to try to do hard tasks. If they failed they were put to death; the suitor who succeeded should win his daughter. The boy agreed to do as he wished. The Chief said, 'The mountain before my house keeps me from seeing the sun in the mornings. You must take it away before you can win my daughter. If you fail you shall be put to death.' The boy said he would take away the mountain that night, but the Chief did not think he could do it.

That night when all the village was asleep the boy went to the foot of the mountain. It was a high granite hill, with great trees growing on its top. The boy took out his box and opened it. The little fairy was dancing as hard as he could, but when he saw the light he stopped and said, 'What do you want?' And the boy said, 'I want you to take away this mountain before morning.' 'It shall be done,' said the little man. Then the boy closed the box and lay down and went to sleep. He slept soundly all night. When he awoke in the early morning the mountain was gone. All around was only a level meadow. The sun was still low in the eastern sky, but all the village could see it. When the Chief awoke, he wondered greatly. He thought he had lost his daughter at last. But he decided to set another hard task for the boy to do.

Soon the boy went to the Chief to claim his bride. But the Chief said, 'You must do another task for me. Not far away there is a village where my enemies live. They have caused me great trouble. You must destroy the village and drive all the people away before you can win my daughter. If you fail to do it to-night, you shall be put to death to-morrow.' The boy agreed to do as he wished. And the Chief thought the boy would surely be killed in making the attempt.

That night the boy set out for the distant village. He ran very fast and soon reached the border of it. Then he took out his box and opened it. The fairy stopped dancing and said, 'What do you want?' 'I want you to destroy this village to-night and drive all the people away,' said the boy. 'It shall be done,' said the fairy. Then the boy closed the box and went to sleep under a tree. He slept soundly all night. In the morning when he awoke, there was no village in sight. All around him was silence; not a sound of life came to him but the sounds of the forest; the village had been destroyed in the night and all its people were now far away. Then the boy went back and told the Chief that he had done the deed. The Chief sent a messenger to see if the boy spoke the truth, and the messenger came back and said that the task had been done. Then the Chief knew that he was beaten. He knew that the boy had very great power which he could not understand, and he said, 'You may take my lovely daughter.' So the boy took the girl as his wife and comrade. The Chief gave them a great lodge to live in and servants to wait on them, and they were very happy.

But their happiness was soon ended for a time. One day the boy went away with many others to hunt far in the forest. He put on a hunting suit, but he forgot to take his magic box along with him. He left it behind in the pocket of his coat. In the house was a wicked servant who wanted the boy's possessions for himself. One day he had seen him opening the box and talking to it. He wondered what his master meant and what was in the box. When his master had gone hunting, the servant went to hang up his clothes. He found the box in the coat pocket. He took it out and opened it. Inside, the little man was dancing as hard as he could. When he saw the light, he stopped and said, 'What do you want?' The servant knew that at last he had found the secret of his master's power. 'What do you want me to do?' repeated the little man. The man-servant said, 'I want you at once to remove this house and all it contains to some place far away.' Then he closed the box. At once there was darkness, and when light came again in a few seconds, the house and all in it were far away in the depths of the forest. The servant was very pleased.

Soon the hunters came back. They had taken much game. When the boy came to where his home had been, he found that his house was gone, and his wife and servants and all his possessions were gone with it. He knew at once what had happened. But he knew how to overcome his wicked servant. He took a magic bow and arrow that his mother had given him before he left his old home long before. Then he went out and shot his arrow into the woods. He ran as fast as he could, following the arrow. He ran so fast that he could follow it in its flight. And he kept under the arrow as it sped on and on. When the arrow dropped far in the forest, the boy stopped. Not far in front of him he saw his own house. He hid among the trees until night came. Then he crept softly to the house. There was not a sound. Everyone was asleep. He went in, and there, sure enough, was his coat hanging on a peg. He slipped it on, and in the pocket he found the magic box. He opened it, and there was the little man dancing as hard as he could. When the cover was lifted, the little man stopped and said, 'What do you want?' The boy said, 'I want you at once to take this house and all it contains back to the village where it was before.' The little man said, 'It shall be done.' Then the boy went to sleep. He awoke in the morning before the others were up, and sure enough the house was back in the village. Then the boy asked the little man in the box to punish the wicked servant. And the servant was sent far away to be a wanderer on the face of the earth; and he wanders about to this day, and he is always looking for something that never comes, and he has always beautiful dreams that never come true.

After that, the boy and his wife lived happily. The boy never again left the box behind him; he kept it always with him. And when he wanted anything, the little fairy always brought it to him. Soon the old Chief died, and the boy became Chief in his place. He travelled the road of Long Life over which the wrinkled old man had come. When he grew old, he asked the fairy in the box to bring him back to the Land of

Youth, but that was the one thing the dancing fairy could not do. So at the end of the long road the old man disappeared over the hill and left his box behind him with the great deeds it had done.

7. The Mouse and the Sun

LONG before the white men came to Canada, and when the animals ruled the earth, a little boy and his sister lived alone on the Canadian plains. Their father and mother died when the children were very young. The children had no relations, and they were left to look after themselves. They lived many miles from other people; indeed they had never seen any people but their parents, they lived so far away. The boy was very small; he was no bigger than a baby. The girl was large and strong, and she had to provide food for both of them and do all the work in the house. She had to take care of her little brother, and she took him with her wherever she went so that no harm would come to him. She made

him a bow and a number of arrows to play with. One day in winter she
went out to gather wood for the fire. She took her little brother with her.
She told him to hide while she walked farther on. She said, 'You will
soon see a flock of snow birds passing near you if you watch. Shoot one
of them and bring it home.' The snow lay deep on the plains, and many
snow birds were flying around looking for food. The boy tried to shoot
them, but his aim was not good, and he was unable to hit any of them.
When his sister came back to him, he had no bird and he was very much
ashamed. But his sister said, 'Never mind. Do not be discouraged. You
will have better luck to-morrow.'

The next day the girl took her brother with her again when she went
to gather wood. She left him behind at the place where he had hidden
himself the day before. Again the snow birds came flying past, searching
for food. The boy shot several arrows at them, and at last he killed one.
When his sister came back to him, he showed her the bird. He was
pleased with his success, and he said, 'I shall try to kill one each day.
You must skin them and when we have enough skins, I shall make a
coat from them.' And his sister promised to do as he wished. Each day
the boy went with his sister and waited for the snow birds to fly past.
And each day he killed one and took it home. They skinned the birds
and dried the skins. Soon the boy had enough bird skins to make a coat,
for he was very small. A few bird skins made his coat. His sister sewed
the skins together and the boy put on the coat. He was very proud of it.

One day the boy said to his sister, 'Sister, we are all alone in the
world. We have never seen any other people except our father and
mother. Are there any other people on the earth?' His sister told him
that she had heard from her mother that other people lived far away to
the east beyond the mists of the prairie, and that others, from whom his
mother had come, lived away to the west beyond the distant hills. The
boy said, 'I should like to see my mother's people if they are anywhere
on the earth.' So one day when his sister was away, he put on his bird-
skin coat and took his bow and arrows and set out towards the distant
hills to see if he could find his mother's people. It was spring-time in
the north country. The sun had melted the snow, and little streams
were flowing and little blades of grass had begun to peep above the
ground. But the earth was soft and wet, and the day was hot, and warm
winds blew over the plains. The boy walked for a long time. By the time
the sun was high up in the sky, he was very tired for he was very small.
He came to a dry knoll and lay down to rest. Soon he fell asleep. As he

31

slept, the sun beat down upon him. It was so hot that it singed his bird-skin coat; then the coat shrank and shrank in the heat until it was only a small patch on his back. When he awoke and stretched himself, he burst his coat in many places, it had grown so tight. He was very cross when he saw how the sun had ruined his coat. He shook his fist at the sun and said, 'I will have vengeance; you need not think you are too high to escape me. I will punish you yet.' He decided that without his coat he could not go any farther to seek his mother's people, and at evening he returned home.

When he reached home, he showed his sister his ruined coat. He was very sad, and for weeks he would scarcely eat a bite. And all the time he spoke bitterly of the sun. His sister tried to comfort him. She told him that next winter when the snow birds came flying south again, he could kill more of them and she would make him another coat. But for a long time he would not be comforted. At last he roused himself. He asked his sister to make him a snare, for he was going to catch the sun. She made him a snare from a buffalo-hide cord, but he told her that it would not do. Then she cut off some of her long black hair, and from it she made a braided noose. The boy said that it would do very well. Then he set out to catch the sun. He travelled many days until he came to the Great Water in the East. It was summer in the north country, and the sun rose early. The boy placed his snare just where the sun would strike the land when he rose at dawn out of the sea, and he watched from a distance. Sure enough, in the morning just as the sun rose out of the sea and came above the earth, he was caught in the snare and held fast. The sun could not rise; he was held fast to the earth. The boy was quite pleased with his success. 'Now,' he said, 'I have punished the sun for ruining my bird-skin coat.' And he returned to his home on the plains.

That day there was no light upon the earth. It was twilight in all the land. The animals were in great fear and wonder. The birds fled to their nests, and only the owl came out to look for food. At last the animals and the birds called a council to see what they could do. They found that the sun was tied to the earth by a snare. They decided that some one must go up close to the sun and cut the cord that held him. It was a very dangerous task, for the heat was very great and anyone who tried to cut the cord would perhaps be burned to death. So they drew lots to see who should go. The lot fell to Woodpecker. And Woodpecker went up and picked at the cord with his bill. He tried hard to cut it, but it was a strong braid of woman's hair and it could not be cut easily. Woodpecker picked and picked at it for a long time. At last his head was so badly burned that he could stand the heat no longer and he had to fly away without cutting the cord. His head was red from the great heat. And ever since, poor Woodpecker has had a red head because the sun singed him when he tried to set him free.

Then the animals called for a volunteer to undertake the task of cutting the snare. Mouse was at that time the largest and strongest animal in the world, and he thought that because of his great strength, it was his duty to attempt the hard and dangerous task. So he set out. When he reached the snare, he tried to cut the cord with his teeth, but the cord was strong and could not be cut easily. The heat was very great. Mouse would have run away, but he was so big and strong that he was ashamed to leave the task, for he thought that the smaller animals would laugh at him. So he stuck to his work and sawed the cord with his teeth, one hair at a time. Soon his back began to burn and scorch and smoke. But he stuck to his task. Then he began to melt away because of the great heat, and the whole top of his body was burned to ashes. But still he stuck to his task for a long time, cutting hair after hair. Finally he cut the last hair; the snare parted, and the sun was at last free to continue his day's journey and give light to the world. And the animals and birds rejoiced greatly over the success of Mouse. But poor Mouse had melted almost entirely away in the great heat. When he went up to the snare, he was the largest animal in the world; when he came down, he was the smallest. And his back was burned to ashes. And ever since, Mouse has been the smallest animal in the world, and his coat has always been the colour of grey ashes, because he was scorched when freeing the sun from a snare in the old days.

8. Glooskap's Country

IN FAR back times many centuries before the white men came from
Europe to live in the New World, Eastern Canada was inhabited by
Indians. They were a mighty race, great in size and strong in battle.
Their descendants live in certain of these parts still, dwelling in settle-
ments of their own apart from the white folk. You may still see them in
their strange tents or wigwams, making arrows and baskets and garden-
seats. Some of them are still fleet of foot and can run many miles without
tiring. But their real greatness has long since gone. They have grown
smaller in size, and they are no longer powerful as in the old days. In
early times they were called the Children of Light, for of all the people
in America they dwelt nearest to the sun-rise. Their great lord and

creator was Glooskap. Where he was himself born, and when, no man knows. From the place of his birth he sailed across the sea in a great stone canoe to the part of America nearest to the rising sun. He landed on the eastern shores of Canada. Far out he anchored his canoe and it was so large that it became an island, and great trees grew upon it. When he needed it, it was always ready to do his bidding, but it always became an island when it was not in use. On the shore of the Atlantic Ocean, Glooskap dwelt many years—ages and ages—until one day he sailed away to the hunting grounds of his fathers far over the sea.

About Glooskap's work many strange tales are told. From his birth and throughout his long life his deeds were very wonderful. He was one of twin brothers, the other being Wolf the son of Wickedness. Glooskap was the son of Goodness. Their mother died at their birth and the two children were left alone. Both had magic power which could keep them from harm, and death could not come to them except in one way. Glooskap could be killed only by a flowering rush, and Wolf only by a fern root; and each alone knew the secret of his own death. Now it was known before Glooskap's birth that he should become the Lord of the Land of the Rising Sun in Canada. But Beaver and Squirrel who were great in those days—and even before his coming—were jealous of his power when he arrived, for they themselves wished to rule the land. They tempted Wolf to kill his brother, and he being the son of Wickedness would have been glad of the chance, but he did not know the secret of his brother's death. One night of bright starlight, Beaver hiding stealthily among the trees as was his custom, heard Glooskap boasting to the stars about his charmed life; he could trust the stars, and he told them that he could be killed only by means of a flowering rush. Then Beaver hurried away to Wolf; he told him that he knew the secret of Glooskap's death and that he would tell it if Wolf would give him what he wished. To this Wolf agreed and Beaver told him what he had heard Glooskap say to the stars. 'What do you want in return for the secret?' asked Wolf. 'Wings like a pigeon,' answered Beaver. But Wolf said, 'You have a tail like a file; what could you do with wings like a pigeon?' And he laughed at him scornfully and would not grant him his wish as he had promised. Thereupon Beaver was very cross and resolved to have vengeance on Wolf. He went quickly to Glooskap and told him that Wolf knew the secret of his death and that he had better be on his guard. The next night Glooskap hid himself among the trees near to Wolf's tent. He heard Wolf boasting to the stars about his charmed life, and telling them the secret of his death—that he could be killed only by a fern root. And Glooskap, fearing for his own life, for he had no faith in the love of Wolf the son of Wickedness, at once slew his brother with a fern root. Then he changed him into a mountain, where he sleeps to this day like a huge hill.

Glooskap then ruled the country alone. But soon he grew lonely without companions and he decided to people his land. He first made the Fairies and the Elves, and sent them to dwell in the meadows and tiny streams and among the hills and caves. Then he took his bow and arrows, and for many days he shot at the ash trees in the forest. And out of the bark of the trees at which he shot there came first men whom he called Indians, the Children of Light. Then came the animals—all that had not before lived in his land—and the birds of the air and the fish of the sea, and he gave them each a name. At first all the animals were very large, so large that the head of the deer could touch the tops of the tallest pines. Even Squirrel could tear down the largest trees in the forest. One day Glooskap called all the animals to him to learn if they were friendly to his people. And he said to Bear, 'What would you do if you should meet a man?' And Bear answered, 'I should eat him up.' And Glooskap sent Bear away to the Northland, far from the dwellings of men, to live on fish from the frozen sea. And he said to Squirrel, 'What would you do if you should meet a man?' And Squirrel answered, 'I should tear down trees on his head.' And Glooskap, fearing for his men because of the strength of the animals, decided to make the animals smaller. So he took Squirrel and smoothed his back with his hand for a whole day, until he became very small as he is now, and he made him carry his tail on his back that he might thereby use up some of his strength; but Squirrel still scratches as in the old days.

Glooskap made all the animals smaller and weaker than they were when they were first created. He gave his people power over them, so that the greatest and strongest of all his creatures was man. The animals became his friends and the friends of his people; they could talk like men and they often spoke to them, and they were eager to obey Glooskap and to help him in his work. Two great wolves became his dogs; he could change their size and make them kind or cruel as he willed. They guarded his tent by day and night and always followed him about, even swimming behind him when he went far away over the sea. The Loons of the beach became his messengers, and one of them—old Tatler— became his chief tale-bearer. They always brought him news from other lands over the water and they also kept him well informed about the deeds of his own people, telling him who were good and who were evil. Fox too brought him tales from places deep in the forest, and was one of his most trusted friends. The Rabbits became the guides of men; one of them—old Bunny—was his scout of the woods, and those who followed him never lost their way. The Partridge built boats for men and animals, until because of the bird's stupidity, Glooskap took away his power. The Whale became his carrier, and old Blob the whale came quickly to his call and carried him on her back when he wished to go far over the sea. The Great Eagle made the winds for him; when she moved her wings the winds blew; she could make them great or gentle as Glooskap commanded, and when Glooskap tied her wings, the winds were still. Each animal and bird had special work to do.

Glooskap's only enemies were Beaver and Badger and Bull Frog. These always plotted against him and tried to destroy his power by stirring up strife among his people. At last he could be patient with them no longer, and he resolved to drive Beaver away. One day when Beaver watched him from a distance, Glooskap scooped up great handfuls of earth and stones and threw them in anger at his enemy, and Beaver in great fear because of Glooskap's great power, fled far away. The earth that Glooskap threw fell into the ocean and became islands. The spot from which Glooskap had taken the earth became a beautiful bay. To the shores of this bay Glooskap moved his tent, and lived there until he left the earth. When Beaver went away, he built a dam from a high place on the south to the shore on the north, and he thought to live there in comfort. But the dam caused the high tides of the sea to overflow the valley, and it was a constant source of trouble and fear to the people who lived near it. Thereupon Glooskap in anger one day broke the dam and pushed part of it out into the sea. The broken part which he moved out became a cape stretching into the ocean, and there you may see it to this day. Then Beaver, knowing that Glooskap was more powerful than he, troubled him openly no more, but frequently by stealth he tried to do him harm.

When Bull Frog was first created, he was given power over all the fresh-water streams in the land. He dwelt in the stream from which Glooskap's people took water for their use—for drinking and cooking. But he too proved false to Glooskap, and grew vain of his own great power. Once, that he might show his skill and win a great reputation among men, he dried up the water in the stream until only the mud

37

remained. The people thirsted without fresh water, and were much distressed, and at last they complained to Glooskap. Glooskap told them not to worry, for he would soon set things right. That he might make sure of Bull Frog's treachery he went himself to the bank of the stream, and there he asked a boy to bring him water to drink. The boy searched for water for a whole day, while Glooskap sat on a log and silently smoked his pipe. At last the boy came back bringing only a small cup, no larger than a thimble, filled with dirty water, and said it was all the water he could get.

Glooskap knew then that his people had told him the truth about Bull Frog's wickedness. In great anger he went himself to the mud where Bull Frog dwelt and asked for water. But Bull Frog stubbornly refused to let the water come forth. Then Glooskap grasped Bull Frog with a mighty grip and squeezed him tight until he crumpled his back and made him soft. With great force he hurled him far out into the mud, and said, 'Henceforth you shall live in dirty water; and you shall always croak with a dry throat, as a punishment for your sins.' Then with his own magic power he brought forth water so that the stream flowed again, and the people all rejoiced. He promised that never again should any creature have power to dry up the streams. And since that time Bull Frog has lived in muddy pools; he still croaks, for his throat is always dry, and to this day his back is wrinkled and crumpled and bears the marks of Glooskap's mighty fingers. And since that day the supply of clear fresh water has never failed in the country and the streams have never dried up.

Glooskap was always kind to his people. He taught the men how to hunt and how to build huts and canoes. He taught them what plants were good to eat, and he told them the names of all the stars. But he did not dwell among his men. He dwelt apart from them in a great tent, but when they sought him they always found him. He never married as they did. There dwelt with him as his housekeeper a very wise old woman; her name was Dame Bear, but Glooskap called her always 'grandmother.' With him too there lived a little boy whom Glooskap always called 'little brother.' And Glooskap gave him a magic root from the forest by the use of which he could change his shape into various forms. Whether or not Dame Bear was really his grandmother or the little boy his brother, no man knows. But both lived with him until his death.

Glooskap and Dame Bear and the little boy lived together for many ages. Glooskap had a magic belt which gave him power over sickness and hunger and danger and death. And anyone on whom it was placed was given the same strange power. And while Glooskap was with them, his people lived very happily. They never wanted for food or clothing. For Glooskap was kind to his people and wished them to be contented and at peace.

9. How Rabbit Lost His Tail

WHEN Glooskap first created the animals in Canada, he took good care that they should all be friendly to himself and to his people. They could all talk like men, and like them they had one common speech. Each had a special duty to do for Glooskap, and each did his best to help him in his work. Of all the animals, the gentlest and most faithful was Bunny the Rabbit. Now, in those first days of his life, Rabbit was a very beautiful animal, more beautiful than he is to-day. He had a very long bushy tail like a fox; he always wore a thick brown coat; his body was large and round and sleek; his legs were straight and strong; he walked and ran like other animals and did not hop and jump about as he does now. He was always very polite and kind of heart. Because of his beauty and his good qualities, Glooskap chose him as his forest guide, his Scout of the Woods. He gave him power that enabled him to know well all the land, so that he could lead people and all the other animals wherever they wished to go without losing their way.

One day in the springtime it chanced that Bunny sat alone on a log in the forest, his long bushy tail trailing far behind him. He had just come back from a long scouting tour and he was very tired. As he sat resting in the sun, an Indian came along. The Indian was weary and stained with much travel, and he looked like a wayfarer who had come far. He threw himself on the ground close to the log on which Rabbit sat and began to weep bitterly. Bunny with his usual kindness asked, 'Why do you weep?' And the man answered, 'I have lost my way in the forest. I am on my way to marry this afternoon a beautiful girl whom her father pledged to me long ago. She is loved by a wicked forest Fairy and I have heard that perhaps she loves him. And I know that if I am late she will refuse to wait for me and that she will marry him instead.' But Rabbit said: 'Have no fear. I am Bunny, Glooskap's forest guide. I will show you the way and bring you to the wedding in good time.' The man was comforted and his spirits rose, and they talked some time together and became good friends.

When the man had somewhat got back his strength, they began their journey to the wedding. But Rabbit, being nimble-footed, ran fast and was soon so far in advance of his companion that he was lost to view. The man followed slowly, catching here and there through the green trees a glimpse of his guide's brown coat. As he stumbled along, thinking of his troubles, he fell into a deep pit that lay close to the forest path. He was too weak to climb out, and he called loudly for help. Bunny soon missed his follower, but he heard the man's yells, and turning about, he ran back to the pit. 'Have no fear,' said Rabbit as he looked over the edge, 'I will get you out without mishap.' Then, turning his back to the pit, he let his long bushy tail hang to the bottom. 'Catch hold of my tail,' he ordered, 'hold on tight and I will pull you out.' The man did as he was told. Rabbit sprang forward, but as he jumped, the weight of the man, who was very heavy, was more than he could bear, and poor Bunny's tail broke off within an inch of the root. The man fell back into the pit with a thud, holding in his hand poor Rabbit's tail. But Bunny in all his work as a guide had never known defeat, and he determined not to know it now. Holding to a strong tree with his front feet, he put his hind legs into the pit and said to the man, 'Take hold of my legs and hang on tight.' The man did as he was told. Then Rabbit pulled and pulled until his hind legs stretched and he feared that they too would break off; but although the weight on them was great, he finally pulled the man out after great difficulty. He found to his dismay that his hind legs had lengthened greatly because of their heavy load. He was no longer able to walk straight, but he now had to hop along with a strange jumping gait. Even his body was much stretched, and his waist

41

had become very slender because of his long heavy pull. The two travellers then went on their way, Bunny hopping along, and the man moving more cautiously.

Finally, they reached the end of their journey. The people were all gathered for the wedding, and eagerly awaiting the coming of the bridegroom. Sure enough, the forest Fairy was there, trying by his tricks to win the girl for himself. But the man was in good time, and he married the maiden as he had hoped. As he was very thankful to Bunny, he asked him to the marriage dance and told him he might dance with the bride. So Rabbit put rings on his heels and a bangle around his neck, after his usual custom at weddings, and joined the merry-makers. Through the forest green where they danced many tiny streams were flowing, and to the soft music of these the dance went on. As the bride jumped across one of these streams during her dance with Bunny, she accidentally let the end of her dress drop into the water so that it got very wet. When she moved again into the sun, her dress, because of its wetting, shrank and shrank until it reached her knees and made her much ashamed. But Rabbit's heart was touched as usual by her plight; he ran quickly and got a deer skin that he knew to be hidden in the trees not far away, and he wrapped the pretty skin around the bride. Then he twisted a cord with which to tie it on. He held one end of the cord in his teeth and twisted the other end with his front paws. But in his haste, he held it so tight and twisted it so hard that when a couple waltzing past carelessly bumped into him the cord split his upper lip right up to the nose. But Rabbit was not dismayed by his split lip. He fastened on the bride's new deer-skin gown, and then he danced all the evening until the moon was far up in the sky. Before he went away, the man and his bride wanted to pay him for his work, but he would not take payment. Then the bride gave him a new white fur coat and said, 'In winter wear this white coat; it is the colour of snow; your enemies cannot then see you so plainly against the white ground, and they cannot so easily do you harm; but in summer wear your old brown coat, the colour of the leaves and grass.' And Bunny gratefully took the coat and went his way.

He lingered many days in the new country, for he was ashamed to go back to his own people with his changed appearance. His lip was split; his tail was gone, and his hind legs were stretched and crooked. Finally, he mustered up his courage and returned home. His old friends wondered much at his changed looks, and some of them were cruel enough to laugh at him. But Bunny deceived them all. When they asked him where he had been so long, he answered, 'I guided a man to a far-off land which you have never seen and of which you have never heard.' Then he told them many strange tales of its beauty and its good people.

'How did you lose your fine tail?' they asked. And he answered, 'In the land to which I have been, the animals wear no tails. It is an aristocratic country, and wishing to be in the fashion, I cut mine off.'

'And why is your waist so slender?' they asked. 'Oh,' replied Bunny, 'in that country it is not the fashion to be fat, and I took great trouble to make my waist slight and willowy.' 'Why do you hop about,' they asked, 'when you once walked so straight?' 'In that land,' answered Bunny, 'it is not genteel to walk straight; only the vulgar and untrained do that. The best people have a walk of their own, and it took me many days under a good walking-teacher to learn it.'

'But how did you split your upper lip?' they asked finally. 'In the land to which I have been,' said Bunny, 'the people do not eat as we do. There they eat with knives and forks and not with their paws. I found it hard to get used to their new ways. One day I put food into my mouth with my knife—a very vulgar act in that land—and my knife slipped and cut my lip, and the wound has never healed.'

And being deceived and envying Bunny because of the wonders he had seen, they asked him no more questions. But the descendants of Rabbit to this day wear a white coat in winter and a brown one in summer. They have also a split upper lip; their waist is still very slender; they have no tail; their hind legs are longer than their front ones; they hop and jump nimbly about, but they are unable to walk straight. And all these strange things are a result of old Bunny's accident at the man's wedding long ago.

10. The Partridge and His Drum

IN FAR back times when only Indians dwelt in Canada, Glooskap, who was Lord and Master of the tribes, chose Partridge from among all his creatures to be the boat-builder for the birds of the sea. Partridge was then a very wonderful bird, very different from what he is today. He dwelt always along the ocean shore, on the banks of great rivers, and he could swim like a duck or a gull. He could change his shape to that of a man. He knew all the country well, and often he wandered far through the woods looking for good trees from which to build his boats. Among all the people he was held in high regard because of his skill. He was always industrious and always busy, and at all hours of the day and late into the night, he could be heard hammering at his canoes, making a sound like a man tapping quickly on a drum. But he lost his reputation through no fault of his own. He no longer builds boats; the power to make the strange sound of his hammering is all that remains with him of his former greatness.

It happened that one very cold day Partridge walked alone over the snow in the deep forest near the shore of a great lake, looking for lumber for his boats. On the bank of a stream he saw four beautiful maidens sitting on the ice braiding their long hair. He knew that they were the nymphs or fairies of the stream, and he watched them from behind a tree. He had long desired to win a stream fairy for his bride, but up to that time he had found it an impossible task, for the fairies were very timid. As he watched them now, he thought to himself, 'Perhaps I can catch one of them and carry her off.' So he stealthily slipped from behind the tree and crept along towards the bank. But the water-nymphs, who could hear the smallest sound, heard his footsteps, and looking around,

they spied him among the trees. 'Oh, oh!' they all cried, and at once they all dropped into the icy water and disappeared.

Now, Partridge, being then a river-dweller and of very great strength, was a good fisherman. Many a time he had caught the slippery harbour seals, and often he had dined plentifully on their meat. He hit upon a crafty trick by which to seize a nymph. He cut a number of branches from a spruce tree, and sticking them upright in the snow on the shore, he hid behind them, and waited for the nymphs to appear again. Sure enough they soon came back and sat again upon the ice braiding their long hair. Partridge put his head over the boughs to take a peep at them so that he might pick out the most beautiful, but again they saw him, and with the same frightened cry, 'Oh, oh!' they dropped quickly into the sea. After them went Partridge, although he knew that the water was very cold. He caught one, but she slipped from his arms, and when he came to the surface, he had only her hair ribbon in his hand.

Now, in those old days water-nymphs in this part of the sea could not live long without their hair ribbons, for the ribbons contained always much of their magic power. Partridge knew this, and he knew too that sooner or later the nymph would wander about on land looking for her lost charm. So he put the ribbon in his pocket and with a light heart he went about his business of seeking wood for his boats. That night when he went back to his tent he hid the ribbon not far from his hand in hope of the fairy's visit; then, pretending to sleep, he closed his eyes and

45

waited. He had not been there long when there came in very softly the beautiful water-nymph in search of her lost ribbon. Now, when a water-nymph sets foot in the dwelling of man or animal without her hair ribbon, she is always powerless. This Partridge knew well. He sprang quickly from his couch, caught her with little trouble, and easily persuaded her to remain with him as his wife. This was against Glooskap's orders, for Glooskap knew that if one of his people married a water-nymph no good could come of it. But Glooskap said nothing.

Partridge and his nymph-wife lived happily enough for a time. But he always feared for her safety when he went far away looking for lumber for his boats, for many evil creatures were always about in the forest. And he always said to her before he went away, 'Keep the doors tightly barred while I am gone, for many wicked people and robbers prowl through the woods, and they will try to enter the tent perhaps to kill you.' And she always promised to be on her guard.

One day Partridge went far away in search of lumber for a new fleet of boats he was then building. In the afternoon he came to a grove of wonderful cedar trees. He wished to examine it carefully, and as night was coming on—for winter nights come early in the Canadian woods— he decided to stay there until the next day. So as the day went down, he made a bed of boughs and went to sleep. He had no fear for his wife's safety, for she had promised to keep the doors barred.

Meanwhile, his wife waited at home for his coming. When the stars came out, she knew that he would not come home that night, and being sleepy she went to bed, first seeing that the doors were securely fastened. She felt very lonely all by herself in the big tent, for Partridge, because of the troublesome noise of his boat-building, dwelt a good distance away from his neighbours. At midnight she was awakened by a loud knocking at the door. 'Open the door,' said a voice outside; 'I am cold and hungry and I have come far.' But mindful of the warning of Partridge, the nymph-wife paid no heed to the call. Now, the voice was that of a wicked sorcerer who always prowled through the forest, and who knew that Partridge was away. He wished to kill and eat the nymph. He was a very clever and sly fellow, and he could imitate the voices of all men and animals to lure people to their death. For a long time after his first call he was silent. Then he knocked again and imitated the voice of the nymph's brothers and sisters, and said, 'Oh, sister, we have followed you for a long time until at last we have found you; open the door to us.' But still the nymph was suspicious and refused to unbar the door. Then the sorcerer imitated her father's voice and called her 'daughter.' But still she would not let him in. At last he talked like her mother, and said, 'Oh, daughter, open the door; I have come far in search of you, and I am very cold and hungry and tired.' The nymph-wife was deceived at last, for she thought the voice was that of her old mother from the stream. Hastily she opened the door. At once the wicked sorcerer—the evil spirit of the woods— pounced upon her, and killing her at a blow, he greedily devoured her like a wolf, until not a bone was left.

The next morning Partridge came home. He found the door of his house open and his wife absent. He wondered greatly, for he remembered her promise, and he could not believe that she had been killed. So he resolved to use his magic power to learn where she had gone. He took his magic wooden plate and filled it with water, and placed it in a corner of the tent while he slept. When he awoke, the dish was full not of water but of blood, and he knew from this sign that his wife had been killed by the sorcerer. He determined to punish her slayer, and taking his axe and his bow and arrows and his magic charm, he left his work and set out in pursuit of the sorcerer. He knew that the sorcerers travelled in pairs; he knew too that they had many tricks by which to escape punishment, and that they could take on various shapes. So he went along cautiously.

By evening he reached a great lone land in the far north where he thought he found traces of two of the evil ones. He came to a large cave which he entered, intending to pass the night there. From a huge rock at the side of the cave a man's foot was sticking. He knew that here was one of the sorcerers who had gone into the rock to sleep as was their custom, leaving his foot sticking out so that his comrade could pull him out when he had slept long enough. Partridge quickly cut off the foot close to the rock, and there the sorcerer was left closed up forever in the stone. There the rock remains to this day. Just as Partridge had finished the cutting, the sorcerer's companion came in, and Partridge knew—for he had seen him often about his tent—that here at last was the murderer of his wife. When the sorcerer saw no foot sticking from the rock, he knew at once that his brother was forever locked up in the stone, and he became very angry. Then he saw Partridge whom he knew to be his brother's slayer, but giving no sign of his knowledge, he received him kindly. He bolted the door of the cave, and then made a great fire thinking to roast Partridge alive and thereby have a good meal. But

Partridge used his magic charm against heat and helped the sorcerer to pile more wood on the fire, saying that he was very cold. Soon the cave grew hotter and hotter until at last its sides became red and the flames shot high to the roof, and even before he knew it the sorcerer was overcome by the great heat. Partridge threw him upon the fire, where he was quickly burned to cinders. Then, well pleased with his vengeance, he returned quickly to his home.

But from that day poor Partridge was never himself again. He sorrowed greatly for his dead nymph-wife, until he became stupid and could not do his work well, but he went faithfully about his duties, finishing the great fleet of boats for the birds and animals. Finally came the day when all were to be launched, and Glooskap and all his people gathered to see the fleet go by. It was a very wonderful sight on a great inland sea. The eagle had a large canoe which he paddled with the ends of his wings; all the birds of the sea and the river had very wonderful boats—the crane and the duck, the snipe and the curlew, the plover and the gull, the wild goose and the loon and the kingfisher. And the boats were all of different colours, each colour the same as that of the bird for whom the boat was made. All the birds were supplied with boats. Even the humming-bird had a tiny canoe of many wonderful colours, and he had a little paddle not larger than a small pin.

Partridge's own canoe was the last to be launched. The people all watched for it in patience and eagerness, for they thought that because he had built such wonderful boats for the other birds, he would have a particularly good one for himself. Now, Partridge had built his own canoe last, while he sorrowed for his dead wife. His brain had been muddled by his great grief. He reasoned foolishly that since a boat with two ends could be rowed in two directions, a boat with no ends at all could be rowed in all directions. So he made his own boat round like a saucer. But when it was launched and he tried to paddle it, he made no headway, for it turned round and round but always stayed in one place. All the people and the birds when they saw it laughed heartily at him and called him 'fool'. Then poor Partridge's grief was increased. He knew that he had forever lost his reputation as a boat-builder among the birds of the sea. He had no wish to dwell longer among them, and he decided to leave them for ever. So he flew far away into the forest, and since that time he has never been seen upon the shore of the sea, nor near a river or lake. He stays on land—far in the deep woods, and he has forgotten even how to fish and how to swim. But he still keeps one remnant of his old life. He still makes a drumming noise as if he is hammering a canoe, and deep in the forest you can still hear his strange sound. You know then that he is mindful of old times when he built boats upon the shore and all day long and far into the night tapped lightly with his hammer.

11. How Summer Came
to Canada

ONCE during Glooskap's lifetime and reign in Canada it grew very cold. Everywhere there was snow and ice, and in all the land there was not a flower nor a leaf left alive. The fires that the Indians built could not bring warmth. The food supply was slowly eaten up, and the people were unable to grow more corn because of the hard frozen ground. Great numbers of men and women and children died daily from cold and hunger, and it seemed as if the whole land must soon perish.

Over this extreme cold Glooskap had no power. He tried all his magic, but it was of no avail. For the cold was caused by a powerful giant who came into the land from the far North, bringing Famine and Death as his helpers. Even with his breath he could blight and wither the trees, so that they brought forth no leaves nor fruit; and he could destroy the corn and kill man and beast. The giant's name was Winter. He was very old and very strong, and he had ruled in the far North long before the coming of man. Glooskap, being brave and wishing to help his people in their need, went alone to the giant's tent to try to coax or bribe or force him to go away. But even he, with all his magic power, at once fell in love with the giant's home; for in the sunlight it sparkled like crystal and was of many wonderful colours, but in the night under the moonlight it was spotlessly white. From the tent, when Glooskap looked out, the face of the earth was beautiful. The trees had a covering of snow that gave them strange fantastic shapes. The sky was filled by night with flashing quivering lights, and even the stars had a new brightness. The forest, too, was full of mysterious noises. Glooskap soon forgot his people amid his new surroundings. The giant told him tales of olden times when all the land was silent and white and beautiful like his sparkling tent. After a time the giant used his charm of slumber and inaction, until Glooskap fell asleep, for the charm was the charm of the Frost. For six months he slept like a bear. Then he awoke, for he was very strong and Winter could not kill him even in his sleep. But when he arose he was hungry and very tired.

One day soon after he awoke, his tale-bearer, Tatler the Loon, brought him good news. He told of a wonderful Southland, far away, where it was always warm, and where lived a Queen who could easily overcome the giant; indeed, she was the only one on earth whose power the giant feared. Loon described carefully the road to the new country. Glooskap, to save his people from Winter and Famine and Death, decided to go to the Southland and find the Queen. So he went to the sea, miles away, and sang the magic song that the whales obeyed. His old friend Blob the Whale came quickly to his call, and getting on her back he sailed away. Now, the whale always had a strange law for travellers. She said to Glooskap: 'You must shut your eyes tight while I carry you; to open them is dangerous, for, if you do, I will surely go aground on a reef or a sand bar and cannot get off, and you may then be drowned.' And Glooskap promised to keep his eyes shut. Many days the whale swam, and each day the water grew warmer, and the air grew gentler and sweeter, for it came from spicy shores; and the smells were no longer those of the salt sea, but of fruits and flowers and pines. Soon they saw in the sky by night the Southern Cross. They found, too, that they were no longer in the deep sea, but in shallow water flowing warm over yellow sands, and that land lay not far ahead. Blob the Whale now swam more cautiously. Down in the sand the clams were singing a song of warning, telling travellers in these strange waters of the treacherous sand bar beneath. 'Oh, big whale,' they sang, 'keep out to sea, for the water here is shallow and you shall come to grief if you keep on to shore.' But the whale did not understand the language of the little clams. And he said to Glooskap, who understood, 'What do they sing?' But Glooskap, wishing to land at once, answered, 'They tell you to hurry for a storm is coming—to hurry along as fast as you can.' Then the whale hurried until she was soon close to the land. Glooskap, wishing the whale to go aground so that he could more easily walk ashore, opened his left eye and peeped, which was contrary to the whale's laws. And at once the whale stuck hard and fast on the beach, so that Glooskap, springing from her head, walked ashore on dry land. The whale, thinking that she could never get off, was very angry, and sang a song of lament and blame. But Glooskap put one end of his strong bow against the whale's jaw, and taking the other end in his hands, he placed his feet against the high bank, and, with a mighty push, he sent old Blob again into the deep water. Then, to keep the whale's friendship, he threw her an old pipe and a bag of Indian tobacco leaves—for Glooskap was a great smoker—and the whale, greatly pleased with the gift, lighted the pipe and smoking it swam far out to sea. Glooskap watched her disappear from view until he could see only clouds of her smoke against the sky. And to this day the whale has Glooskap's old pipe, and sailors often see her rise to the surface to smoke it in peace and to blow rings of tobacco smoke into the air.

When the whale had gone, Glooskap walked with great strides far inland. Soon he found the way of which Loon had told him. It was the Rainbow Road that led to the Wilderness of Flowers. It lay through the land of the Sunrise, beautiful and fresh in the morning light. On each side were sweet magnolias and palms, and all kinds of trees and flowers. The grass was soft and velvety, for by night the dew was always on it; and snow and hail were unknown, and winds never blew coldly, for here the charm of the Frost had no power.

Glooskap went quickly along the flower-lined Rainbow Road, until he came to an orange grove where the air was sweet with the scent of blossoms. Soon he heard sounds of music. He peered through the trees, and saw that the sounds came from an open space not far ahead, where the grass was soft and where tiny streams were flowing and making melody. It was lilac-time in the land, and around the open space all kinds of flowers in the world were blooming. On the trees numberless birds were singing—birds of wonderfully coloured feathers such as Glooskap had never heard or seen before. He knew that he had reached at last the Wilderness of Flowers, of which old Tatler the Loon had spoken. He drew deep breaths of honeysuckle and heliotrope and countless other flowers, until he soon grew strong again after his long voyage.

Then he crept close to the edge of the open space and looked in from behind the trees. On the flower-covered grass within, many fair maidens were singing and dancing, holding in their hands chains of blossoms, like children in a Maypole game. In the centre of the group was one fairer than all the others—the most beautiful creature he had ever seen —her long brown hair crowned with flowers and her arms filled with blossoms. For some time Glooskap gazed in silence, for he was too surprised to move or to utter speech. Then he saw at his side an old woman—wrinkled and faded, but still beautiful—like himself watching the dance. He found his voice and asked, 'Who are those maidens in the Wilderness of Flowers?' And the old woman answered, 'The maiden in the centre of the group is the Fairy Queen; her name is Summer; she is the daughter of the rosy Dawn—the most beautiful ever born; the maidens dancing with her are her children, the Fairies of Light and Sunshine and Flowers.'

Glooskap knew that here at last was the Queen who by her charms could melt old Winter's heart and force him to go away, for she was very beautiful and good. With his magic song he lured her from her children into the dark forest; there he seized her and held her fast by a crafty trick. Then, with her as a companion, he began his long return journey north by land. That he might know the way back to the Wilderness of Flowers, he cut a large moose hide, which he always carried, into a long slender cord, and as he ran north with Summer, he let the cord unwind behind him, for he had no time to mark the trail in the usual way. When they had gone, Summer's children mourned greatly for their Queen. For weeks the tears ran down their cheeks like rain on all the land, and for a long time, old Dawn, the Queen's mother, covered herself with dark mourning clouds and refused to be bright.

After many days, still holding Summer in his bosom—for she loved him because of his magic power—Glooskap reached the Northland. He

53

found none of his people, for they were all asleep under the giant's power, and the whole country was cold and lonely. At last he came to the home of old Winter. The giant welcomed him and the beautiful girl, for he hoped to freeze them both and keep them with him always. For some time they talked together in the tent, but, although he tried hard, the giant was unable to put them to sleep. Soon old Winter felt that his power had vanished and that the charm of the Frost was broken. Large drops of sweat ran down his face; then his tent slowly disappeared, and he was left homeless. Summer used her strange power until everything that Winter had put to sleep awoke again. Buds came again upon the trees; the snow ran down the rivers, carrying away the dead leaves; and the grass and the corn sprang up with new life. And old Winter, being sorrowful, wept, for he knew that his reign was ended, and his tears were like cold rain. Summer, the Queen, seeing him mourn and wishing to stop his tears, said: 'I have proved that I am more powerful than you; I give you now all the country to the far north for your own, and there I shall never disturb you; you may come back to Glooskap's country six months of every year and reign as of old, but you will be less severe; during the other six months, I myself will come from the south and rule the land.' Old Winter could do nothing but accept this offer gracefully, for he feared that if he did not he would melt entirely away. So he built a new home farther north, and there he reigns without interruption. In the late autumn he comes back to Glooskap's country and reigns for six months, but his rule is softer than in olden times. And when he comes, Summer, following Glooskap's moose-hide cord, runs home with her birds to the Wilderness of Flowers. But at the end of six months she always comes back to drive old Winter away to his own land, to awaken the northern world, and to bring it the joys that only she, the Queen, can give. And so, in Glooskap's old country Winter and Summer, the hoary old giant and the beautiful Fairy Queen, divide the rule of the land between them.

12. How Turtle Came

ON THE shores of a great water in Canada is a land where Indians once dwelt. In the days of French rule it was a garrisoned fort. The remains of the old moat and ramparts and stockade are still seen in the centre of what is now a large green meadow; but they are now overgrown with grass, and should you go there, on summer days you can see children playing upon them, picking wild flowers and making daisy chains, unmindful of the past fortunes of the spot on which they play. Behind you across the river which empties here is a city in modern dress. Before you is the sea with two little islands not far away resting in the summer haze upon its bosom. Moaning gas-buoys toss about in the gentle roll of the waters; by night red beacon lights lift their bright heads all about to light the sailor's road; summer cottages nestle on the beach before you; the hum of modern life is in your ears and the sight of it is in your eyes as you stand to-day upon the cliff.

But it was not always so. Long before the coming of the white race, before beacon lights and cities and summer cottages were known, this land was the home of Indians. Many of their descendants live there still, at peace with the white folk who took their lands and their forests. They are the remnants of Glooskap's people. It was here, on the beach in the little cove, that the Turtle was first created and where he first dwelt. Long ago, after the white men came, he fled from these waters; and although his descendants are still sometimes caught by fishermen off the coast, neither he nor his children nor any of his tribe ever went back to the place of his creation. But the place of his birth is still pointed out.

It was in Glooskap's time that the Turtle came into being. There dwelt in the land an old Indian, a lazy, poor, and by no means beautiful man. As a hunter he had been of no value; he lived alone; and now he had come to the end of his life with little of the world's goods to his credit. But although he was poor, he was of a merry heart and a good nature, and he was well liked by all. Now, the chief of the tribe had three beautiful daughters who were much sought for by the young men of the village, all of whom wished to win their love. The eldest was the loveliest in the land; her name was Flower of the Corn. The old Indian would gladly have made one of these girls his wife for he was tired of living alone, but she on her part thought him worthless, and he on his part feared that if he wooed her, her many other suitors would be jealous and would perhaps take his life. So the old man kept his secret to himself and continued his sad existence.

It happened that one day Glooskap came into the land to see his people. Of all the tents in the village he chose that of the old man as his resting place, for he had known him a long time and liked him because of his good nature and his merry heart. He was not with him long before he knew his secret, that he loved Flower of the Corn; and he also learned of his fear to woo her. Glooskap encouraged him and urged him to make his wishes known to the chief. But the old Indian said, 'I am old and poor and I have no good clothes to wear, and I know that I should meet only with scorn.' But Glooskap placed upon him his magic belt, and at once the old man became young and handsome; he also gave him fine clothes. Then he sent him to the chief's home. And the old man said, after the fashion of Indians when they wish to marry, 'I am tired living alone. I have come for your eldest daughter.' And the old chief, when he saw him so beautiful because of Glooskap's magic power, could not refuse his request and Flower of the Corn became his bride.

As the old man had feared, the young men of the village were very angry because he had won so beautiful a wife, and they resolved to do him harm. At first they tried to take vengeance on Glooskap, for as they had seen little of him they did not know of his great power. A great wedding feast was held for the old man and his bride, to which all the young men were invited. Two of the most jealous sat next to Glooskap, one on each side, and during the feast they plotted to kill him. But Glooskap heard them plotting against his life and he knew that the time had come for him to show his strength. So at the end of the wedding feast, as he arose from the table he turned to each one and tapped him gently on the nose. When each rubbed the spot that Glooskap had touched, he found that his nose had disappeared. In great shame and anger they fled from the feast, and never afterwards dwelt among men. One of these was Toad; the other was Porcupine. And since that time neither Toad nor Porcupine has ever had a nose and their faces have always been flat because of Glooskap's touch at the banquet long ago.

Some days after the wedding feast, a great festival was held in the village. Glooskap knew that here again an attempt would be made upon the old Indian's life by his jealous enemies. He feared too that after he had gone from the village his old friend would surely be treacherously killed, and, as the time of his going away was at hand, he resolved upon a plan to save him from danger. He told the old man that at the festival his enemies would try to trample him under their feet during a game of ball. And he gave him a magic root which, if he ate it before the game, would give him power to jump high when they crowded in upon him. Sure enough, in the game of ball the young men surrounded the old man and watched for a chance to crush him. Twice he jumped high over their heads and escaped unhurt. But the third time when he jumped he stuck upon the top of a tent and could not get down.

Inside the tent sat Glooskap quietly smoking his pipe and waiting for this very thing to happen. He made a smouldering fire from which the smoke rose in great clouds and passed out at the top of the tent around the old man, and he smoked and smoked great pipefuls of tobacco until far into the night. And the old man hung to the tent poles, dangling in the smoke until midnight. He hung there so long that from the smoke of the smouldering fire and that of Glooskap's pipe, his old skin became as hard as a shell. And Glooskap said to him, 'I have done this thing for your own good. I fear that if I leave you here, after I have gone your enemies will kill you. I make you now chief of the Tortoise

57

race and your name shall be called Turtle; hereafter you may roll through a flame of fire and you will not be burned nor will you feel pain, and you may live in water or on land as you prefer. And you shall have a very long life; and although your head be cut off you shall live nine days afterwards. And when your enemies throw you into the fire or into the water you need have no fear.' Then he took him down from the tent pole.

The next day the old Indian's enemies, angry because he had escaped at the festival, built a great fire in the forest, and seizing him as he walked alone in the woods, they threw him upon it. But he went to sleep in the flame and when he awoke he called for more wood, telling them that he was very cold. They wondered greatly, and after plotting together they resolved to throw him into the sea. They carried him far out in a canoe and dropped him overboard, and went ashore well pleased with their work, for they believed that at last they had taken vengeance. The next day was a day of great heat. At low tide when some of his enemies looked out to sea they saw basking in the sun on a sand-bar far away a strange figure. They were curious, and they rowed out to see what it was that shone so brightly in the sun. When they reached the sand-bar after paddling a long time they saw that it was the old Indian. There he was, sunning himself on the sand-bar, his hard smoked back shining in the bright light. As they came near, he said, 'Good day,' and grinning at them mischievously, he rolled lazily off the sand-bar and disappeared in the water.

Glooskap before he left the island, used his magic power to change Flower of the Corn in the same way and he sent her into the sea to live with her husband. And he gave her power to lay eggs in the sand. And the two lived happily for many long years, and raised up a mighty race. But still the Turtle rolls sideways into the sea like his old ancestor if men come near him as he suns himself on the sand. And you can still see on his back the marks of Glooskap's smoke. When the white men came, he left the land of his creation, but his descendants to this day live to a great age and grow to a great size along the Atlantic coast.

13. The First Mosquito

WHEN Glooskap lived with his people it happened once that the tribes grew jealous of his power. This jealousy was not because of any evil in themselves; it was prompted by a wicked sorceress who during the absence of Glooskap prevailed upon the people to do him harm. Some said that the sorceress was angry because she had once loved Glooskap and he had refused to return her love; others said that she was much older than Glooskap, that before his birth she had herself ruled the earth for a long time, and that when Glooskap came he had put an end to her reign. The truth of the matter no man knows, but it is certain that she was very powerful and that she always watched for a chance to harm Glooskap.

Her chance came when Glooskap went for six weeks on a hunting trip far into the forest. She then told the people that he was neglecting them, and she soon persuaded them to pack up and leave him, for she believed that he would perish if he were left alone. When the people went away, they took with them Dame Bear, Glooskap's old grandmother, and his little brother, whom Glooskap had left behind. The band journeyed hastily across the land to the sea; then they sailed in their canoes to a great island, where they stopped and set up their tents. And the sorceress left the road they travelled well guarded by evil beasts and dragons who, she hoped, would kill Glooskap if he tried to follow them. She made Dame Bear and the little boy her slaves, and compelled them to do much hard work. She gave them but little food and but scanty clothing, so that they were soon very miserable.

When Glooskap came back to his home at the end of six weeks, he found that his people had disappeared. His friend Fox, who had watched slyly the people's departure and the wicked woman's tricks, told him all that had happened. Glooskap did not blame his people, for he knew that their going away had been brought about by his old enemy. But that he might teach his people the folly of their act—for he knew that they would now be very hungry and poor—he tarried alone in his home-land for many years before he set out to find them and to take vengeance on their wicked leader. Then, taking his magic belt and his two dogs, he set out upon his long journey. He went across the sea to another land, and then he travelled eastward, his dogs following close behind him. Here he was far from the road that his people had travelled, and there were no dragons to bar his progress.

Soon he came to a village where the people were friendly. He heard from an old man and woman about the road along which the sorceress and his own people had passed. The old man told him of the dragons ahead of him and of the evil, hideous creatures that had been left to guard the way. But Glooskap, unafraid, and trusting in his dogs and his magic belt, set out along the enchanted road. At last he came to a narrow pass in the hills watched over by two terrible dogs. He put his magic belt around the necks of his own dogs for a moment, and at once they grew to an immense size; and they easily killed the beasts of his enemy, and he passed on unharmed.

After some hours he came to a high hill. At the bottom was a large tent in which he knew, from the tale of the old man of the friendly village, that a wicked man lived with his two beautiful daughters. He knew too that they waited his coming, for prompted by the sorceress they wished to kill him. As he looked down from the top of the hill, he saw the two daughters approaching afar off. They were very beautiful and fair; but Glooskap remembered the old man's warning and he resolved to be on his guard. One of them carried in her hands a string of costly beads. They met him with pleasant smiles and invited him to the tent below the hill; and they tried to place the beads about his neck to show him their great love. But Glooskap knew that the beads were enchanted, and that if he placed them around his neck he should lose his strength and power. So he set his dogs upon the girls, and the dogs were so terrible because of his magic belt that the girls ran away in great fear; as they ran, they dropped the string of beads, without which they had no power. Glooskap picked up the beads and then cautiously entered the tent of his enemies. On a couch of skins near the door the old man was dozing, and before he could rise, Glooskap placed the beads about his neck and killed him with a blow. Then he went on his way. He met with many enemies on this evil road, but by the aid of his dogs and his magic belt and the enchanted beads he overcame them all and was unharmed.

At last he reached the sea, and he looked over the dark water to another land and wondered how to get across. Finally, he sang the magic song that the whales always obeyed. Old Blob the Whale came quickly to his call, and getting on her back he sailed away to the eastward. His two dogs swam close behind Old Blob. The Whale soon brought him to the land where he knew that his people dwelt. He sprang ashore, his dogs following him, and set out with long rapid strides in search of his enemies. At the end of a few hours' journey he found traces of old camp-fires, and he knew that his people were not far away. At last he reached the place where they were living. In the distance he saw a camp, which because of his magic power he knew to be that of the sorceress. Near by was his little brother, whom the wicked sorceress had made her slave; he was pale and much worn, and he was clad only in rags; he was seeking wood for a fire, and as he gathered up the dry sticks he cried, and sang a song of lament—'Where is Glooskap, my big brother? Alas! he is far away, and I shall never see him again.' Then Glooskap took pity on his little brother, and gave a signal that the little boy knew well. And his brother, turning around, spied Glooskap behind the trees afar off, and running to him cried out with joy, for he knew that help had at last come.

But Glooskap knew that to overcome his great enemy and to free his people, he must be very careful and use his craftiest tricks. He told his little brother to be silent, and to tell no one but Old Dame Bear, the grandmother, that he had come. He sent him back to his hard work in the camp, and promised that when the twilight came he should be freed. And he said, 'Do what you can to make the wicked woman angry, for when anger comes to her, her power leaves her; when you are sent to rock her baby to sleep at twilight, snatch it from its cradle and throw it into the camp-fire. Then run to me where I hide here among the trees; take Dame Bear with you, and all will be well.'

His little brother then went back to his hard work in the woman's tent and told Dame Bear what he had seen and heard. And the two waited patiently for the twilight. At the sunset hour the little boy, still supperless, was sent by the sorceress to rock her baby to sleep. For the first time in his long separation from his big brother he worked with joy, and without hunger, for he knew that he would soon be free. Suddenly he snatched from the cradle-hammock the woman's baby—a

61

wicked child like her mother—and hurled her into the camp-fire. Then, taking Dame Bear by the arm, he ran towards Glooskap's hiding place. The baby howled with pain and cursed loudly as she had heard her mother do, and rolled herself out of the fire. And the sorceress was very angry, and muttering dire threats she ran after the boy and Dame Bear. They soon reached Glooskap, who sprang from his hiding place, his magic belt around him. When the sorceress saw Glooskap, she was more angry than before, so that her strength left her and she was powerless. Yet she gave battle.

Glooskap tore up a huge pine tree from its roots and hurled it at his enemy. It entered her side and stuck there, and although she tried with all her might she could not draw it out. Glooskap could now have killed her with a blow, but he did not wish to do that. He wanted to let her live in misery, and to give her a greater punishment than death. And so, yelling with pain and shame, the sorceress ran back to her tent, while Glooskap took Dame Bear and his little brother to his own camp among the trees and gave them food. He knew now that the battle was over, for it had long been known that if the wicked woman's side was once pierced her power would never return.

When Glooskap's people heard that he had come, they rejoiced greatly, for they were hungry and cold. The sorceress had failed to provide food for them, and they were tired of her wicked and cruel rule which was very unlike that of Glooskap. But Glooskap tarried before making friends again with them, and remained for many days in his own camp in the trees watching them from afar. His dogs guarded his grove and kept all away except Dame Bear and his little brother. Meanwhile, the wicked sorceress in pain with the pine tree in her side moved about in great anger, but as her power was now gone, the people refused longer to obey her. And they all laughed at her because of the pine tree sticking in her side. At last, being very angry, she said, 'I do not wish to live like this when my power is gone. All the people laugh at me because of the pine tree sticking in my side. I wish that I might change to something that would always be a plague and a torment to man, for I hate mankind.' Glooskap heard her wish, although he was afar off, and with his magic power he changed her at once to a mosquito. Then he forgave his people, and as they were hungry he gave them much food and drink, for he had killed many moose in the land. And the people all rejoiced and promised never again to forsake him or to be jealous of his power.

Then Glooskap gathered his people on the shore of the great ocean, and calling the whales, his sea carriers, he bade them carry him and his people from this land back to their old home. There they settled down again in peace. But to this day the wicked sorceress roams over the earth as a mosquito; and the pine tree in her side is a sharp sting. She is never at rest, but she shall always remain as she wished, a torment to mankind. The only thing on earth she dreads is fire and smoke, for she still remembers that the throwing of her baby into the fire long ago caused the outburst of anger that in the end deprived her of her strength. And by fire and smoke in the summer twilight men still drive her and her descendants from their dwellings.

14. The Moon and His Frog-Wife

WHEN Glooskap first reigned upon the earth, what is now the Moon shone by day and what is now the Sun shone by night. Their work was exactly opposite to what it is to-day, for the present Moon was then the Sun and the present Sun was then the Moon. The Moon was then very red and bright; the Sun was pale and silvery. At that time the Sun—the present Moon—kept very irregular hours, and was very careless about his work. Sometimes he rose very early in the morning and set very late at night; at other times he rose very late and went to bed very early. For weeks in the winter he refused to shine at all, and even when he did appear at his work he gave very little warmth and he might just as well have been covered in his clouds. The Moon—the present Sun—was, on the other hand, always faithful to his duties.

At last the people grew tired of the Sun's strange actions and irregularities. They protested loudly against his methods of work, until in the end they sent some of their number to complain to Glooskap. Glooskap rebuked the Sun, but the latter answered that he had done his work as well as he could, and that his accusers were merely his enemies. Glooskap had really been too busy to notice the Sun's way of working; so, that he might treat all with fairness, he said to the accusers: 'Charge the Sun formally and openly with neglect of his duty; I will call a great meeting of all my people; we will hold a trial to judge him; I myself will be the

64

judge; whoever wants to give evidence may do so, and the Sun may make his defence.' To this all the people and the Sun agreed.

Now, in those days the Sun had many wives. With some of them he was far from happy, for often they sorely tormented him and tried his patience, and a few of them he would gladly get rid of if he could. One of his scolding wives was Frog. She had a crumpled back and a wrinkled face and a harsh voice; she was always jumping about, and with her of all his wives he was on the least friendly terms. When she heard that her husband was to be tried before Glooskap on a serious charge, she wished to be present at the trial, for she was very inquisitive. But the Sun said, 'This trial is for men, not for women; your place is at home and not in the courts of warriors; you must not come.' The Frog-wife pleaded to be allowed to go, but the more she pleaded the more sternly the Sun refused his permission. However, being a woman, and not to be outdone by a man, she resolved to go to the trial whether her husband permitted it or not, and she decided to steal into the court quietly after the trial had commenced.

At last the day of the trial arrived. The great court-tent was filled with Glooskap's people. In the centre of the platform sat Glooskap, and near him sat the Sun, eager to defend himself from the charges of his enemies. When the trial was well advanced, and the evidence had nearly all been taken, the Sun's Frog-wife appeared suddenly at the door. All the seats were filled, but Glooskap with his usual politeness arose to find her a place. But when the Sun saw her there contrary to his wishes, he was very angry. He looked at her sternly with a frown, making at her a wry, twisted face; and drawing down his right eyelid, he said to Glooskap, 'Oh, Master, do not trouble yourself to find her a seat; let her sit on my eyelid; that is a good enough seat for her; she can hang on there well enough, for she always wants to stick to me and follow me wherever I go.' And at once the Frog-wife jumped to his eyelid and sat there quite comfortably.

Then the trial went on. Because of the Sun's clever defence of himself he was declared 'not guilty' of the charges against him. It was decided by the judge, Glooskap—and all the people, even the accusers, agreed—that under the circumstances he had done his work as well as he could, and that he deserved neither blame nor punishment. But at the close of the trial, when the Sun attempted to go back to his work, he could not get rid of his Frog-wife. He tried with all his might but he could not shake her off. She stuck fast to his eyelid and stubbornly refused to leave her seat, and she said that henceforth she would stay with him to see that he did his work well. All the people pulled and tugged and coaxed, but they failed to move her. The strongest men in the land came, but even they could not pull her away. Then the people lamented and said to Glooskap: 'She covers the side of the Sun's face and hinders his work; she makes him ugly; we must not have our Light of Day disfigured like this and bright on one side only; all the world will laugh at us. What are we to do?' And they were in great sorrow and distress.

But Glooskap in his wisdom found a way out of the difficulty. He said: 'Be not troubled, O my people! We will make the Moon and the Sun exchange places; the Moon, who is still perfect and unharmed, shall become the Light of Day instead of Night, and shall take the name Sun. The Sun shall become the Light of Night instead of Day, and shall take the name Moon; for at night it will matter little if one side of his face is dark; and his Frog-wife hanging to his eyelid will by night be little noticed.' To this the people all agreed. And so the Sun was changed with the Moon to shine by night, and the Moon was changed with the Sun to shine by day.

So now when the Moon—the old Sun—first appears at his work, he holds away from the earth the side of his face to which his Frog-wife is hanging, for he is very much ashamed of his appearance. And when he turns his head full upon the earth, you can still see, when the sky is clear, his black Frog-wife hanging to his right eyelid and covering one side of his face. And always when his month's work is nearly done he turns his head abruptly in a frantic effort to shake her off, but he never succeeds. She hangs there always, and because of his Frog-wife's curiosity he shall never shine again by day.

15. Glooskap and the Fairy

ONE day Glooskap was in his tent with his old Grandmother. They heard a great noise. 'A very big man is coming,' said Glooskap, 'I hear his footsteps.' Time passed but no one came. Soon they heard a great noise again. 'He must be a *very* big man,' said Glooskap; 'the earth is trembling under his tread, for the calves of my legs are shaking; he is coming nearer.' Soon there was a knock at the door. 'Come in,' said Glooskap. In came a little fellow no bigger than a man's thumb. 'You walk very heavily and make a great noise for so small a man,' said Glooskap. 'Yes,' said the little fellow; but not another word would he say.

They sat silent for a long time. Then Glooskap tried to put his strange little caller to the test. 'Take something to eat,' he said, and he passed him a plateful of food. With his magic power he made the plate very heavy, and he thought that the little man could not hold it but would let it fall on his toes. But the little fellow took it easily, and held it while he ate all it contained. When he had finished eating, he passed it back. But it had grown so heavy because of the little man's power that Glooskap could hardly hold it up.

Then they went outside. It was blowing very hard. 'It is a windy day,' said Glooskap. 'Oh no,' said the little fellow, 'it is very calm and pleasant; I should like to have a sail on the sea.' Glooskap had a very large heavy canoe. He thought it would be fun to send the little fellow sailing in it, for he thought he could not paddle it. He told him there was a canoe on the beach and that he might take it for a sail. The little man thanked him and went to the beach. Glooskap went back to his tent on the high cliff to watch what would happen. Soon he saw the little man out on the sea in the big heavy canoe. Then he untied the wings of the great Wind Bird, and the winds blew harder than ever and the waves rolled high. But the little man weathered the storm all right; he seemed to be enjoying his sail, and after a time he came ashore safely.

When he came in, Glooskap said, 'Did you have a good sail?' 'Very good,' replied the little man, 'but I like stronger winds and a rougher sea.' And Glooskap wondered much. Then they went outside again. It was still blowing hard. The little man blew through his nostrils, and the wind from them blew so hard that the grass fell down before it, and Glooskap was knocked head over heels and had to put his arms around a big tree and hold on tight to keep from blowing over the cliff. Then the little man stopped blowing, and they agreed to end their contest and to rest together. Glooskap knew that the little man was the strong Fairy of the forest of whom he had long heard. The Fairy gave him new power to overcome evil, and then went back to the land-of-little-people from which he had come.

16. The Passing of Glooskap

GLOOSKAP, the magic master of the Indian tribes along the Atlantic coast of Canada, had very great power for many ages. But as he grew old, his power gradually grew less. He had done in his long lifetime many great and noble deeds. He had freed his land of all the mighty monsters that had inhabited it before his coming. No evil beasts nor serpents nor dragons were now found near his home, and there were no longer cruel giants in the forest hard by. He had made his people happy. But, strangely enough, his people showed him but scanty gratitude. When he grew old they became evil, and they were not as faithful as in the days of his youth and strength. Even the animals grew treacherous. His dogs, once loyal, were no longer eager to do his bidding, and one stormy day as he fished for porpoises they stubbornly refused to obey his command to head off the fish. Thereupon, in anger, he changed his dogs into a stone island, now a rocky light-housed island on the Atlantic coast. All around him he saw signs of faithlessness, and often he was in great sorrow because of his people's ingratitude.

One afternoon in the autumn, Glooskap walked alone by the ocean, thinking silently of his people's evil ways and of his own vanished strength. Behind him the tall trees rose on the hills, their leaves now turned to a mass of many colours, yellow and red under the autumn sun. Here and there clusters of red autumn berries peeped through the dying leaves. On the high bank long stalks of golden-rod nodded their faded heads; the grass was withered brown, and from its depths came the doleful sounds of crickets. Before him lay the sea, still and idle and grey in the soft mellow light. Subdued noises came from the tents near by, where his people, busy and expectant, were making arrows for the great annual autumn hunt, for the hunter's moon had come. Otherwise, a strange silence—the silence of Nature's death—filled the air. Glooskap knew, as he moodily walked along the beach, that Summer had gone, that she had fled from the Northland, following the moose-hide cord he had placed for her along the Rainbow Road to the Wilderness of Flowers. Closing his eyes, he could see her again in all her beauty as he had really seen her many years before when he had first found her dancing among her children, the Fairies of Flowers and Light. All the incidents of his long journey in search of her came back to him—the sail with Old Blob the Whale; the Southern Cross in the sky; the song of the clams under the golden sands; the lilac country with its magnolia and jessamine; the fair maiden dancers on the green; and Summer herself with her brown hair and her blossoms. Even his lost youth and his vanished strength seemed to come back to him. He could feel on his old cheeks again the soft air of the Southland; he could hear the music of its tiny streams; and he opened his nostrils wide in fancy to pleasant odours from scented flowers. And as he dreamed of the old days, he was lonely for Summer his Fairy Queen; for although he was a great warrior he had a woman's tender heart. Somehow, on this autumn day he was filled with a strange feeling of melancholy such as he had never known before. He could not shake the feeling from him. It brought him a deep sense of coming danger which he could not explain.

Suddenly he was aroused from his dreaming by the appearance of his messengers, the Loons, who were still loyal to him. They had been away many days in search of news, and now they came to him over the water uttering strange cries that sounded like foolish laughter. Glooskap knew from their cries that they brought unwelcome tidings. When they met him on the beach they said, 'Oh, Master, we bring you a sad message. From away across the ocean a race of strange pale-faced men is coming, smaller in size than our people but more powerful. One of their number is more than a match for a score of your best warriors, for they carry with them many deadly weapons the like of which you have never seen. They are coming in wonderful ships greater than your canoes. They will take all your lands, and will kill those of your people who refuse to submit to their rule.' The Loons would have continued their story, but Glooskap wished to hear no more. He understood now the cause of his melancholy dread. He knew that the pale race of which the Loons had spoken was the race of which he had long heard, and that the white men were coming at last. He knew too that it would be useless to stay to give them battle. His reign on earth, he knew well, was ended for a time and now he must go away. Far out to sea was another hunting ground to which he must sail to join his fathers. It was a place, he had been told, pleasanter by far than his old home on the shores of the great water—a place to which good warriors went when their work on earth was done. So he returned silently to his tent to get ready for his long journey.

That night he called all his people to the gathering-place. He told them that he was going away, far away, miles and miles over the sunlit sea. Not one of them should go with him. He would be away, he said, many long years, but some day he would come back. He told them nothing of the message of the Loons, nothing of the white men's coming. But he offered as a parting gift to grant them each one last wish. And at once all the people wished for what they most desired, and all their requests were granted; for Glooskap's great power returned for a brief space before he went away.

The people's wishes were very strange and varied. An old man who had been of little value as a hunter asked that he might be great in the killing of game. And Glooskap gave him a magic flute, which when played upon won the love of women, and brought the moose and caribou to his side to meet their death. And the old man, with not a care in his heart, went his way, for he knew now that he should always have food. A young Indian asked that he might have the love of many people. Glooskap gave him a bag very tightly tied; he told him not to open it until he reached his home, and then his wish would be granted. But the youth, being curious, opened the bag on the way. At once there flew from it numberless girls, all of whom strove for his affection, until in the struggle they trampled him to death. What became of the people no man knows. Another, a gay and frivolous fellow, asked that he might always amuse people. Glooskap gave him a magic root from the forest which would cause anyone who ate it to amuse all whom he met; he told him not to eat it until he reached his home, and then his presence

71

would always be like sunshine to all. But he, being curious, ate the root on the way. For a time he amused all who met him, so that they all laughed and were of a merry heart. But soon, because he had not heeded Glooskap's command, the people grew tired of him and no longer laughed at him. And he grew weary of himself and found no pleasure in his power, which now no longer moved people to laughter. And his life became a burden until in despair he killed himself in the forest. And Old Night Hawk, the evil spirit of the night, came down from the clouds and carried him away to the dwelling place of Darkness and he was never afterwards heard of among men. Another wished to become a Fairy of the Forest. Glooskap washed him in the sea, and put a magic belt around his waist, and at once he became a Fairy Prince dwelling among the Elves. And he gave him a small pipe which made wondrous music, and to this day you can hear his pipe on sunny days in the meadows.

But the wish that was most difficult to gratify, for it tried Glooskap's greatest power, was that of a youth who wanted to win a beautiful girl for his wife. She was the daughter of a powerful chief, who placed such hard work and cruel tasks on all who desired her that they died in attempting them. Glooskap gave him his stone canoe and bade him sail away to the chief's home; he gave the Fairies of the Deep charge over him, and he tied the wings of the great Eagle, the Wind Bird, so that there might be no wind during his voyage. He gave him also a magic belt and taught him a magic song, both of which should help him in his need.

Soon the youth came without mishap to a large island, the home of the girl he loved. He hid the canoe in the trees and set out inland. At the end of a long road he reached the village where the cruel chief and his daughter lived. He said to the chief, after the fashion of Indians when they want to marry, 'I am tired of the lonely life; I have come for your daughter.' The chief replied that the youth might have his daughter if he could do certain feats of strength. The youth knew that these were the feats the attempt of which had cost many before him their lives, but trusting to Glooskap's help, he consented. The chief told him he must slay a great horned dragon that lived in the forest hardby, and that he must bring the dragon's head to his tent on the following morning.

In the night the youth went to the dragon's den. Over the mouth of it he placed a great log; then standing near it he sang the magic song that Glooskap had taught him. Soon the dragon came out in answer to the magic call; he waved his head all about looking for the sound; then he placed his head over the log to listen. At once the youth severed the creature's head with a blow of his axe, and taking it by one of its great horns he brought it in the morning to the chief's camp. And the chief, greatly surprised, said to himself, 'I fear he will win my daughter.' There were other difficult feats to try the young man's courage, but all of them he did without harm to himself, and with great wonder to the old chief.

Finally, the chief used one of his last and hardest tests. He said, 'There is a man of my tribe who has never been beaten in running; you must race with him and beat him if you would win my daughter; you must both run around the world.' The old man was sure that here at last the youth would fail. But the youth put on the magic belt that Glooskap had given him, and when all the people were gathered to watch the contest, he met his rival without fear. He said to the chief's runner, 'What do men call you?' And he answered, 'I am Northern Light; and what do men call you?' The youth answered, 'I am Chain-Lightning.'

The starting signal was given by the chief, and the two rivals set out on their race. In a moment they were out of sight, away behind the distant hills. The people all waited patiently for their return. Soon the youth, Chain-Lightning, appeared; he had been around the world, but he was not breathing hard and he was not even tired from his long run. There was yet no sign of his rival. Late in the evening Northern Light came in; but he was very weary, and as he came near he trembled and tottered. He confessed that he had not been all around the world; he had turned back, for Chain-Lightning had gone too fast for him, yet he was very tired. He admitted his defeat. The people wondered greatly at the power of the victorious youth. And the old chief said, 'I fear he has won my daughter.'

There was still a final test. The chief said, 'There is a man of my tribe who has never been overcome in diving and swimming under water. You must strive with him and defeat him if you would win my daughter.' And the youth agreed. Again he put on the magic belt and met his rival without fear. When they met by the sea the youth asked the chief's swimmer, 'What do men call you?' And he replied, 'I am Black Duck; and what do men call you?' He answered, 'I am Loon.' When the chief gave the signal they dived and swam under water. In a few minutes Black Duck rose again, for he was out of breath; but the people waited in wonder many hours before Loon rose; and when he came up he was not tired, but laughed heartily. And the old chief, well content, said to him, 'My tests are ended; you have won my daughter.' That night the great wedding feast was held; and the youth taking with him his bride, set sail for his home in Glooskap's canoe.

A few of those who asked gifts, Glooskap punished before he went away, because of their foolish requests. One who came was very tall and proud of his good looks. He always covered his moccasins with bright beads, and wore coloured coats, and sprinkled himself with strange perfumes, and on the top of his cap he wore a long feather. He asked Glooskap to make him taller and straighter than any of his fellows. And when Glooskap heard his wish, to punish him for his pride he changed him at once to a pine tree. He made him very tall and straight until his head rose above the forest. There he stands to this day, the high green feather in his cap waving always in the wind. And when the wind blows you can still hear him singing with a moaning voice, 'I am a great man, I am a beautiful Indian, taller than my fellows.' Many others Glooskap punished, but all who had diseases he healed, and sent away happy.

When Glooskap knew that the wishes of all the good people who had obeyed his commands had been granted, he was ready to set out on his last journey. One day on the shore of the wide ocean he made a great feast to which all his people came and all the animals with them. But it was not a merry gathering, for they knew that they met with Glooskap for the last time before his long absence. In the late autumn afternoon, when the feast was ended, Glooskap prepared to leave them. He threw his kettle into the sea, for he would need it no more, and it became an island. And he tied one wing of the Wind Bird, so that after he had gone away the gales would not blow so strong on the Atlantic coast as they had blown in his lifetime. And he talked long to his people and smoked his last pipe with them and gave them good advice; he spoke of his going away, but of the land to which he was going he would say nothing; he promised that some day after many years had passed he would come again among them. Then in the evening a great stone canoe came over the ocean, guided by two of the Children of Light. And Glooskap, seeing it, said, 'It is now the sunset hour, and I must leave you.' Many of his people, his good followers who throughout his lifetime had been faithful to him, begged him to allow them to go with him. But he answered, 'No; this last great journey I must make alone, for no man can come with me or help me.' And just at the turn of the tide as the sun set behind the distant hills, he embarked in the great stone canoe and sailed far out to sea with the ebbing tide, singing as he went a strange sad song. His people and all the beasts looked after him until in the deepening twilight they could see him no more; but long after they had lost sight of him, his song came to them, weird and doleful, across the water; gradually the sounds grew fainter and fainter, until when night came they died entirely away. Then a strange silence fell upon the earth. The beasts mourned until they lost the power of speech; they fled into the forest in different ways, and since that time they have never met together in peaceful council as in the olden days, and they have never spoken like men. The Great Owl departed in sorrow, and hid himself in the deep forest; since that time he has seldom appeared by day, but at night he always cries, 'Koo-koo-koo,' which in the Indian language means, 'I am sad, I am sad.' And the Loon, Glooskap's old messenger, wanders up and down upon the beach calling for his master with loud wild cries. And Glooskap's people grow smaller and smaller in number because of their Master's absence, and they slowly waste away until some day they too shall vanish from the earth.

So Glooskap sailed away over the sea to the distant hunting grounds of his fathers. There he lives still in a great long tent, where he is making arrows, preparing for his last Great Battle. And when the thunder rolls and the lightning flashes those of his people who still remain on earth know that he is angry; where the sea sparkles most brightly in the sunlight or moans most dismally in the storm, they know that Glooskap is there; when the phosphorescent lights appear at night upon the sea, they know that he is working late by the strange light; and when there are no stars, they know that Glooskap lies asleep, taking his rest. But when his great tent is filled with arrows, Glooskap will come back to fight his last battle and overcome the evil creatures of the world; he will then bring back the Golden Age of happiness to earth; and his people in hope and patience still await his coming.

17. The Indian Cinderella

ON THE shores of a wide bay on the Atlantic coast there dwelt in old times a great Indian warrior. It was said that he had been one of Glooskap's best helpers and friends, and that he had done for him many wonderful deeds. But that, no man knows. He had, however, a very wonderful and strange power; he could make himself invisible; he could thus mingle unseen with his enemies and listen to their plots. He was known among the people as Strong Wind, the Invisible. He dwelt with his sister in a tent near the sea, and his sister helped him greatly in his work. Many maidens would have been glad to marry him, and he was much sought after because of his mighty deeds; and it was known that Strong Wind would marry the first maiden who could see him as he came home at night. Many made the trial, but it was a long time before one succeeded.

Strong Wind used a clever trick to test the truthfulness of all who sought to win him. Each evening as the day went down, his sister walked on the beach with any girl who wished to make the trial. His sister could always see him, but no one else could see him. And as he came home from work in the twilight, his sister as she saw him drawing near would ask the girl who sought him, 'Do you see him?' And each girl would falsely answer 'Yes.' And his sister would ask, 'With what does he draw his sled?' And each girl would answer, 'With the hide of a moose,' or 'With a pole,' or 'With a great cord.' And then his sister would know that they all had lied, for their answers were mere guesses. And many tried and lied and failed, for Strong Wind would not marry any who were untruthful.

There lived in the village a great chief who had three daughters. Their mother had long been dead. One of these was much younger than the others. She was very beautiful and gentle and well beloved by all, and for that reason her older sisters were very jealous of her charms and

76

treated her very cruelly. They clothed her in rags that she might be ugly; and they cut off her long black hair; and they burned her face with coals from the fire that she might be scarred and disfigured. And they lied to their father, telling him that she had done these things herself. But the young girl was patient and kept her gentle heart and went gladly about her work.

Like other girls, the chief's two eldest daughters tried to win Strong Wind. One evening, as the day went down, they walked on the shore with Strong Wind's sister and waited for his coming. Soon he came home from his day's work, drawing his sled. And his sister asked as usual, 'Do you see him?' And each one, lying, answered 'Yes.' And she asked, 'Of what is his shoulder strap made?' And each, guessing, said 'Of rawhide.' Then they entered the tent where they hoped to see Strong Wind eating his supper; and when he took off his coat and his moccasins they could see them, but more than these they saw nothing. And Strong Wind knew that they had lied, and he kept himself from their sight, and they went home dismayed.

One day the chief's youngest daughter with her rags and her burnt face resolved to seek Strong Wind. She patched her clothes with bits of birch bark from the trees, and put on the few little ornaments she possessed, and went forth to try to see the Invisible One as all the other girls of the village had done before. And her sisters laughed at her and called her 'fool'; and as she passed along the road all the people laughed at her because of her tattered frock and her burnt face, but silently she went her way.

Strong Wind's sister received the little girl kindly, and at twilight she took her to the beach. Soon Strong Wind came home drawing his sled. And his sister asked, 'Do you see him?' And the girl answered 'No,' and his sister wondered greatly because she spoke the truth. And again she asked, 'Do you see him now?' And the girl answered, 'Yes, and he is very wonderful.' And she asked, 'With what does he draw his sled?' And the girl answered, 'With the Rainbow,' and she was much afraid. And she asked further, 'Of what is his bowstring?' And the girl answered, 'His bowstring is the Milky Way.'

Then Strong Wind's sister knew that because the girl had spoken the truth at first her brother had made himself visible to her. And she said, 'Truly, you have seen him.' And she took her home and bathed her, and all the scars disappeared from her face and body; and her hair grew long and black again like the raven's wing; and she gave her fine clothes to wear and many rich ornaments. Then she bade her take the wife's seat in the tent. Soon Strong Wind entered and sat beside her, and called her his bride. The very next day she became his wife, and ever afterwards she helped him to do great deeds. The girl's two elder sisters were very cross and they wondered greatly at what had taken place. But Strong Wind, who knew of their cruelty, resolved to punish them. Using his great power, he changed them both into aspen trees and rooted them in the earth. And since that day the leaves of the aspen have always trembled, and they shiver in fear at the approach of Strong Wind, it matters not how softly he comes, for they are still mindful of his great power and anger because of their lies and their cruelty to their sister long ago.

18. The Boy and His Three Helpers

AN INDIAN boy lived alone with his parents in the Canadian forest. His parents were very old, and the boy took care of them and hunted and provided them with food. He was always kind to them, and they told him that because of his goodness to them he would never lack happiness and good fortune. But soon his parents died, and the boy was left alone in the world. He lived far from other people, and now that his parents were gone, he decided to leave his old home and find friends elsewhere. One day before he left home, while he was hunting he killed a raven with his arrow. When he picked up the bird from the snow it was bleeding, and red blood stained his black, glossy feathers. He looked at the dead bird and said, 'I wish I could find a comrade whose hair is as black as the raven's wing, whose skin is as white as the snow, and whose lips are as red as these blood stains.' As he spoke, an old man came along and said, 'I will help you to find such a comrade. I have heard of your goodness.' So he gave the boy a belt and told him to wear it always, and that it would bring to him those who could help him. Then he went away and the boy went back to his own home.

The next day he left his old home and set out to see the world beyond the hills. He was not merry as he went on his way, for he did not gladly leave all behind him. As he went along he met a man on the trail. One of the man's legs was bent up at the knee, and his foot was tied to his thigh, and he hopped along on one foot. The boy said, 'Why are you hopping along on one foot?' The man said, 'If I did not tie up my leg, I would run so fast that I would be around the world in a few seconds. I know that you are in search of a beautiful comrade. I have come to go along with you.' Then he untied his leg, and in a moment he was out of

79

sight. In a few seconds he came back from the opposite direction. He had been around the world. So the man and the boy went along together.

The next day they met a man on the trail with his nose covered up. The boy said, 'Why do you keep your nose covered?' The man said, 'If I did not keep my nostrils covered, I would blow so hard that there would always be a whirlwind where I am. You are in search of a beautiful comrade. I have come to help you.' Then he uncovered his nostrils, and at once there was such a wind that trees were torn down and the man and the boy were knocked head over heels. So the three went along together.

The next day they saw a man in the forest who was cutting down a hundred trees with one blow of his axe. He said to the boy, 'You are in search of a beautiful comrade. I have come to help you.' So the four went along together. Soon they came to a village where a great chief lived. The chief had a beautiful daughter; her skin was as white as snow, her lips were as red as blood, and her hair was as black and glossy as the raven's wing. The boy said, 'She shall be my comrade. I must win her.' So he went to the chief and made known to him his wishes. But the chief said, 'The task of winning my daughter is difficult and dangerous. The men of your party must do very hard feats of strength. If they fail, they shall all be put to death. If they succeed, you may have my daughter. But I do not want to give her to a stranger.' The boy agreed to attempt the difficult feats and to risk his life and the lives of his party in the effort.

The first feat was a test of speed between one of the boy's party and one of the chief's. The boy untied his friend's leg, and the two rival runners set out on their race. They were to run around the world. The boy's runner came in far ahead and won the race. The next feat was a test of strength in moving rocks down a mountain side. The boy took the Wind-Blower to the mountain top. He uncovered his nostrils, and the contest began. The Wind-Blower blew so hard that the rocks on his side of the hill were all blown down in an instant, and he won the contest. Then the chief said, 'The next and last contest is a test of skill and strength in building a house from trees in the forest. I want to see how quickly you can build a house for my daughter.' Then the Pine-Chopper went to work, striving with the chief's builder. With one blow of his axe he felled a hundred trees. Then he trimmed them, and he had the house completed before his rival had trees enough cut down. Then the chief said, 'You may take my daughter.'

After the wedding feast the four men and the bride set out on their journey home. The chief gave them a canoe and told them to go home by sea as the way was shorter. So one morning they set out. But when they were far out on the ocean, they saw a great storm coming behind them on the water. The chief had sent it after them; he hoped to drown them all, for he would rather see his daughter dead than wedded to a stranger. But before it reached them, the Wind-Blower rose in the canoe, and uncovered his nostrils and began to blow. Soon his breath met the wind-storm and there was a great struggle. But he soon overcame the storm and forced it back. The sea around them remained calm, and they reached the land unharmed. Then the Pine-Chopper built a house for the boy and his bride. The boy thanked his three friends for their help. They told him that if he ever needed them again they would come quickly to his aid. Then they went on their way. The boy and his bride lived happily in their new home. But he always kept the old man's belt near him to aid him in times of need.

'I
wish I
could find
a comrade
whose hair is as black as
the raven's wing,
whose skin is as white as
the snow,
and whose lips are as
these blood stains.'

19. The Duck with Red Feet

A HUNTER in old times lived on the bank of a river far away in the Canadian forest. He passed all his days in the deep woods where he had great success in catching and killing game. There was no better hunter then he in all the country. Every evening he returned to his home, bringing his day's catch with him. His father and mother were both dead and he had no sister. He had only one brother. This brother was very small. He was so small that the hunter kept him in a little box; when he went away in the morning to hunt, he always closed the box up tight so that his little brother could not get out, for he feared that if he got out harm would come to him. Every night he took him out of the box to give him food, and the little man was so hungry that he always ate a great lot of food. The little man slept always with his brother, but every morning he was carefully locked up in the box. And in time he grew very tired of his prison.

One evening as the hunter came down the river from his hunting journey he saw a very beautiful girl sitting on the bank of the stream. He decided he would catch her and take her home to be his wife, for he was lonely. He paddled to the beach as silently as he could, but she saw him coming and she jumped into the water and disappeared. She went to her home at the bottom of the river and told her mother that the hunter had tried to catch her. But her mother told her that she should not have run away. She said, 'The hunter who tried to catch you was intended to be your husband. You must wait for him to-morrow and tell him you will be his wife.'

The next night as the hunter came down the river, the girl was again sitting on the bank. He paddled over as he had done on the evening before, but this time she did not run away. She said, 'I have been waiting for you. You may take me for your wife.' And the man, well pleased with his beautiful prize, placed her in his canoe and took her home. He did not tell her of his little brother in the box. He cooked a beaver for the evening meal. He and his wife ate half of it, but he placed the other half away in the cupboard. Then he told his wife to go to sleep, and she went to bed and soon fell asleep. When she awoke in the morning her husband had gone for his day's hunting, for he had to leave early to go a long distance into the forest. She found too that the half of the beaver he had put in the cupboard was gone. And she wondered what had become of it.

That evening when her husband came home, he cooked another beaver for their meal. Again they ate one half of it, and the man placed the other half of it to one side. But not a word did he say of his brother in the box. Then the man sent his wife to bed as on the previous night, and soon she was fast asleep. When she awoke in the morning, her husband was gone for his day's hunting. The half of the beaver which he had placed to one side was also gone, but she knew he had not taken it. She was afraid, and all day she wondered where the meat had gone. She decided that she would find out what had happened to it.

That night when her husband came home, he cooked half a small moose for their evening meal. They ate part of it, and the man placed the remainder of it to one side as usual. Then he told his wife to go to sleep. She went to bed and pretended to sleep, but she stayed wide awake, peeping through half-closed eyelids. When her husband thought she was sleeping soundly, he unlocked a little box that stood on a low shelf, and took out a little man and gave him the moose meat he had put aside. The little man ate every bit of it. He looked very strange. He was all red from head to heels, as if he were covered with red paint, and he said not a word. When he had greedily eaten all the meat, the man washed him and combed his hair and then put him back in the box and locked him up. The woman wondered greatly at this strange happening,

83

but she could not keep from laughing heartily to herself because of the funny appearance of the little red man.

The next day the man left early for his day's hunting. When she was sure he was far away, she thought she would take a peep at the queer little red man in the box. She found the key hanging on the wall, and opened the box and called to the little man to come out. But he would not come. He seemed to be very much afraid of her. She coaxed him to come out, but he refused. Then she caught him and pulled him out. He looked at her for a long time, but he would say not a word. Then he ran to the door, which was open, and with a sudden jump he sprang into the air and disappeared. The woman called to him but he would not come back. He was never seen again. The woman was very much afraid. But she was more frightened when she looked at her hands. They were all red because she had caught the little red man, and many red spots were on her arms and on her feet where the red colouring from the man had dropped. She tried to wash off the red spots, but she could not remove them. She washed and rubbed her hands all day, but the stains would not come off. When her husband came home in the evening, he knew when he saw her red hands what had happened. He knew that his brother of the box had gone. And he was very angry. He seized a rod and ran at her to beat her. She was afraid he would kill her, and she ran to the river and jumped in to go back to her old home. But as she reached the water, she was changed from what she was. At once she became a Sheldrake Duck. The red spots remained on her, and the sea could not wash them off. And to this day the Sheldrake Duck has red stains on her feet and feathers, because she was curious and took the funny little red man from the box in the olden days.

20. The Northern Lights

ONE autumn day in old times a woman and her infant son were lost in the Canadian woods. The woman was going back to her home from a long journey, and in some strange way she wandered from the path. The more she walked about, the more confused she became, and for many days she searched for the right road, but she could not find it. All the time she lived on berries and on the little food she carried. At last she found a cave in the woods, and she decided to use it for a home. She had not been long in the cave when a large bear came in, and she knew then that she had taken refuge in a bear's den. She thought the bear would kill her and her child. But the bear was good. He looked upon them as his own kind and soon they all became friends. The bear hunted during the day, and each night he brought to the cave much meat, which the woman cooked. So they lived comfortably through the long winter.

After a time the woman's child grew to be a very strong boy. The bear taught him to wrestle, and after a few weeks' practice the boy could throw down his teacher. And the mother said, 'He will be a great warrior,' for she knew that his strength was more than human. When the boy grew large and strong enough to take care of his mother, they decided to try to find the way back to their old home. So one day they said goodbye to the bear, and set out on their journey. After many hardships and dangers they reached their native village where the people, who had thought them dead, received them with great rejoicing. The boy continued to grow in strength until the people said they had never seen anyone so powerful. There was no limit to his strength.

One day the boy said to his mother, 'I am going to travel far away until I find other men who are as strong as I am. Then my strength will be tested and I will come back to you.' His mother agreed that he should go, and one morning he set out on his strange journey. He came to the bank of a river, and there he saw a man standing not far ahead of him. As he looked, a large canoe came drifting down the river, filled with people. They had lost their paddles. One of the people called to the man on the bank and asked him to help them to land. The man put out a long pole and placed the end of it under the canoe, and lifted the canoe and all the people to the beach. 'There,' thought the boy, 'is a man as strong as I am.' Then the boy ran to the spot and picked up the canoe full of people and carried it up to the bank. He spoke to the man and told him of his own great strength. Then he said, 'We are two strong men. Let us go along together until we find a third man as strong as we are.' The man agreed, and he went along with the boy. They travelled far that day, and in the afternoon they came to a country of high rocky hills. It was a lonely and silent place, and no people seemed to be living in it. At last they saw a man rolling a large stone up the side of a mountain. The stone was as large as a house, and the mountain was very steep, but the man rolled the stone up with ease. He had rolled it half way up when the two strangers came along. The boy picked up the stone and threw it to the top of the mountain without difficulty. And the roller-man looked at them with great wonder. Then the boy told him of the strength of himself and his comrade, and said, 'We are three strong men. Let us go hunting together.' The man agreed, and the three went along together.

They built a house for themselves, to live in while they hunted. They agreed that only two of them should go away at once to hunt, and that the other should stay at home to look after the place and to prepare the evening meal. They decided that each should stay at home in his turn. The next day, the man of the river bank who had lifted the canoe stayed at home. Towards evening he got ready for the coming of his comrades, and he cooked a good meal to have waiting for them. Just as he had finished cooking it, a small boy came in and asked for food. He was very small and worn and ragged, and the man pitied him and told him to eat what he wanted. The boy ate and ate until he had eaten all the food prepared for the three strong men. Then he went away and disappeared in the side of the mountain. When the two hunters came home they were very hungry, and they were cross when they heard that their meal had all been eaten up. And they vowed vengeance on the little glutton who had taken all their food.

The next day it was the turn of the stone-rolling man to stay at home. In the evening he cooked a good meal for himself and his comrades. But before the hunters came home, the little boy came in again and asked for food. He looked so small and worn and he cried so bitterly that the man did not have the heart to send him away, and he told him to eat what he wanted. The boy ate and ate until not a scrap of food was left. Then he laughed and went out and disappeared in the mountain. When the two hunters came home, they were again very cross to find that their food had all been eaten up by a tiny boy.

The next day the strong boy stayed at home, while the canoe-lifter and the stone-roller went hunting. In the evening the small boy came again, just as he had done on the two previous days. He wept and asked for food. The strong boy told him to eat what he wanted. He ate and ate as before, until he had eaten up the whole meal. Then he got up to go out. But the strong boy caught him and held him fast. There was a long struggle, for the tiny boy was very powerful, and he was almost a match for the strong boy. But at last he was thrown down, and he pleaded for his life. The strong boy said he would spare him on condition that he would take him to his home. He wanted to see what kind of a place he lived in. And the small boy agreed. Then the strong boy went with him to the side of the mountain. When they reached it, the little boy said, 'I am the servant of a terrible giant, who has never been defeated in battle. I think you can overcome him. Take this stick and beat him with it, for it is the only thing that can give him pain.' Then he gave him a stick that lay on the ground, and they went on to the giant's cave in the side of the hill. When they went in, the giant sprang upon the strong boy. There was a long fight. It lasted for a whole day, and at last the strong boy overcame the giant and beat him dead with the magic stick. Then the little boy said, 'I will reward you for freeing me from my terrible master. I have three beautiful sisters, and you may have whichever one you want for your wife.' He took the strong boy to his home in a cave far down in a valley on the other side of a mountain, and there they found the three beautiful girls. The strong boy took the youngest one for himself, and he took the other two for his two comrades. When they came out of the cave, the strong boy found that they would have a very hard path to climb up the steep side of the mountain. Then luckily, as he thought, he saw his two strong comrades standing on the top of the high cliff far above him. They saw him and the three girls far below them. He called to them to let down a rope, and said, 'The three girls I have with me cannot climb the steep path. You must pull them up.' So the men above let down a strong cord and the strong boy sent up the two oldest girls first, one at a time. Then, before sending up his own choice, the youngest, he thought he would test the loyalty of his comrades. They were standing far back from the top of the cliff, holding the rope, and they could not see the boy and the girl below. The boy tied a heavy stone to the end of the rope, and called, 'I am going up next. Pull away.' The men pulled and pulled until they had drawn the weight near the top of the cliff. Then they cut the rope, and down crashed the stone to the bottom of the cliff, where it broke into many pieces. The men above hoped that they had killed their comrade. They did not think that he had meant the two fairy wives for them, so they decided to kill him. But they were outwitted by the boy and the stone. 'That is a fine way to reward my kindness,' said the boy to his girl companion when he saw the stone in pieces on the rocks. As he spoke he looked up and saw the two fairy girls running away from the two men above, who were left all alone. Then with the magic help of the little boy, the girls' brother, the strong boy at once punished the two men by making them follow the girls. They followed them on and on, but they never found them. And they still follow them; they wander always, and they are never at rest.

Then the strong boy left the little boy behind him to look after himself, and he took his fairy wife and climbed up the path and went to live far away in the forest. For a time they lived very happily. One day the boy said, 'I am going back to my old home to see my people. You must wait here, and in a few days I shall come back.' The girl did not want him to go; she feared he would forget her; but he told her that he must go. Then she said, 'When you reach your home, a small black dog will meet you at the door. It will jump to lick your hand. But do not let it touch you. It is an evil spirit in disguise, and if it licks your hand you will forget all about me and you will not come back to me.' The man promised to be on his guard, and he set out for his native place, leaving his wife behind him. Soon he reached his home, and as he opened the door, sure enough the black dog of which his wife had spoken jumped towards him. Before the strong boy could turn aside, the dog licked his hand as his wife had said. Then he forgot all about his old life in the forest; and he lived with never a thought of the fairy girl he had left behind him far away.

His wife waited long for him to come back. Then she knew that her husband had forgotten her because of the black dog, and late in the autumn she set out to find him. Soon she came to the place where he dwelt. It was morning, and she decided to hide until night, and then go to his home. She went to a stream that ran beside the village, and climbed into a tree that stretched out over the water. Near by was an old house in which an old man lived. The old man came to the brook for water, and as he bent down to fill his pail, he saw the face of the beautiful girl in the tree reflected in the stream. He called to her to come down from the tree. He had never seen a creature so lovely. He brought her to his tent and gave her food, and he told her that her husband had gone far up the river to hunt. In the evening she went along the river to wait for her husband as he came home. When she saw him coming in his canoe, she sat on the bank of the stream and sang her magic song. It was a song of wonderful melody, such as only fairy maidens can sing, and the sound went far over the water and charmed all who heard it. When her husband heard the song, he stopped to listen. He soon knew that the music was that of his fairy wife of the forest, for no one else on earth could sing so wonderful a song. Then his old life in the forest came back to his mind, with memories of the two strong men and the tiny boy and the three fairy girls. And he remembered his wife to whom he had promised to return. Then he paddled his canoe to the bank, and found his wife, and they were happy again. It was a cold autumn night and the moon was full, and his wife said, 'We must not stay here. This is a wicked place where men forget. If you stay here, you will forget me again.' Then she shuddered when she thought that her husband might forget her again, and he shuddered when he thought that he might lose her again. And they continued to tremble in fear. Then she said, 'We must go to another land. It is a more beautiful land than this. It is the Land of Eternal Memory where men and women never forget those they loved. I know where it is. We will go to it.' Then she sang her magic song, and at once a great bird came through the air to where they sat. And still trembling in fear lest they should forget each other, they sprang to the bird's back, and the bird carried them up to the sky. And there they were changed into Northern Lights. And you can still see them, with their children around them, on autumn nights in the north country, beautiful in the northern sky. And they still tremble when they think of the Land of Forgetfulness they have left and of the pain it caused them in the old days of their youth.

21. The Boy and the Robbers' Magical Booty

A VERY rich Seigneur lived once in a large town. He had three beautiful daughters and one son. The son was but a baby. The Seigneur wasted his money in wicked living. He spent much of his time in feasting and drinking and gambling. His wife and daughters were much troubled. Soon his money was all gone. But he decided that he would have to get more somewhere, for he wished to continue in his evil ways of living. One day he met a man in the fields. The man said, 'I have heard of your beautiful daughters. Will you give me the eldest for my wife?' The Seigneur said, 'You may have one if you pay me a great sum of money.'

So the man paid the money and took the eldest girl away. Then the Seigneur went back to his old ways. He spent his money on worthless friends, and he was idle for a long time. Soon his money was all gone. One day in the fields he met another man. The man said, 'I have heard of your beautiful daughters. Will you give me the oldest one at home for my wife?' The Seigneur said, 'You may take her if you will give me a great sum of money for her.' The man paid him the money and took the second girl away. Then the Seigneur spent this money as he had spent all the rest. Soon it was all gone, and he looked for more. Again he met a man in the fields, and he sold him his youngest daughter for a great sum of money. So the three girls were sold to strangers. No one knew where they had gone or what had become of them. Their mother often wept over them. Only her little baby boy was left with her. The Seigneur soon died because of his wicked life, but he had not used up all the money he had received for the third girl, and he left some of it behind. When the little boy grew up he went to school. His mother had told him nothing of his three lost sisters. But his playmates in school told him, for they had heard their parents speak of them. They told him that his father had sold them, and that no one knew where they were. When he asked his mother about it she would not tell him at first; but at last she told him all, and she wept because she did not know where her daughters had gone.

The boy decided to go in search of his sisters. His mother said goodbye to him and wished him good luck. He passed through a lonely forest. As he went along, he came upon three robbers sitting on a grass plot under the trees. They were quarrelling about something. The boy stood and watched them. He heard one of the robbers say, 'The boy will decide for us.' And the others agreed. They called the boy to them, and one of them said, 'We have here a coat, a sword, and a pair of shoes which we have stolen. All these things have magical power. The coat can make its wearer invisible; the shoes can make the wearer run faster than the winds; and the sword can overcome all enemies. We cannot agree on how to divide the booty. We want you to be umpire in our dispute and decide for us.' The boy said he would decide the question, but first he must think about it. Then the robbers set about preparing their evening meal. One gathered wood for a fire; another went to a stream for water; and the third looked after the food. When their backs were all turned to the boy, he put on the strange coat and shoes and took the sword. At once he was invisible. The robbers soon prepared their meal, and looked for the boy. He was nowhere to be seen, and the magical coat and shoes and sword had gone with him. Then they knew that he had outwitted them, and they were very angry.

The boy waved his sword and wished himself at the home of his eldest sister. Away he went at once, running like the wind, and in an instant he stood before a very large house. He went in and asked to see the mistress of the place. When she came to him he called her 'sister.' But she greeted him coldly, and said, 'I have no brother big enough to travel.' But he told her of her old home, and soon convinced her that he was indeed her brother. She was very glad to see him. She told him that her husband was a very wonderful man who could do wonderful deeds. Soon her husband came home. He was pleased to see his brother-in-law, and they all had a very happy time together for several days.

Then the boy decided to go on and find his second sister. When he was leaving, his brother-in-law gave him a scale from a fish's back, and said, 'This has very wonderful power. If you ever get into trouble, speak to it and it will bring you help from the sea.' Then the boy waved his sword and wished himself at the home of his second sister. At once he stood before a great house. The mistress received him coldly, just as her elder sister had done, until he convinced her that he was indeed her brother. She told him that her husband was a very wonderful man who had great power. Soon her husband came home and greeted him kindly, and they had a happy time together for many days.

Then the boy decided to go on and find his youngest sister. Before he left, his second brother-in-law gave him a small lock of soft wool, and said, 'This has great power. If you ever get into trouble, speak to it and it will bring you help from the fields.' Then the boy waved his sword and wished himself at the home of his youngest sister. She received him as the others had done; but he soon convinced her that he was her brother, and he found that her husband was a man of great power.

The boy stayed with them a long time. Then he decided to set out to find a wife. His sister told him that in a town far away lived a very rich Seigneur who had two beautiful daughters. He said, 'I will go and win the younger.' Before he left, his third brother-in-law gave him a small feather, and said, 'This has wonderful power. If you ever get into trouble, speak to it and it will bring you help from the air.' Then the boy waved his sword and wished himself at the house of the rich Seigneur. And at once he reached the village, going faster than the winds. Before going to the Seigneur's house he went into a house on the

93

border of the village. Two old women were there. They received him kindly. He told them he had come far to seek the Seigneur's younger daughter. They said, 'The Seigneur's elder daughter is to be married tomorrow, but she will not be long with her husband.' 'Why?' said the boy. They wondered at the boy's ignorance. They said, 'Have you not heard of the Giant of the Sea-cave?' He said he had not. Then they took him to the window, and pointed to a high cliff far across the bay. The waves were breaking at its base and the spray dashed high on its side. But he could see a hole like a door in the face of the cliff. One of the old women said, 'In that cave lives the Giant of the Sea. As soon as a girl is married in this land, he carries her off to the cave and she is never heard of again. His cave is full of brides. He cannot be killed, for he keeps the secret of his life hidden where no one can find it. He is the terror of all the country.' The boy said nothing, but he decided to kill the giant.

The boy then went on to the Seigneur's home to see the wedding of the Seigneur's elder daughter. There was a great gathering, and there was much rejoicing, for the people did not think that the giant would carry off the Seigneur's daughter. But during the wedding feast the bride disappeared and was seen no more. The people knew that the giant had taken her, and there was great sadness.

Then the boy went to the Seigneur and told him that he wanted to marry his younger daughter. The Seigneur said, 'Little good it will do you to marry her, for she will be carried off at once by the Giant of the Sea.' 'But I can kill the giant,' said the boy. 'No man can do that,' said the Seigneur. Then the boy convinced him of his power, and the Seigneur consented to the marriage. The next day the wedding feast was held. There was but little gladness, for the people knew that the Seigneur's only remaining child would soon be stolen away by the Giant of the Sea. Sure enough, at the feast, the bride disappeared; she was taken to the giant's cave. There was much sadness among the people, but the boy said, 'To-morrow I will go and bring her back.'

The next day the boy put on his magical coat and shoes and took his sword and went to the giant's cave. The hole in the cliff was closed up and he could not enter, but he cut a hole in the rock with his sword and went in. He found himself in a very large room. Many women sat around in a circle, all sad and weeping, but all very beautiful. In the circle sat his own wife. At the back of the cave sat the terrible Giant of the Sea. They could not see the boy because of his magical coat. Soon the giant said quickly, 'There is a wedding in the town,' and disappeared. Then the boy made his presence known to his wife. He told her to ask the giant when he came back where the secret of his life was hidden. He told her not to fear, for he would rescue her. He had time to say but few words when the giant came back, bringing a bride with him. Then the boy's wife said to the giant, 'Where do you keep the secret of your life?' He said, 'No one has ever asked me that before, and since you are the first to ask me, I will tell you. I keep it in a box far out in the sea. It is in an iron box. There are seven boxes, one inside the other. It is in the inside box.' Then he told her the exact spot where the box was hidden. Then she said, 'Where do you keep the keys?' He said, 'They are hidden beside the box.'

When the boy heard this, he went away from the cave and sat on the shore. He took out his fish-scale and told it what he wished, and at once help came to him from the sea, as his brother-in-law had promised. A large whale swam to him and said, 'What do you want?' The boy said, 'Bring me the iron box and the keys that lie at the bottom of the ocean.' He told him where to find them. At once the whale went off, and soon returned with the box and the keys. But the keys were rusty and the boy could not open the lock. Then he took out his lock of wool and told it what he wished, and at once help came to him from the fields. A large sheep came running to him and said, 'What do you want?' The boy said, 'Break open this box and each box you find inside.' Then the sheep butted with his horns the outer box until he broke it, and butted each one until he broke them all. When he broke the last one the boy was not on his guard, and the giant's secret of life flew out and escaped into the air. Then the boy took out his feather, and told it what he wished. At once a great bird like a goose came flying through the air, and said, 'What do you want?' The boy said, 'Bring me the giant's secret of life; it has just escaped from the box and is flying in the air.' The bird flew away and soon came back with his prisoner—the giant's secret of life—and the boy killed it with his magical sword. Then he went to the cave. He was still invisible. The giant had lost his power, for the secret of his life had been found and killed. So the boy easily killed him with his sword. Then the boy removed his magical coat and showed himself to the brides who sat in the cave. He brought them all back to the Seigneur's home and their husbands came and claimed them. The Seigneur gave the boy a large house near to his own, and there the boy and his wife lived happily. And the boy sent for his mother, and brought her to live

95

with him and his wife. Soon the Seigneur died. He left all his money and his possessions to the boy, and the boy became Seigneur in his stead, and was lord of all the land. He lived to be very old, and he did many wonderful deeds with the sword and the shoes and the coat which he had taken from the robbers in the forest.

22. The Coming of the Corn

IN OLD times there dwelt on the shores of a great lake a mighty warrior. His people had all been driven far away inland by hostile tribes, but he remained behind to roam over the islands in the Lake and to send his people word of any approaching attack. His wife was dead; she had been killed by treacherous foes. He had two little boys, and he kept them with him in his wanderings by the Lake. He was a great magician as well as a man of great strength and he had no fear in his heart. The islands in the Lake were haunted by spirits or 'manitous,' but the man was not afraid of them, and with his boys he paddled his canoe up and down, watching for signs of his foes. Each night he landed in a cove, and pulled his canoe far up among the trees, and slept in the woods out of the sight of travellers. But he found it very hard to get game and fish, and often his boys were very hungry.

One morning at dawn of day he rose and went to find food for breakfast. He left his little boys asleep under the trees. He walked through the forest until he came suddenly upon a wide and open red plain. There was not a tree or a rock or a blade of grass upon it. He set out across the plain, and when he reached the middle of it, he met a small man with a red feather in his cap. 'Where are you going?' said the little man. 'I am going across the plain to the woods on the other side,' said the man; 'my boys are hungry without food, and I am looking for game.' 'How strong are you?' said the little man. 'I am as strong as the human race,' said the man, 'but no stronger.' 'My name is Red Plume,' said the little man; 'we must wrestle. If you should make me fall, say to me "I have thrown you"; if you should overcome me you will never want for food, for you will have other nourishment than fish and game.' They smoked their pipes for a long while, and then they wrestled. They wrestled for a long time. The warrior was growing weak, for the little man was very strong. But at last he threw Red Plume down and cried, 'I have thrown you.' And at once the little man disappeared. When the warrior looked on the ground where his opponent had fallen, he saw only a crooked thing like an acorn, with a red tassel on it. He picked it up and looked at it, and as he looked, a voice from it said, 'Take off my outside covering; split me into many parts, and throw the parts over the plain; scatter every bit of me; throw my spine near the woods. Then in a month come back to the plain.' The warrior did as he was told, and then went back to his boys. On the way he killed a rabbit and cooked it for breakfast. He did not tell his boys what he had seen.

At the end of a month he went alone again to the plain. In the place where he had scattered the pieces of the strange object, he found blades of strange grass peeping green above the ground. And where he had thrown the pieces of the spine near the wood, little pumpkins were growing. He did not tell his boys what he had found. All summer he watched for his foes, and in the autumn he went again to the place where he had thrown down the man of the Red Plume. The plain was covered with Indian corn in the ear, and there were also pumpkins of great size near the woods. The corn was golden yellow, and red tassels grew from the top of the ears. He plucked some ears of corn and gathered some of the pumpkins and set out to find his boys. Then a voice spoke from the corn. He knew it at once to be the voice of the man of the Red Plume. It said, 'You have conquered me. If you had failed, you would still have lived, but often you would have hungered as before. Henceforth you shall never want for food, for when game and fish are scarce you will have bread. And I will never let the human race lack food if they keep me near them.' So corn came to the Indians in olden times, and never afterwards did they want for food.

When the man came to his boys, he told them what he had found. He ground some of the corn between stones, and made bread from the meal, and he cooked a pumpkin and ate it. Then he thought of his poor old father and mother far away beyond the hills, perhaps without food. So that night he took his boys and travelled far through the forest until he found his parents. He told them of his meeting with the man of the Red Plume and of the coming of the corn. And he brought them back with him to the 'manitou' islands near the shores of the great lake. And ever afterwards the fields were fruitful and corn was abundant and never failed in the land where Red Plume fell.

23. The Dance of Death

ONCE long ago there lived on the banks of a beautiful Canadian river a powerful Indian tribe. In the tribe was a very handsome young man, very brave and a great hunter. He was loved by a young Indian girl who was likewise very beautiful. But the young man repulsed her love; he was a great warrior; he was busy getting ready for the autumn and winter hunt and he had little time for such nonsense as love. He frankly told the young girl that he did not love her and that she must follow him no more.

Now, the young girl was very angry, for she was proud and beautiful and of a high temper, and she was little used to have her desires refused. She had a very strange power which the Spirit of the Night had placed in her cradle at her birth. It was a power by which she could do great harm to mankind, but she had never used it in all her life. But now in her anger she said to the young man as he went away with his comrades, 'You may go; but you will never return as you go.' The young man gave no heed to her words; he neither cared for her nor feared her, and with a merry heart he went his way with his companions.

One day many weeks later, when they were far away in the North Country in the land of ice and snow, the young man became suddenly ill. Then he went raging mad with what the Indians call the wild 'madness of the woods.' The girl's strange power was upon him. In the band of hunters was the young man's older brother, a very strong and powerful man. He knew what ailed his brother. He went to the river and sang the strange weird song that calls the Evil Spirit of the Stream to man's assistance. Now this was a very dangerous thing to do, for the Spirit of the Stream had no love for cowards; but the man being brave had no fear, as he wished to save his brother's life. After the usual custom, he dared the Evil Spirit of the Stream to come to him. Soon the monster appeared in answer to the challenge, its great eyes shining like

fire on the water and its horns rising above the surface. It asked the man
what he wished, and the man answered, 'I wish you to help me; I wish
my brother to be in his right mind again and free from the maiden's
wicked power.' Then the monster said, 'You may have what you wish if
you are not afraid'; and the man said that he feared nothing. And the
monster asked, 'Do you fear me?' And the man said 'No.' Then said the
monster, 'Take hold of my horns and scrape them with your knife.'
The man did as he was told, and he scraped and scraped until he had
taken a handful of powder from the monster's horns.

The monster wondered at the man's bravery and said, 'Go to your
camp now; put half the scrapings into a cup of water and give it to your
brother to drink; put the other half in another cup of water and give it
to the maiden to drink when you go back home, and all will be well.'

Then the Indian returned to the camp and did as the monster had told him, and his brother drank the powdered water and soon got back his senses and his strength.

When the hunt was ended, the band returned home. It was night in the spring-time when they reached their village; the snow had already left the ground and the trees were in bud. In a great tent in the village the annual Spring Dance was in progress, and all the people of the place were gathered. Among them was the maiden lover dancing merrily with the rest. None of the hunting band entered the tent, but they watched the dance from outside the door. The elder brother had mixed a drink as the Evil Spirit of the Stream had told him, by placing the remainder of the powder in a cup of water. And he stood at the door waiting for his chance to give it to the girl. The night was hot and still, and he knew that the dancers would soon grow warm and thirsty. At last the maiden lover came to the door to breathe the cool night air; the man passed her the cup, and without looking at him or knowing him she took it and gladly drained it dry because of her great thirst; then she went back to the dance.

Then a very strange shadow came upon her. When she began to dance she was a young and beautiful girl, the loveliest of all the maidens in the land. But after she had drunk the magic cup she grew gradually older. Her friends noticed the change and stood rooted with terror; the tales of their parents came back to their memories; they knew that the girl was now passing through the Dance of Death from which no power could save her. Their fears were well founded. At each turn of the dance, a year was added to the girl's life; the colour faded slowly from her cheeks; her shoulders slowly stooped; wrinkles appeared upon her face; her hands trembled as if palsied; her feet lost their nimbleness and her tread was no longer light. She was growing old in the Dance of Death. Yet she was unconscious of it all, and her life ebbed away without her knowing it. At last she reached the end of the room, tottering to the music of the dance; but old age was now upon her, and she fell dead upon the floor. Her power over the young man was forever ended, for the Spirit of the Stream had brought about the Dance of Death. 'She will trouble you no more,' said the elder Indian to his brother as he gazed upon the shrunken face and form, 'her dance is forever ended.' The people wondered greatly at the strange happening and their merry-making was hushed; and since that day the Indians in silent fear still point you on the river to the scene of the Dance of Death.

24. The First Pig and Porcupine

A MAN and his wife lived once long ago in the Canadian forest. They lived far away from other people, and they found it very lonely. They were very poor, for game was not plentiful, yet they were always happy and contented. They had only one child, a boy, whom they loved well. The boy grew up to be very strong and clever. But he was often lonely without any companions but his parents. The birds and the animals of the woods were his friends, because he was kind to them and they looked upon him as a comrade. At last he grew tired of his lonely life. He longed for adventure. So one day he said to his parents, 'I am going far away to see other men and women and to do great deeds.' His parents did not want to let him go at first, for they would be very lonely without him. But they knew that he could never become great where he was, and they consented to let him go.

The next morning he set out on his journey. He travelled all day. At night he slept on the ground under the stars. In the morning Rabbit came to where he lay and woke him up. Rabbit said, 'Hello, friend; where are you going?' 'I am going to find people,' said the boy. 'That is what I want to do too,' said Rabbit; 'we shall go together.' So they went on together. They travelled a long distance through the forest. They crossed many small streams and climbed many hills. At last they heard voices through the trees, and soon they saw not far in front of them an Indian village. Rabbit hid among the trees, but the boy went forward alone to see the people. The people were all kind to him and gave him food and asked him to stay with them. But they were all very sad and many of them were weeping. The boy asked them what was the matter. They said, 'The Chief has a very beautiful daughter, and word has come to us that to-morrow a great giant is coming to eat her up. It will be useless to send her away, for the giant will follow her. He is a very terrible monster and cannot be killed.' Then they continued to weep and lament.

The boy went out to the woods and told Rabbit what he had heard. He said, 'We had better go on our way so that we may be far off when the giant comes.' But Rabbit said, 'No. Go back to the people and tell them you can save the Chief's daughter. Have no fear. When night comes bring the girl here to me and I will save her.' So the boy went back to the people and told them not to fear, for he would save the girl from the giant. They laughed at him at first, for everyone who had attempted to stop the giant had been killed. But when they saw that the boy was quite sure of his power, they listened to him. They went to the Chief and told him what the stranger had said. Then the Chief sent for him and said, 'If you can save my daughter from the giant, she shall be yours.'

When evening came, the boy brought the girl to where Rabbit was waiting. Rabbit had a little carriage ready, drawn by two little squirrels. When he spoke to the squirrels they grew until they were as large as dogs. They all got into the carriage, the boy and the girl and Rabbit, and away went the squirrels. It was a clear summer night and the moon was full. The road was hard, and they ran along rapidly over the road among the trees, and soon they reached a village far away. They came to a tent on the bank of a stream. The boy went in and found only an old woman. She said, 'Death is not far away from you. The giant is close on your heels.' Then she wept. She told them to go to the river, for her husband was there. So they went to the river. Rabbit and his squirrels stayed behind to see what the giant would do. The boy and girl found an old man fishing from the bank. He said, 'Death is not far away from you, for the giant is close on your tracks. But I will help you.' He sprang into the water, and lay there and spread out his arms and legs. Then he said, 'Stand on my back.' So they stepped on to his back. They feared at first that they would fall off; but at once he grew as large as a big canoe, and he swam with them across the river. When they landed on the other side they turned to look at him and they saw then that he was old Sea Duck, the boy's friend. He pointed to a high mountain. 'Go to the mountain,' he said, 'and there you will find Rabbit.' Then he swam away.

The boy and the girl went towards the mountain. But they heard the giant roaring behind them and splashing in the stream as he crossed. When they reached the foot of the mountain, he was almost upon them. At the foot of the mountain Rabbit was waiting for them. The side of the mountain was very steep. It was almost perpendicular. Rabbit took a long pole and held it up. 'Climb this,' he said. As the boy and the girl climbed, the pole lengthened until they stepped from it to the top of the mountain. Rabbit climbed up after them with his squirrels. The giant saw them all from the foot of the mountain and climbed up the pole after them. But when he was near the top, the boy pushed the pole out and it fell backwards, taking the giant with it. The giant was killed by the fall. Then the boy and the girl and Rabbit got into the squirrel carriage. They went quickly down the other side of the mountain, and over the moonlit road until they came to the girl's native village. When they reached the border of the village, Rabbit said, 'Now, old friend, good-bye. I must go away. But if ever again you are in trouble, I will help you if I can.' Then Rabbit and his squirrels went away. The boy brought the girl back to the Chief's home. The people all wondered greatly to see her alive. The Chief said to the boy, 'You may have her as your wife.' So they were married and a great wedding feast was held.

But two young men of the girl's village were very angry because the girl had married a stranger. Each wanted her for himself. So they decided to kill her husband. They asked him to go fishing with them far out to sea. The next day the boy went with them to the deep-sea fishing place. It was a long sail. When they were almost out of sight of land, the boy's enemies threw him overboard before he could defend himself, and sailed away leaving him struggling in the water. The boy called for help. Not far away was a small island, and from the beach came a large white Sea Gull in answer to his cries. When Sea Gull saw his plight he said, 'Have no fear, old friend, I will help you.' Sea Gull flew away and the boy lay on his back and floated with the tide. Soon Sea Gull came back carrying a long cord. He let down one end of it and told the boy to hold on to it tight. Then he said, 'It is a long swim to the island. But I will tow you there.' And Sea Gull towed him to the island, and left him there, saying, 'I am very tired after such a long pull. I can go no farther. Good-bye, old friend. Others will help you.'

As the boy sat shivering on the island beach, Fox came along. 'Hello, old friend,' said Fox. 'What are you doing here?' The boy told him what had happened, and said, 'I am very hungry.' Fox said, 'I have no food for you, but I can help you in another way.' Then Fox picked a blade of grass from the bank and said, 'Eat it.' The boy ate it and at once he was changed into a horse and ate grass until he was full and his hunger had left him. When Fox saw that he was full, he gave him another blade of grass, and said, 'Eat it.' He ate it and at once he was changed back to a boy. Then Fox said, 'When night comes, I will take you home, for there is no boat on the island.' So they waited for the evening. When night came and the moon came out they went to the water's edge. They could see the lights of the village far away across the sea. 'Catch hold of my tail,' said Fox, 'and hang on tight.' The boy caught Fox's tail and Fox swam away, towing the boy behind him. The sea was very rough, and the waves ran high, and the boy thought he would never reach the land. But he held on tight and after some hours they came to the shore. Fox said, 'Good-bye, old friend. I must go no farther. But if you are ever again in trouble, call me and I will help you.' Then Fox ran away along the beach.

The boy made a fire and dried his clothes and then went to the village. The people all wondered greatly to see him alive. They thought he was dead. They said, 'Tomorrow one of the men who took you fishing is to marry your wife. He told her you had drowned yourself because you were sorry you had married her. Then he asked her to be his wife and she consented.' The boy went to his old home and there found his wife. She was very frightened when she saw him, for she thought he had come back from the land of the dead. He told her of the treachery of the two men. She wept, but he said, 'Do not weep, but rejoice, for I shall punish the two men tomorrow. There will be no wedding feast for them as they expected.' The next morning the boy went to the Chief, his father-in-law, and told him what had happened. The Chief said, 'Put the two men to death.' But the boy said, 'No, I have a better form of punishment.' Then he called Fox. When Fox came, he said to him, 'Bring me two blades of grass that can change men into beasts, such as you used to change me yesterday.' Fox ran away and soon came back with the grass. The boy took the two blades, and went to the men who had tried to drown him. He said, 'Here is some sweet grass I found under the sea. Taste it.' And each took a blade and ate it. At once they were changed. One became a pig and the other became a porcupine, and both had coarse hair or bristles all over them, and they had noses of a strange and funny shape. The boy's punishment of his enemies was then complete. He said, 'Live now despised by men, with your noses always to the ground.' So the first pig and the first porcupine appeared upon the earth.

25. The Shrove Tuesday Visitor

IN OLDEN times in Canada, Shrove Tuesday, the day before the beginning of Lent, was more strictly observed than it is to-day. The night was always one of great merriment and feasting. Boys and girls of the villages and country places gathered there for the last time before the long period of quiet. They danced until midnight, but the youth or maiden who dared to dance after the hour of twelve was henceforth followed with little luck. This rule was not often broken, for when it was broken the Spirits of Evil always walked the earth and brought disaster to the youthful dancers.

In a remote village on the banks of a great river there dwelt in the seventeenth century a French peasant, a kind and devout old man. He had but one child, a daughter. She was a handsome girl, and naturally enough she had many suitors among the young men of the place. One of these she prized above all the others, and she had promised to become his wife. On the evening of the Shrove Tuesday before the date set for the wedding, as was the custom the young people of the village gathered at her home. It was a simple but joyous gathering, the last which the girl could attend before her marriage. Right merrily the dance went on, and all the guests were in high spirits. Soon after eleven o'clock a sleigh drawn by a great coal-black horse stopped at the door. It contained but one man. Without knocking at the door, the newcomer entered. The rooms were crowded, but the rumour soon spread whisperingly around that a new presence had appeared, and the simple villagers strove to get a look at the tall figure in fine clothes. The old man of the house received the stranger kindly and offered him the best he had in his home, for such was the custom in the old days. One thing the gathering particularly noted—the stranger kept his fur cap on his head, and he did not remove his gloves; but as the night was cold this caused but little wonder.

After the silence caused by the stranger's entrance the music swelled, and again the dance went on. The newcomer chose the old man's daughter as his partner. He came to her and said, 'My pretty lass, I hope you will dance with me tonight, and more than once, too.' 'Certainly,' replied the girl, well pleased with the honour, and knowing that her friends would envy her. During the remainder of the evening the stranger never left her side, and dance after dance they had together. From a corner of the room the girl's lover watched the pair in silence and anger.

In a small room opening from that in which the dancers were gathered was an old and pious woman seated on a chest at the foot of a bed, praying fervently. She was the girl's aunt. In one hand she held her beads, with the other she beckoned to her niece to come to her.

'It is very wrong of you,' she said, 'to forsake your lover for this stranger; his manner is not pleasing to me. Each time I utter the name of the Saviour or the Virgin Mary as he passes the door, he turns from me with a look of anger.' But the girl paid no heed to her aunt's advice.

At last it was midnight, and Lent had come. The old man gave the signal for the dance to cease. 'Let us have one more dance,' said the stranger. 'Just one more,' pleaded the girl; 'my last dance before my marriage.' And the old man wishing to please his only child—for he loved her well—consented, and although it was already Ash Wednesday the dance went on. The stranger again danced with the girl. 'You have been mine all the evening,' he whispered; 'why should you not be mine for ever?' But the girl laughed at his question. 'I am a strange fellow,' said the stranger, 'and when I will to do a thing it must be done. Only say yes, and nothing can ever separate us.' The girl cast a glance towards her dejected lover in the corner of the room. 'I understand,' said the stranger. 'I am too late; you love him.'

'Yes,' answered the girl, 'I love him, or rather I did love him once,' for the girl's head had been turned by the attentions of the stranger.

'That is well,' said the stranger; 'I will arrange all, and overcome all difficulties. Give me your hand to seal our plight.'

She placed her hand in his, but at once she withdrew it with a low cry of pain. She had felt in her flesh the point of some sharp instrument as if the stranger held a knife in his hand. In great terror she fainted and was carried to a couch. At once the dance was stopped and the dancers gathered around her, wondering at the sudden happenings. At the same time two villagers came in and and called the old man to the door to see a strange sight without. The deep snow for many yards around the stranger's horse and sleigh had melted in the hour since his arrival, and a large patch of bare ground was now showing. Terror soon spread among the guests; they spoke in whispers of fear, and shrank from the centre of the room to the walls as if eager to escape; but the old man begged them not to leave him. The stranger looked with a cold smile upon the dread of the company. He kept close to the couch where the girl was slowly coming back to life. He took from his pocket a beautiful necklace, and said to her, 'Take off the glass beads you wear, and for my sake take this beautiful necklace.' But to her glass beads was attached a little cross which she did not want to part with, and she refused to take his gift.

Meanwhile, in the home of the priest, some distance away, there was a strange happening. While he prayed for his flock the old priest had fallen asleep. He saw in his slumber a vision of the old man's home and what was happening there. He started quickly from his sleep and called his servant and told him to harness his horse at once, for not far away a soul was in danger of eternal death. He hurried to the old man's home. When he reached there, the stranger had already unfastened the beads from the girl's neck and was about to place his own necklace upon her and to seize her in his arms. But the old priest was too quick for him. He passed his sacred stole around the girl's neck and drew her towards him, and turning to the stranger he said, 'What art thou, Evil One, doing among Christians?' At this remark terror was renewed among the guests; some fell to their knees in prayer; all were weeping, for they knew now that the stranger with the stately presence and the velvet clothes was the Spirit of Evil and Death. And the stranger answered, 'I do not know as Christians those who forget their faith by dancing on holy days. This fair girl has chosen to be mine. With the blood that flowed from her hand she sealed the compact which binds her to me for ever.'

In answer, the old curé struck the stranger hard across the face with his stole, and repeated some Latin words which none of the guests understood. There was a great crash, as if it thundered, and in a moment amid the noise the stranger disappeared; with his horse and sleigh he had vanished as mysteriously and quickly as he had come.

The guests were long in recovering from their fear, and all night they prayed with the curé that their evil deeds might be forgiven. That she might be cleansed from her sins and that her promise to the stranger might be rightly broken, the girl entered a convent to pass the remainder of her life. A few years later she died. And since that day in her little village on the banks of the great river, the Shrove Tuesday dancers have always stopped their dance at midnight; for youths and maidens still keep in mind the strange dancer in the fine clothes who wooed the peasant's only daughter and almost carried her off.

26. The Boy of Great Strength and the Giants

ON THE banks of a mighty river near a great lake in the West, there lived in old times a boy who was very small in size. As he grew older he did not grow larger, and he remained very tiny. He lived alone with his sister, who was older than he. His sister looked upon him as a child and made him toys to play with. One day in winter he asked his sister to make him a ball to play with on the ice of the river. And she made him a ball out of strong cord. The boy played on the ice, throwing the ball in front of him and running after it as it rolled to see if he could catch it. At last the ball went very far in front of him and the wind blew it along so that it did not stop rolling. He followed it a long distance and he saw in front of him four giant men lying on the ice spearing fish. When he came close to them, they looked at him and laughed, and one said, 'See what a tiny mite is here,' but they did not speak to him. The boy was very cross because they had laughed at his small size, and he thought, 'I shall teach them that I am powerful although I am small.'

As the boy passed them on his way back, he saw four large fish lying on the ice beside them. He took the one nearest to him and ran away as fast as he could. When the giant who owned the fish looked up, he saw the boy running away, and he said to his companions, 'The small boy has stolen my fish.' When the boy reached home, his sister asked him where he had got the fish, and he answered that he had found it on the ice. 'How could you get it there?' she asked, but he would not answer; he merely said, 'Go and cook it.' So they cooked it and ate it for their evening meal.

The next day the boy played again on the ice of the river. The giant men were again fishing. When he came up to where they were, his ball rolled into a hole through which they fished. He asked one of the men to hand him his ball, but the man laughed at him and pushed the ball under the ice with his spear. Then the boy caught the man's arm and twisted it until he broke it, for he had great strength; he picked his ball from under the ice and went home. The man with the broken arm called his comrades and showed them what had happened, and they all swore that they would kill the boy.

The next day the four giant brother fishermen set out to find the boy. Soon they reached his home among the rocks on the bank of the river. The boy's sister heard the noise of their snow shoes on the crusted snow as they came near, and she ran into the house in great fear. But the boy said, 'Have no fear; give me something to eat.' She gave him food on a dish which was made from a magic shell, and he began to eat. Just then the men came to the door and were about to push it open when the boy turned his dish upside-down and at once the door was closed with a large stone. Then the men tried to crack the stone, and at last they made a small hole in it. One of them put his eye to the hole and peeped in, but the boy shot an arrow into his eye and killed him. Then the others, not knowing what had caused their brother to fall, peeped through the hole, and each one was killed in his turn by an arrow shot through his eye.

Then the boy went out and cut them into small pieces, and as he did so he said, 'Henceforth let no man be bigger than your pieces are now.' So men became of their present size, and they have never since grown to giant stature.

When the springtime came, the boy's sister made him new bows and arrows. He took one of the arrows and shot it far out into the lake. Then he swam out after it, while his sister in fear watched him from the shore and called to him to come back. But he cried loudly, 'Fish of the red fins, come and swallow me.' And at once a great fish came and swallowed him. Then his sister tied an old moccasin to a strong cord and fastened it to a tree that grew out over the lake. And the fish said to the boy, 'What is that floating in the water?' And the boy said, 'Take hold of it and swallow it.' The fish swallowed it and was held fast to the tree by the cord. Then the boy took hold of the line and pulled himself and the fish to the shore. His sister cut the fish open and let the boy out. Then they cut up the fish and dried it, and the boy told his sister never again to doubt his strength, for although he was small he was very powerful. And since that time, men have never grown larger than he, but although small they have had power over all other creatures.

27. The Strange Tale of Caribou and Moose

Two widows lived side by side in the forest. Their husbands had long been dead. Each widow had a little boy. One boy was called Caribou; the other was called Moose. One springtime the widows were gathering maple sap to make sugar. The two boys played at home. They talked of the great forest, and decided to travel, to see the big woods and the mountains far away. In the morning they set out on their journey. They walked all day, and in the evening they came to a camp far away in the woods. The camp was that of the Porcupines. The Porcupines were kind to the boys, and gave them food. In the morning they gave them new moccasins, and told them the road to follow. The road, they said, had many giants.

The boys travelled all day without mishap. At last they came to the edge of the wood where the giants lived. Here they met a woman. She was half Indian, for her mother was an Indian woman who had been carried off by a giant. Her mother had long been dead. The woman they met knew that the boys were of her mother's people, and she treated them kindly. She told them that ahead of them were three great giants they would have to overcome before they could pass on their way. She gave them a box containing two dogs. The box was very small; it could be hidden in one hand. The dogs were no bigger than a fly, but when they were rubbed with the hand they grew very large and cross; and the more they were rubbed, the larger and crosser they became. The dogs were to be used, she said, to defeat the first giant. Then the woman told them of the second giant. She said he was very terrible, and that his head was covered with great toads, the poison of which would kill any one who touched them. She told them that the giant would ask them to kill a toad because it hurt his head, hoping thereby to poison them. She warned them not to touch it, and she gave them some cranberries, and told them to crush the cranberries in their hands when the giant made his request and the noise would make the giant think they were crushing the poisonous toad. Then she told them of the third giant; and she gave them a knife with which to overcome him. It was a very wonderful knife that could not be turned aside from anything it attacked.

Then the boys went on their way. Soon they saw the first giant standing by the side of the path. He rushed at them as if to kill them; but they opened their magic box and took out the dogs. They rubbed them until they grew very large and cross, and when the giant came near they let them loose. The dogs soon killed the giant, and the boys went on their way, leaving the dogs to go back to the woman who gave them. Soon they came to the second giant. He was very ugly and terrible, and he had long hair covered with toads. He met the boys kindly, hoping to deceive them. Then, just as the woman had told them, he said, 'Something hurts my head. Do you see what it is?' And they said, 'Yes, it is a great toad.' 'Kill it,' said the giant. Then the boys put their hands close to his head and crushed the cranberries the woman had given them, and the giant thought the noise was that of the crushing of the toad. The boys then went on their way. The giant was well pleased, for he thought they would drop dead very soon because of the poison, and that next day he would find them and have a good meal. Soon the boys came to the third giant. He was very terrible, and he attacked them at once. But one of the boys drew the magic knife and plunged it into the giant's breast. The giant could not turn it aside; it pierced his heart, and he fell dead. Then the boys knew that they were safe.

The next morning the boys decided to separate, and to go each his own way. Moose went north, and Caribou went south. By-and-by Moose came to a tent where dwelt a woman with one daughter. The daughter wished to be married, but her mother was jealous of her daughter's charms, and she killed every suitor who wooed her daughter. Her mother had the power of a witch, which she had received from the Evil Spirit of the forest. The daughter loved Moose when she saw him. She warned him that her mother would try to kill him. Moose asked the mother if he might have the daughter as his wife, and the mother said, 'Yes; but first you must do whatever I bid you.' To this Moose agreed. When he went to bed, the daughter warned him to be on his guard. The mother put a thick skin over him for a blanket, covering him all up. Then she went to get another, saying that it was a cold night. Moose knew he would soon smother without air under the thick skins when she piled them over him, and while she was gone he cut a hole through the skin with his magic knife so that his nose would go through it. The woman came back with other skins, and covered him with a great many, but in each skin Moose cut a hole over his nose so that he might get air. The woman left him, believing that he would smother in the night, for she did not want her daughter to wed; but Moose breathed freely and slept soundly.

The next morning the woman uncovered him, thinking that he was dead; but Moose said he had slept well. The woman wondered greatly, and resolved upon another plan to kill him. A great tree grew near the tent. It was hemlock, and bigger than a haystack at the bottom. It had thick bark which was loose at the top. The woman gave Moose a long pole and told him to knock down the bark. Moose took the pole and knocked a piece off, but as it fell he jumped from under it, for he could jump far. The heavy bark fell with a great crash. Then he knocked off all the bark until the tree was stripped, but he was unharmed. The woman wondered greatly. She resolved upon another plan to kill him. The next day she took Moose to an island far off the coast. There were no trees on the island. They left their canoe on the beach and walked inland. The woman said, 'Wait here awhile; I will come back soon.' Then she went back to the beach. She took the canoe and paddled home, leaving Moose behind. 'Now,' she said, 'he will starve, for he cannot get off the island, and there is nothing there to eat.' When Moose came back to the beach, after waiting a long while, he saw the canoe a mere speck on the water far away. He was much troubled, for he thought that now he would surely die, and he cried loudly. But the sea-gulls flying above the beach heard his cries, and two large gulls came down to him. They told him not to cry, for they would save him. One went to each side of him and told him to take hold and hang on. So he put an arm around each gull's neck, and they rose into the air with him and flew over the sea. Moose was very frightened when he looked down at the water. But the gulls took him home safely. He sat a long time on the beach, and then the woman came paddling her canoe from the island. When she reached the land, Moose said, 'What kept you so long? I have been waiting for you a long time.' But he did not tell her how he had come home. The woman was so surprised she did not know what to say. But she resolved upon another plan to kill him.

The next day she invited Moose to a wrestling match on a high hill. The hill was full of stones. Moose decided that to save his own life he must kill the woman, because he had had enough of her treachery. They wrestled, and Moose let the woman throw him down, but because he was agile he saved himself from a great fall. He let her throw him a second time, but again he was unharmed, to her great surprise. The contest was three falls. The woman was sure she could kill him the third time. But the third time, Moose threw her down so hard that her back was broken on the stones. Then he tossed her high in the air, and she fell so hard that she was broken in pieces. Moose was then free from danger. He married the woman's daughter; but he was not very happy. The daughter was like her mother and caused him trouble, for she was often very wicked. She was a great fisher, and went often to the streams to fish. She could go under the water and stay a long time and then bring up fish in her hands. One night in winter she went down through a hole in the ice to fish. It was very cold, and while she was down, the hole froze over and she could not get out. She called to Moose to break the ice, but Moose was glad to be rid of her and he would not let her out. So she was drowned in the stream.

Moose never married again, and ever afterwards he lived a lonely life. He did not like company any more. That is why he is usually seen by himself, and why he usually travels alone in the forest. But Caribou, on the other hand, likes company, and that is why he is usually seen with five or six others of his kind, and why he seldom travels alone.

28. Jack and His Wonderful Hen

JACK lived with his parents in a remote part of Canada. He had no brothers or sisters. His parents were very poor, and their only possession was a goat that supplied them with milk. When the boy grew up, he decided to go out into the world and earn something to make his parents more comfortable in their old age. So one day he said, 'I am going far away to look for work that you may be able to buy better food.' His parents did not want him to go, for he was their one source of happiness; but he would not listen to their pleading. With no money and something of a heavy heart he went on his way. It was summer in the land, and when he came out of the forest into the open country he saw people in the meadows making hay. Soon he came to a very large farm where a number of men were busy. He asked the man in charge for work. The man said, 'How long do you want to work?' Jack answered, 'A week.' The man hired him, and he went to work. He was a great worker, and in a week he had done as much as one of the other men could do in a year. The man was pleased with his work.

At the end of the week Jack asked for his wages. The man gave him a little money in part payment, and an old hen for the other part. Jack was very cross. He said, 'I don't want a hen; I want money. Little good an old hen can do me!' But the man would not give him more money. He said, 'The hen will lay eggs for you. She will lay two dozen eggs a day—an egg every hour.' So Jack with much disgust took the old hen, for he could do no better, and went home. His parents were glad to see him again, and to get the money he had earned; but they laughed at his old hen. But at the end of a day, when she had laid two dozen eggs, they were well pleased.

In a week Jack said, 'I am going away again to earn more money.' This time his parents were not troubled. They knew he could take care of himself. He said, 'I will take the old hen with me and sell her for a great price.' So one morning he set out. He went through the forest with his old hen under his arm. He passed again by the meadows where men and women were making hay, but he did not ask for work. As he passed, the people looked at his hen and laughed, but he went along unheeding. He soon came to the town where the Seigneur lived, and he went to a house where he got food and lodging for himself and his old hen. He left the hen there and went to the Seigneur's house. He told the Seigneur that he had a wonderful bird, and offered to sell her to him. 'Go and bring me the bird,' said the Seigneur. But when Jack brought the old hen to him the Seigneur was very angry. 'Little good an old hen like that will do me,' he said. But when Jack told him that she could lay twenty-four eggs a day, he said, 'If that is true you may have your price. We will keep her for a day and test your word.' So they locked the old hen up for a day. At the end of that time she had laid twenty-four eggs, and the Seigneur wondered greatly. He said, 'How much do you want for your hen?' Jack answered, 'Whatever you wish to pay me.' The Seigneur gave him much money, and Jack, well pleased with his bargain, went home. His parents were glad to have him back, and to get the money he had got for the old hen. They began to live very comfortably.

At the end of a few weeks Jack decided to go away again. He said, 'Let me take the old goat and sell her. We can do without her milk.' He thought that since he had sold the hen so well, he could make a good sale of the goat. His parents agreed to his wishes. So one morning he tied ribbons and flowers around the old goat's head and covered her with a many-coloured blanket, and set out, leading her behind him. He went along through the forest. It was harvest time, and he passed great farms where reapers were busy cutting yellow grain. But he did not ask for work. The people all looked with wonder at his goat as he passed, but he spoke to no one. Soon he came to the town where the Seigneur lived. He brought his goat to the Seigneur and offered to sell her to him, and the Seigneur gave him much money for her. Then she was placed in a yard with the Seigneur's other animals. The yard was always guarded by two keepers.

Jack decided not to go home at once. He planned to steal the goat back and take her home. Then he would have the goat and much money too. So he bought a large quantity of food, put it in a basket, and carried it to the animal yard. When the two keepers saw him coming, they ran to him to send him away, for no one else was allowed at night near the yard. But Jack said, 'The night is long and cool. The Seigneur

sent me to you with this basket of food.' The keepers were well pleased with the food, and they sat down and had a good meal. They ate until they were full. Jack said, 'If you want to sleep for an hour, I will watch. I like to sit in the moonlight.' The harvest moon was full, and the night was as bright as day. The two keepers thanked Jack for his kindness, and lay down on some straw, and were soon fast asleep because of their hearty meal. Jack waited until they were sound asleep. Then he took the old goat and walked quietly away, leading her behind him. The town was all asleep. There was not a sound anywhere. Soon he reached the open country without meeting anyone, and passed by rich harvest fields until he came to the forest. Then he followed the forest path in the bright moonlight, and reached his home before morning. His parents were glad to see him again so soon and to get his money. But when he told them that he had sold the old goat and stolen her back they were very angry, and his father said, 'No good can come of it. The old goat will bring you to a sad end.'

After a few days Jack decided to set out again to seek his fortune. He took the stolen goat with him. Before he was out of the forest he came upon a man camped in a green place under the trees. The man asked him who he was. Jack said, 'I am a servant of the Seigneur. I take care of his beautiful goats. He gave me this one for myself.' The man liked the goat very much, and asked Jack what he would take for her. But Jack said he would not sell her. Then Jack asked him who he was. The man said, 'I am a robber. If you will come with me, we will soon be very rich.' So Jack agreed to join him. They went along together for some days. But the robber always had his eye on the goat. One night as they slept on the bank of a stream, the robber killed Jack with a blow and threw his body into the river. He wanted his goat. Then he took the old goat and went on his way. Poor Jack's stolen goat had brought him to a sad end.

29. The Sad Tale of
Woodpecker and Bluejay

A SISTER and brother lived alone in a house in the forest. Their father
and mother were dead. The boy had a strange magic power which had
been given to him by his parents. The two children loved each other
very deeply. The brother cared well for his sister and protected her
from all danger. He knew that the forest had many evil creatures who
would be glad to carry off his sister if they could. The brother often
went far away to hunt. He was often gone for many days. When he went
away, he always said to his sister, 'Keep the door barred while I am
gone, and do not speak to anyone.'

One day the brother went far away into the forest. He would not be
home till evening. He said to his sister, 'Keep the door barred; do not
eat until I come back, and do not speak to anyone.' Then he went his
way into the woods. The sister forgot her brother's warning. It was a
hot day, and she opened the door for air. Soon Otter appeared at the
door. The girl spoke to him and he came in. Otter spoke to her, but she
remembered the warning of her brother and she would speak no more.
Otter talked and asked her questions, but she would not answer. Then
Otter became very angry. He determined to make her speak. He caught
her roughly and pulled down her hair. Her hair was very long and
beautiful and as black as the raven's wing. He dragged her by the hair
to the fire, as if he would burn her, and said, 'You will speak, you will
speak or I will kill you.' But she would not speak. Then he cut off her
hair, hoping that she would cry out. But still she refused to utter a
sound. Then he ate her food. He ate everything in the house, for he was
a great eater. But still she said not a word of protest. Then Otter went
away in disgust and rage, babbling loudly as he went.

But just as Otter left the house, the girl's brother was coming home.

He saw Otter through the trees, and he knew that harm had been done. He came to the house, and through the door he saw his sister with her hair cut short. When he came in, he asked her what was the matter. She told him what had happened. He was very cross, and he scolded her for leaving the door open and for speaking to Otter. He said, 'You did not heed my warning. Why did you not run out when Otter came in?' But the girl said, 'It would have done no good; he would have followed me and caught me.' And the man said, 'Why did you not wish for me?' for each had power to bring the other home at once by a wish. But his sister said, 'I was so frightened I did not think of it.' 'Why do you cry?' the brother asked. 'Because he hurt me,' she answered, 'and because he cut off my beautiful hair.'

Then the brother took pity on her. He comforted her and said, 'Do not cry for that; I will make your hair grow beautiful again. But your good name is lost; you can never get that back; you have disobeyed my orders; you have talked to a wicked man.'

Then he dressed his sister in good clothes, and washed and combed her hair. And as he combed it, it grew longer and longer and more beautiful than before, and the girl was comforted. Then he made paint from roots. He made red paint and blue paint. And he painted her face and head red, and painted his own face and head blue. Then he watched for Otter that he might take vengeance. Soon he saw Otter going to the lake to fish. Otter went down under the water. The brother went to the shore of the lake and sang his magic song. And at once the lake froze over. Otter felt the cold underneath the water, and he came up in great haste. He bumped his head on the ice and broke the ice; then he stuck his head through the hole to see what had happened. But as he looked, the water froze around his neck, and he could get neither under the ice nor upon it. He was held fast, and the brother killed him by breaking his head with a stout stick.

Then the brother went home and told his sister that he had taken vengeance and had killed Otter. And he said, 'Now, you and I must part.' His sister cried and pleaded to be forgiven, but he said, 'We must part; we cannot dwell longer among our people; they know you have disobeyed me and have done evil.'

Then they said good-bye. And the brother said, 'You go south-west; I will go north-east; and soon we shall be changed from what we are.' Then they parted and went in different ways as he had said. And at once by his magic power they were changed, and she became a Woodpecker

124

and he became a Bluejay. And her head is still red because of the paint he put on her; and he is still blue because of the paint he put on himself. But although they parted, they are still mindful of each other. She always taps on the trees to let her brother know that she is still alive, and he calls, 'I am here; I am here,' to let her know that he still lives. But he keeps more to the north country, and often in the autumn when the other birds fly south, he remains behind to spend the winter in the north.

30. The Stupid Boy and the Wand

THREE brothers lived with their mother in the forest. They had no sisters; their father was dead, and their mother was an invalid. The youngest boy was very stupid and silly; he was always doing foolish things, and he could never be trusted to do anything in the right way. His two brothers provided for the home, and worked to get food and clothing for themselves and their mother. While they were away, the youngest boy was left in charge of the house and his sick mother. But each night when the two older boys came home, they found that their brother had made many mistakes during the day. Sometimes he gave all the food in the house away to beggars. So they often beat him. But his mother always said, 'He will do better yet.' His brothers were more cruel to him each day. One day when they were away, an old woman came to the door and asked for food and clothing. The boy worked hard to give her what she asked for, but when his brothers came home they only beat him for his pains.

That night the boy ran away from home. He decided that he would endure his brothers' cruelty no longer. So he went into the forest with a sad heart and slept under the trees. In the morning the old woman to whom he had given food the day before came along. He was crying bitterly, for he was hungry and cold. She asked him why he cried, and he told her of his brothers' cruelty. 'Never mind,' she said, 'we will bring happiness out of your sorrow.' She gave him a little wand, and told him to carry it with him always and that it would bring him good fortune. Then she told him to go back home and that all would be well. So he put the magic stick under his coat and went home. He reached home early, and his brothers and mother did not know he had been away.

Before they went away to work, his brothers told him to look after the pigs all day. Soon after they had gone, a rich drover came along wanting to buy pigs. The boy said he would sell all he had for a good sum. He first cut off the pigs' tails and placed them in a heap. He sold the pigs to the man and gave the money to his mother. Then he took the tails and went to the swamp near the river and stuck them in the mud. When his brothers came home they asked about the pigs. The boy said they had run to the swamp and had sunk into the mud. The brothers went to the swamp, and there were the tails sticking up from the mire. They pulled each one, and each tail came up. The brothers thought the tails had broken off and that the pigs were sunk in the mud. And they were very angry at the boy.

The next day they decided to drown him and thus get rid of him. So they placed him in a bag and brought him to the river when the tide was out and the beach was bare. They dug a hole far out in the sand and buried him. They thought the tide would come in over the hole and drown him. When they had gone away, the boy waved his wand and at once the pigs he had sold to the drover came grunting over the sand. He called to them to root up the mud where he lay, and he promised them good food if they would obey him. So they rooted in the sand until the bag was uncovered. Then he kicked a hole in the bag and crawled out. He killed a pig, placed it in the bag and buried it. Soon the tide came in and covered the hole, and the boy hid near his home all night.

The next day when the tide was out and the beach was bare again, the brothers went down to the spot where they had buried the boy. They wanted to dig him up and bury him in a better place. But when they dug up the bag and opened it, they found only a dead pig. They went home in great wonder, but when they reached the house, the boy was sitting on the doorstep laughing at them. Then they decided to try again to kill him. They placed him in a strong bag and set out with him to a high waterfall; they planned to throw the bag into the river above the falls, and he would be dashed to pieces on the rocks as he was carried over. As they went along, they were hungry, and at noon they left the bag on the side of the road and went into a place to eat. While they were eating, the rich drover who had bought the pigs came along driving a herd of cattle and a flock of sheep. He gave the bag a kick as he passed. The boy called to him, and he stopped and asked what he was doing in the bag. The boy said, 'My brothers and I are going on a robbing tour. They hide me in the bag and leave me where much money can be taken. No one else knows that I am in the bag, and it will never be found out where the money has gone.' The drover said he would like to go along too. But the boy said, 'My brothers will not let you. But you and I can work together unknown to them. You take my place in the bag and I will follow at a distance. My cruel brothers will not know, and when you have taken the money, I will let you out and we will run away together.' So the drover took the boy's place in the bag. The boy told him not to utter a sound. Then he ran away and found the drover's cattle and took charge of them.

Soon his brothers came out of the eating-place. They gave the bag a kick and thought that the boy was still in it. Then they went on their way. When they came to a spot above the waterfall, they tossed the bag far out into the stream. It was carried over the falls, and the poor drover was never seen again. Meanwhile the boy had sold all the drover's cattle and sheep. He went home with a large sum of money and gave it to his mother. When his brothers arrived home, he met them at the door and laughed at them. Then his brothers decided to make no further attempt to kill him, for they saw that it would be of no use. They asked him to let them join him, for they knew that in some way he had received strange power. So the three set out one morning together. As they went along through the forest, a band of robbers fell upon them, and killed the two brothers. But because of his wand, the boy escaped. That night he came upon the robbers' house. The robbers were sitting inside counting out their money. The boy went in with his wand and killed them all. He took their money and went home to his mother. Then he went back to the forest and roused his two brothers from their death sleep. And they all went home and lived happily and comfortably ever afterwards.

31. The Blackfoot and the Bear

ONE summer long ago, when the Blackfeet Indians roamed freely over the Canadian plains, the son of one of the Chiefs decided to go off alone to seek adventure. He wanted to be a great man like his father, and he thought he could never become great if he always stayed at home. He said to his father, 'I am going away far to the West, beyond the mountains. I have heard that our Indian enemies who live there have many fine horses. I will bring some of their horses back to you.' His father loved his son well, for he was his only child. He knew that it would be a very dangerous journey, and he tried to persuade his son not to go. But the boy said, 'Have no fear for me. If I do not come back before the frost is on the prairies, do not be worried about me. But if I do not come before the snow lies deep on the plains, then you will know that I have gone forever and that I shall never come back.' His father knew that only by attempting dangerous deeds and doing hard tasks could his son become great. And although he was loath to see him go, he said goodbye and wished him good luck.

It was summer in the north country when the boy set out. He took a number of companions with him. They travelled towards the Great Water in the West, and in a few days they passed through the foothills and then beyond the mountains. Soon they came to a great river. They saw the trail of Indians along the bank. They followed the trail for many days, and at last in the distance they saw the camps of their enemies. Then they stopped where they would be hidden from their enemies' sight. That night a new summer moon was shining in the sky, and by its light they could see many horses around the distant camp. The moon disappeared early. When it had gone and the night was quite dark, the young man went to the camp to get the horses. He went alone and told his comrades to wait for him. Soon he came back driving many horses. But his enemies had heard him driving the horses and they set out in

130

pursuit of him. When he reached his own camp, he called to his comrades to ride for their lives. All night they rode with their horses. When
morning broke, the fleeing Blackfeet could see the dust of their pursuers
far behind them. For days they rode with their enemies not far away.
They passed at last through the mountains and out again into the
rolling foothills. The plains were before them, and already they could
feel the wind of the prairies. They thought they were now safe.

But their pursuers slowly but surely gained on them. Soon they were
close upon them, and a shower of arrows told the Blackfeet that they
would have to fight. The Blackfeet saw on the trail ahead of them a
lonely pine tree. It was surrounded by scrubby trees and shrubs. To
this spot they fled. They dug a pit and tried to defend themselves. But
their pursuers surrounded the spot and shot their arrows into it. All the
young Chief's comrades were soon killed, and when night came on he
alone remained alive. He was wounded and weary, but he lay silent in
the pit. Then his pursuers built fires all around the place where he lay
to prevent his escape and to drive him out of his hiding place. As the
fires crept closer, the young man thought that he must surely die. Then
he prayed to the Spirit of the Storm that rain might fall, and he used all
the charms he carried with him to try to bring rain. Soon a heavy rain
began to fall and the fires were put out. The night became very dark, for
the sky was covered with storm clouds. In the darkness the young man
crawled through the trees and soon reached the open plain. He crawled
north into the foothills and hid in a cave in the hills. He covered the
front of the cave with grass and boughs and lay hidden out of sight. For
many days and nights he lay there waiting for his wounds to heal. At
night he crawled out and gathered berries and roots for food. But his
wounds did not heal rapidly. He grew weaker and weaker, and at last
he was unable to leave the cave. He waited for death. He thought of his
home far away to the south-east, and of his people's fear and worry for
him, for the snow would soon be deep on the plains.

One day when the snow was falling and he knew that winter had
come, he heard footsteps outside the cave. He thought that an enemy
had found him. The footsteps drew nearer, and soon a huge form
appeared at the door. It was not an Indian, but a bear. The young man
knew then that the cave was the bear's winter home.

He thought that the bear would eat him. But the bear only sniffed
and smelled him all over. The man said, 'Are you going to kill me or
to help me?' The bear said, 'I will help you. I will take you home to

your people. We will start in a few days.' Then the bear licked the man's
wounds. The man said he was very hungry, and the bear said he would
go out and get food. So he went off and soon came back with a grouse
in his mouth. The man ate the grouse and felt better. Each day the bear
brought him food, and licked his wounds so that they healed. At last,
one morning the bear said, 'To-day I must take you home. Get on my
back and hold on tight, and I will soon carry you to your people.' So
the man climbed up on the bear's back and held on tight to his long
hair. And the bear trotted off towards the man's home. For many days
he ran over the plains. Each night he rested and caught food to feed
himself and the man. At last they came one night to the top of a ridge
in the plains. From here, as the young man looked, he could see not far
away the camps of his people near a broad winding river. The bear said,
'Now you see your home-land. We shall camp here to-night. To-morrow
you must go on alone, and I shall go back to the hills.' So in the morning
the bear got ready to go back. He said, 'The snow is lying deep on the
hills. I must hurry and find a den for the winter.' The man was sorry to
see him go. He said, 'You have been very kind to me. Can I do anything
for you in return for your kindness?' And the bear answered, 'You can
do one thing for me. Tell your people what I have done for you. And
tell them never to kill a bear that has gone to its den for the winter. Tell

them always to give a bear a chance to fight or to run for his life.' Then the bear said good-bye and trotted away towards his winter home in the distant hills, and the man walked on to his people on the plains. He told his people of his adventures and what the bear had done for him. And since that day the Blackfeet of the Canadian plains will not kill a bear that has gone to its den for the winter. They still remember the favour asked by the bear in return for his kindness to their ancestor in the old days.

32. The Boys and the Giant

THREE little boys were hunting in the Canadian woods in old times. They pretended to be big like men. A giant was prowling about looking for food. He saw the boys through the trees. He thought he would catch them and have a good meal. So he slapped his hands together rapidly and made a noise like a partridge drumming. The little boys heard the noise. They thought it was a partridge, and they went towards the sound. The giant caught them. He picked each one by the heels and struck the head of each on the ground. He thought they were all dead. Then he put them in a big birch-bark bag, put it on his back, and started home, well pleased with the thought of the nice meal he was going to have.

But the ground on which he had struck the boys' heads was soft.

The boys were only stunned by the blow. And after the giant had walked a little way, the boys came to life again. But they made no sound. One of the boys had a little hunting knife made of stone. The giant walked under the trees, and the branches rattled on the birch-bark bag. When the branches rattled, the boy cut a hole in the bag, and the giant could not hear the noise of the cutting. The boys slipped through the hole, one after the other. Then they ran home as fast as they could.

The giant was very strong. He had not felt the weight of the boys on his back. And he did not notice a difference in the weight when they slipped out. When he reached home, he left his load outside. One of his brothers was waiting for him. The giant said, 'I have a good fat meal outside in my bag. Come out and see it.' When they opened the bag, it was empty. The giant was very cross. But with his brother he sat before the fire to eat greedily what food he had in his cave.

When the boys reached home, they told their people what had happened to them. The people set out to find the giants. Soon they came to their cave. The giant and his brother were sleeping before the fire after their hearty meal. The people hid in the trees and shot at the giants. An arrow struck the old giant. He awoke and said to his brother, 'I have a stitch in my side.' But soon a shower of arrows struck them and they fell dead, and the place was troubled no more by giants.

CANADIAN FAIRY TALES

To the memory of my father
descendant of Canadian pioneers
who upheld the old tradition
and used the ancient speech

Introduction

CANADIAN FAIRY TALES

PROFESSOR MACMILLAN has placed all lovers of fairy tales under a deep debt of obligation to him. The fairy tale makes a universal appeal both to old and young; to the young because it is the natural world in which their fancy delights to range, and to the old because they are conscious again of the spirit of youth as they read such tales to their children and grandchildren over and over again, and rejoice in the illusion that after all there is not a great difference of age which separates the generations.

The fairy tale makes this universal appeal because it deals with the elemental in our natures that is the same in every age and in every race. In the Canadian Tales which Professor Macmillan has so admirably gathered from Indian sources, we find the same types of character and scenes of adventure that we do in the tales of the German forests, of Scandinavia, England or France.

There is in us all an instinctive admiration for the adventurous spirit of the fairy tale which challenges the might that is cruel and devastating, and for the good offices of the fairies which help to vindicate the cause of the noble in its conflict with the ignoble, right with wrong.

The origin of the fairy tale is to be traced always to the early stages of civilization, and it is very gratifying to be assured from time to time that man possesses certain natural impulses which spring from an inherent sense of honour, and the desire to redress the wrongs of the world.

Professor Macmillan has been successful in presenting the Indian folk-lore in a most engaging manner. The stories have all the delightful charm and mystery of the Canadian forests; they have penetrated into the heart of nature, but also into the heart of man.

JOHN GRIER HIBBEN

139

Preface

CANADIAN FAIRY TALES

THE tales in this collection, like those in 'Canadian Wonder Tales', were gathered in various parts of Canada—by river and lake and ocean where sailors and fishermen still watch the stars; in forest clearings where lumbermen yet retain some remnant of the old vanished voyageur life and where Indians still barter for their furs; in remote country places where women spin while they speak with reverence of their fathers' days. The skeleton of each story has been left for the most part unchanged, although the language naturally differs somewhat from that of the story-tellers from whose lips the writer heard them.

It is too often forgotten that long before the time of Arthur and his Round Table these tales were known and treasured by the early inhabitants of our land. However much they may have changed in the oral passing from generation to generation the germ of the story goes back to very early days beyond the dawn of Canadian history. Canada is rich in this ancient lore. The effort to save it from oblivion needs no apology. Fairy literature has an important place in the development of the child mind, and there is no better fairy lore than that of our own country. Through the eyes of the Indian story-teller and the Indian dreamer, inheriting his tales from a romantic past, we can still look through 'magic casements opening on the foam of perilous seas in fairy lands forlorn'; we can still feel something of the atmosphere of that mysterious past in which our ancestors dwelt and laboured. The author's sincerest hope in publishing this volume is that to the children of today the traditions of our romantic Canadian past will not be lost in our practical Canadian present.

CYRUS MACMILLAN

MCGILL UNIVERSITY,
MAY, 1921

33. How Glooskap Made the Birds

ONCE upon a time long before the white men came to Canada there lived a wicked giant who caused great trouble and sorrow wherever he went. Men called him Wolf-Wind. Where he was born no man knows, but his home was in the Cave of the Winds, far in the north country in the Night-Night Land, and there men knew he was hiding on calm days when the sun was hot and the sea was still, and on quiet nights when not a leaf or a flower or a blade of grass was stirring. But whenever he appeared, the great trees cracked in fear and the little trees trembled and the flowers bent their heads close to the earth, trying to hide from his presence. Often he came upon them without warning and with little sign of his coming. And then the corn fell flat never to rise again, and tall trees crashed in the forest, and the flowers dropped dead because of their terror; and often the great waters grew white and moaned or screamed loudly or dashed themselves against the rocks trying to escape from Wolf-Wind. And in the darkness of the night when Wolf-Wind howled, there was great fear upon all the earth.

It happened once in those old times that Wolf-Wind was in a great rage, and he went forth to kill and devour all who dared to come in his path. It chanced in that time that many Indian families were living near the sea. The men and women were fishing far off the coast. They were catching fish to make food for the winter. They went very far away in small canoes, for the sea had long been still and they thought there was no danger. The little children were alone on shore. Suddenly as the sun went down, without a sign of his coming, out of the north came Wolf-Wind in his great rage looking for prey, and roaring loudly as he came. 'I am Wolf-Wind, the giant,' he howled, 'cross not my path, for I will kill all the people I meet, and eat them all up.' His anger only grew as he stalked along, and he splashed and tossed the waters aside in his fury as he came down upon the fishermen and fisher-women far out to sea. The fishers had no time to get out of his reach or to paddle to the shore, so quick was Wolf-Wind's coming, and the giant caught them in his path and broke up their boats and killed them all. All night long he raged over the ocean looking for more fishers.

In the morning Wolf-Wind's anger was not yet spent. Far away in front of him he saw the little children of the fishers playing on the shore. He knew they were alone, for he had killed their fathers and mothers. He resolved to catch them and kill them too, and after them he went, still in a great rage. He went quickly towards the land, roaring as he went and dashing the waters against the rocks in his madness. As he came near the beach he howled in his anger, 'I will catch you and kill you all and eat you and bleach your bones upon the sand.' But the children heard him and they ran away as fast as they could, and they hid in a cave among the great rocks and placed a big stone at the mouth of the cave and Wolf-Wind could not get in. He howled loudly at the door all day and all night long, but the stone was strong and he could not break it down. Then he went on his way still very angry and still roaring, and he howled, 'I will come back and catch you yet. You cannot escape from me.'

The children were very frightened and they stayed long in the cave after Wolf-Wind had gone, for far away they could still hear him howling and crashing in the forest. Then they came out. They knew that Wolf-Wind had killed their fathers and mothers on the sea. They ran away into the forest, for they thought that there they would be safe. They went to the Willow-Willow Land where they found a pleasant place with grass and flowers and streams. And between them and the north country where Wolf-Wind lived were many great trees with thick leaves which they knew would protect them from the giant.

But one day Wolf-Wind, true to his promise, came again in a rage to find them. He came into the land killing all he met in his path. But he could not catch the children, for the trees with their thick leaves kept him away. They heard him howling in the forest far distant. For many days in the late summer he tried to find them but their home was close to the trees, and the great branches spread over them and the thick leaves saved them, and only the sun from the south, coming from the Summer-Flower country, could look in upon them. Try as he could with all his might old Wolf-Wind could not harm them although he knew that they were there; and they were always safe while they lived in the Willow-Willow Land.

Wolf-Wind was more angry than ever because of his failure, for he liked to feed on little children, and his rage knew no bounds. He swore that he would have vengeance on the trees. So he came back again and he brought with him to aid him another giant from the north country who had with him a strange and powerful charm, the Charm of the Frost. And the two giants tried to kill the trees that had saved the little children. But over many of the trees they had no power, for when they came, the trees only laughed and merely swayed and creaked and said, 'You cannot harm us; we are strong, for we came at first from the Night-Night Land in the far north country, and over us the Charm of the Frost has no power.' These were the Spruce and the Fir, the Hemlock and the Pine and the Cedar. But on the other trees Wolf-Wind had vengeance as he had vowed. One night when the harvest moon was shining in the sky he came without warning, and with the help of the giant bearing the Charm of the Frost he killed all the leaves that had kept him from the children, and threw them to the ground. One after one the leaves came off from the Beech and the Birch, the Oak and the Maple, the Alder and the Willow. Some fell quickly, some fluttered slowly down, and some took a long time in dying. But at last the trees stood bare and cold against the sky and there was stillness and sadness in the forest. And Wolf-Wind laughed and played in silence through the leafless branches with the giant from Night-Night Land. And he said, 'Now I have overcome the leaves that kept me away, and now when I please I can kill the children.' But the children only moved closer to the strong and sturdy trees that had come at first from the far north country and over which the Charm of the Frost had no power, and Wolf-Wind could not reach them and they were still for ever safe from the giants.

The children were very sad when they saw what Wolf-Wind had done to their friends and protectors, the trees. Summer had gone back to the Southland following as she always did the Rainbow Road to her home in the Wilderness of Flowers. It was lonely now in the forest and silent; there was not a whisper in the trees; there were no leaves, for it was autumn and Wolf-Wind had killed them all.

At last it came to that time of year when Glooskap, who ruled upon the earth and was very great in those days, gave his yearly gifts to little children. And he came into the land on a sled drawn by his faithful dogs to find out for himself what the children wished for. And the children all came to him each asking for a boon. Now Glooskap had great power upon the earth in that old time. He could always do what he willed. And the little children whom Wolf-Wind had tried to harm in his rage came to Glooskap, the Magic Master of gifts, and they were all very sad because the leaves had gone.

'What do you wish?' said Glooskap. 'We wish nothing for ourselves,' said the children, 'but we ask that the leaves that were killed by Wolf-Wind because they saved us from his rage be brought back to life and put back again in their old home in the trees.' Glooskap was silent for a long time and he sat and thought as was his custom, and he smoked hard at his mighty pipe, for he was a great smoker. Now in that time there were no little forest birds upon the earth, for Glooskap had not yet brought them into being. There were only the birds that dwelt near the sea and over whom Wolf-Wind had no power—Sea-gull and Crane, Wild Duck and Loon, Kingfisher and Brant and Curlew. These only laughed at the giant in his rage and screamed in mockery as they flew from him and hid when he came, among the shallows or the rocks or the thick grass in the marshes. And there were also the sturdy birds that dwelt with men and worked for them, giving them eggs and food. These were Hen and Goose and Duck and Wild Turkey. They gave men food, but they were not fair to look upon; they waddled along and could not fly well and they made no sweet music upon the earth, for their song was a quack and a cackle.

Glooskap decided to bring other birds into the world, not to give food but to bring happiness to the children on the days when summer dwells in the land, with their pretty feathers and their pleasant songs. So after he had smoked long in silence he hit upon a plan. And he said to the children asking for their yearly gifts, 'I cannot bring back to the trees the leaves that Wolf-Wind has killed and stripped off, for it is now too late. But I will take the fallen leaves and change them into little birds. And the birds shall never forget how they were born. When autumn comes they shall go with summer far away to the Summer-Flower Land, but in the spring-time they shall always come back and they shall live as close as they can to the leaves from which they have sprung. And they shall nest, most of them, in the trees under the leaves, and even those that nest in the grass shall love the trees and linger in them. And they shall all be beautiful in colour like the leaves that gave them birth; and they shall have power to rest at times upon the air like a leaf fluttering; and the voice of the air and the laughing waters shall

be in their throats and they shall sing sweet songs for little children. And I give the children charge over them to keep them from harm just as the leaves which gave them birth have saved the little children from the giants. And I will give the trees that Wolf-Wind has stripped power to bring forth new leaves every spring-time so that when Summer comes back from the Wilderness of Flowers the trees shall not be bare. And although Wolf-Wind may strip them off when the Giant of the Frost comes with him from the Night-Night Land they shall always be replaced in the spring-time. And I will take away much of Wolf-Wind's power so that he can no longer harm little children as wickedly as he has done before.'

Glooskap waved his magic wand as was his custom, and at once great flocks of little birds sprang from the ground where the fallen leaves had lain. And they twittered and sang in a great chorus and flew back to the trees. They were of beautiful colours like the leaves that had given them birth. There were Robin Red-breasts and Thrushes all brown and red, from the red and brown leaves of the Oak. And there were Finches and Humming-birds all yellow and green and brown from the leaves of the Alder and the Willow, and they glowed like willows in the sun-light and fluttered like a leaf upon the air. There were Yellowbirds and Canadian Warblers from the golden Beech and Birch leaves. And there were Scarlet Tanagers and Orioles and Grosbeaks all of changing colours, red and purple and brown, from the leaves of the Canadian Maple. And they all sang to the children and the children were all very happy again.

Then Glooskap sent the little birds all away to a warm country until the rule of the Giant of the Frost from the Night-Night Land was over, for it was winter in all the land and it was very cold. But in the spring-time the little birds always come back from the Summer-Flower Land. And they build their nests among the trees as close as they can to their kindred, the leaves from which they came. And all day long they sing among the leaves for little children. At daybreak they wake the children with their choir of dawn, and at twilight they lisp and twitter to lull the children to sleep. And at night they hide among the leaves from Wolf-Wind and are very still with never a twitter or a song. For they do not forget that they are the children's gift from Glooskap and that they came from the leaves stripped from the trees by Wolf-Wind because the leaves saved the little children from the giant long ago.

34. Rabbit and the Grain Buyers

ONCE long ago when the Indians lived in Canada before the white men came, Rabbit was very lazy. He had worked long for Glooskap, the great ruler of the people, as a forest guide, but his toil was not appreciated or rewarded. He saw all the other animals idling their time away, taking their ease all day long, and doing nothing but filling their bellies with food, and sleeping all the afternoon in the hot sunshine. And he said, 'Why should I work for other people when nobody works for me? I will take mine ease like all the other animals.' So he sulked in his little house for a long time and could not be coaxed or driven to do any work. But as he was a lonely fellow who always lived by himself with very few friends in the world except little children, he soon got tired of this lazy life. For by nature he was industrious and energetic and he always liked to be doing something or prowling alone in the forest. So he said, 'I must find some work to do or I shall surely lose my wits. But it must be labour that brings profit to myself and not to other people.'

For a long time Rabbit puzzled his brains thinking on a business or a profession to follow. But nothing seemed to be to his liking. At last one day he saw some Indians trading skins and knives. One was selling and others were buying and they seemed to be making a great deal of money without doing very much work. Rabbit thought that here indeed was an easy way to make a living. Then he saw Duck coming along carrying a basket of eggs. He said to Duck, 'How do you get along in the world? You seem to do nothing but eat and cackle and swim in the pond. You never seem to work.' And Duck said, 'I lay eggs and sell them in exchange for corn. Why don't you lay eggs? It is all very easy.' But Rabbit knew that Duck was only laughing at him, and that he was not meant to make a living in that way.

147

Then he met Bee on the forest path and he said, 'How do you make a living, you wandering bee? You do nothing but gad about all day long, going from flower to flower dressed in your good clothes of yellow and black and always singing your tuneless song?' And Bee said, 'I make honey and wax and sell them. I have a great store for sale now. Why don't you do as I do? I am always happy. I always sing at my work, and what's more, my song is not tuneless. And just for your impudence, take that.' And so saying he stung Rabbit on the nose and went on his way, singing his droning song. Rabbit rubbed his nose in the earth to ease his pain and he swore vengeance on Bee, for he knew that Bee too was only laughing at him. But he could think of no way to make an easy living, for he had nothing to sell but his coat, and he could not very well barter that, for winter would soon be coming on. He was very angry and troubled and he envied Duck and Bee their good fortune because of their eggs and honey and wax.

At last he thought of the Indians he had watched buying and selling skins. 'I have it,' he cried, 'I have it. I will become a great merchant. I will be a great trader. I will live on a farm where they grow corn and vegetables, and I will steal them and sell them to the other animals and thereby make a great store of money. I shall be very rich in a short time.' So, very happy, he went to a field near which was a vegetable garden. And in it were growing Indian corn and all kinds of grain which he knew the other birds and animals would gladly buy. So he made a sign and put it up in front of his house, and it said, 'Buy Rabbit's corn, the best in all the land; it will grow without rain; there is only a small quantity left. Orders taken here.' Then he sat in his house and waited.

Soon many buyers began to arrive. They were curious, and they wanted to see what kind of a merchant Rabbit would make. Rabbit explained to them that he was only an agent, that they must pay him their money, and he would take it to the farmer, and deliver their grain at his house one week from that day. The buyers paid him the money and went away, for they were afraid the farmer would kill them if they went themselves for the corn. They left a great store of money with Rabbit. That night when the moon rose over the hills Rabbit went to the field of corn nearby. But the farmer had spied him thieving that afternoon, and he had placed around his corn a fence of strong netting which poor Rabbit could not get through. And he had also placed around the field many watch-dogs which growled and snarled and frightened thieves away. Night after night Rabbit tried to slip into the

field, but without success, and the week passed and still he had no corn for the customers who, he knew, would soon be arriving for their goods. And meanwhile he had spent all their money and he knew they would all fall upon him and kill him if he failed to keep his word and deliver their purchases.

At last when the day agreed on arrived, he saw his customers coming for their grain. And he hoped that his tricks would save him as they had saved him many times before. He sat in his yard playing his flute, when Earth-Worm, the first customer arrived. 'Good day,' said Rabbit. 'Good day,' said Earth-Worm, 'I have come for my corn, for a week has gone by.' 'Very good,' said Rabbit, 'but first we shall have dinner. It will be ready in a few minutes. You must be hungry after your long journey.' As they sat waiting for their dinner they saw Duck, another customer,

149

waddling up the path with her basket on her neck. And Rabbit said, 'Will not old Duck who comes here want to eat you up?' And Earth-Worm said, 'Yes, yes, where shall I hide?' and he was much excited. 'Hide under this clam-shell,' said Rabbit. So Earth-Worm crawled under the clam-shell and sat very still, trembling for his life.

When Duck arrived, Rabbit said, 'Good morning.' 'Good morning, Mr Merchant,' said Duck, wishing to be polite. 'I have come for my corn, for it is the appointed day of delivery.' 'True, true,' said Rabbit, 'but first we shall have dinner. It will be ready in a few minutes. It will be an honour for me to have you dine with me.' As they sat waiting for their dinner, Rabbit said, 'Would you care to eat an Earth-Worm before your dinner? It would be a good appetizer for you.' And Duck said, 'Thank you very much. I am very fond of Earth-Worms.' Rabbit lifted the clam-shell and poor Earth-Worm was quickly gobbled up by Duck. And Rabbit, laughing to himself, thought, 'Now I am getting rid of my customers.'

As Rabbit and Duck sat talking, they saw Fox trotting up the path. He was another customer coming for his corn. And Rabbit said courteously, 'Madam, I see your old enemy Fox approaching. He will probably wish to eat you up; you had better hide.' And Duck with her feathers all ruffled with excitement said, 'Yes, yes, where shall I hide?' And Rabbit said, 'Hide under this basket.' So Duck crawled under the over-turned basket and sat very still.

Fox soon came in and said, 'Good day, Rabbit. I have come for my corn, for I am in sore need of it to catch chickens, and the seven days have passed.' 'You are very punctual,' said Rabbit, 'but first let us have dinner. It will be ready in a few minutes. It will make you stronger to carry your heavy load.' As they sat waiting for their dinner, Rabbit said, 'Listen, Fox. Would you care to eat a fat Duck now? It would be a tasty bit for you before you dine.' And Fox said, 'You are very kind. I always like to eat a Duck before my dinner.' Rabbit knocked over the basket and Fox quickly devoured poor Duck until not a feather remained. And Rabbit laughed to himself and said, 'Surely I am getting rid of my customers very easily.'

As Rabbit and Fox sat talking over old times in the forest, they saw Bear coming lumbering up the path, tossing his head from side to side, and sniffing the air. And Rabbit said, 'Bear is in a bad temper today. I wonder what can be the cause.' And Fox said, 'This morning I stole all his honey and he saw me running away.' 'He scents you here,' said

Rabbit, 'will he not kill you if he finds you? Perhaps you ought to hide.'
'Yes, yes,' said Fox, 'but where shall I hide?' 'Hide in this box,' said
Rabbit, and Fox sprang into the box, and Rabbit closed down the lid.

When Bear arrived he said gruffly, for he was in a bad temper, 'Good
day, Rabbit. I have come for my corn and I must have it quickly, for
I must be on my way. It is the appointed time.' 'It is indeed the
appointed time,' said Rabbit, 'but first we shall have dinner. It will be
ready in a few minutes and I never let a wayfarer leave my house without first taking nourishment. I have today a dish of fresh fish which you
like very well, and we have never yet dined together.' And Bear agreed
to wait and his gruffness left him at the thought of his good meal, for he
was a great fish-eater, and he talked pleasantly. Then Rabbit said, 'I
have a secret to tell you. Let me whisper it.' He put his mouth close to
Bear's ear and said, 'Old Fox, the sly thief who stole all your honey this
morning is hiding in the box by your side. He came here to boast about
his theft and he laughed loudly to me as he told me how easily you were
cheated. He called you Lack-Brains.' Bear was very angry and at once
he knocked the lid from the box and killed Fox with one blow of his
powerful paw. And Rabbit said to himself, 'What luck I am having;
there is another of my customers gone.' But he wondered how he was
to get rid of Bear, and he scratched his head in thought.

While Bear and Rabbit sat talking, they saw Rabbit's last customer,
the Hunter, coming along. Bear would have run away, but it was too
late. 'Will the Hunter not want to kill you?' said Rabbit, glad to think
that here was the end of poor Bear. 'Indeed he will,' said Bear. 'Oh
dear, oh dear, where shall I hide?' 'Hide under my bed in my house,'
said Rabbit. Poor Bear quickly dashed into the house and crawled
under Rabbit's bed with great difficulty for he was very fat and the bed
was very low and he had to lay himself out flat on the floor, but he was
comfortable in the thought that he would soon escape. When Hunter
arrived he said, 'Good day, Rabbit, I have come for my corn, for my
children need bread.' 'You shall have it,' said Rabbit. 'But first we must
have a bite to eat. I have not very much to offer you, but I can give you
in a few minutes some hot pancakes and fresh maple syrup.' The Hunter
was well pleased with the thought of such a good meal and he said he
would be glad to wait. Then Rabbit said, 'Would you like some bear
meat for your children, and a good warm bear skin for your hearth?'
And the Hunter said, 'Indeed I would. But in these days such luxuries
are hard to find.' And Rabbit said, 'Oh no, they are not; under my bed

in my house, a good fat bear is hiding. He is lying flat on his back, and you can easily kill him.' The Hunter hurried to the house, and sure enough there he found Bear hiding under the bed, flat upon his back. He killed him with a blow and skinned him and cut him up into small pieces and put the meat and the skin into a bag to take home to his children. But while he was about it, Rabbit slipped away into the forest, saying to himself, 'Now I have got rid of all my customers and I am safe. But the life of a merchant is not to my liking. I will not be a trader any more. I will gather corn for myself, but not to sell to others.' And he ran quickly away and hid himself in a dense thicket.

When the Hunter went to look for Rabbit, he could not find him, nor was he able to find his grain. And although he thought he had fared pretty well by getting so much bear meat, he swore vengeance on Rabbit for his deceit, and to this day he searches for him, and if he meets him, he will not let him escape. And Rabbit lives by himself and keeps away from the Hunter as far as he can, for he fears him because of the trick he played upon him in the olden days.

35. Saint Nicholas
and the Children

Two little children lived with their old grandmother in a remote place in the Canadian forest. They were twin children—a boy and a girl, Pierre and Estelle by name—and except for their dress it was not easy to tell them apart. Their father and mother had died in the spring-time, and in the summer they had left their old home because of its many sad memories and had gone to live with their old grandmother in a new home elsewhere. In this new home in the forest where they now lived they were very poor, but they were not unhappy. Times were hard, and there was very little food to be had no matter how well their old grand-mother worked; but they caught fish in the streams and gathered berries and fruit and birds' eggs on the wooded hills, and somehow throughout the summer they kept themselves from want. But when late autumn came and the streams were frozen over and the berries were all gone and there were no eggs, for the birds had all flown south, they were often hungry because they had so little to eat.

Their grandmother worked so hard to provide for herself and the children that at last she fell very sick. For several days she could not leave her bed. And she said, 'I want meat broth to make me well and I must have good meat to make it. If I do not get meat I can have no broth, and if I do not get broth I shall not get well, and if I do not get well I shall die, and if I die you two children will surely starve and die too. So meat and meat alone can save us all from starvation and death.' So the two children, to keep themselves and their grandmother alive, set out one morning in search of meat to make the broth. They lived far from other people and they did not know where to go, but they followed the forest path. The snow lay deep on the ground and sparkled brightly in the sunlight. The children had never before been away from home alone and every sight was of great interest to them. Here and there a rabbit hopped over the snow, or a snowbird hovered and twittered overhead, all looking for food like the children. And there were holly-berries growing in many places, and there was mistletoe hanging from the trees. And Pierre when he saw the holly-berries and the mistletoe said, 'Saint Nicholas will be soon here, for the trees are dressed and ready for his coming.' And Estelle said, 'Yes, Saint Nicholas will be soon here.' And they were both very glad thinking of his coming.

As they went along in the afternoon, they came upon an old man sitting at the door of a small house of spruce-boughs under the trees close to the forest path. He was busy making whistles, whittling willow wands with a knife and tapping gently on the bark until the bark loosened from the wood and slipped easily off. The children stood and watched him at his strange work, for he had merry twinkling eyes, and a kindly weather-beaten face, and thick white hair, and they were not afraid.

'Hello,' said the old man.

'Hello,' said Pierre, 'why are you making willow whistles?'

'I am making them for Saint Nicholas,' said the old man; 'he is coming soon for his yearly visit; indeed he is already in the land; when he makes his rounds he always gives whistles, among other things, to good children, and I must have a great store of them ready for him when he comes, for there are many children to supply.'

Then he went on whittling busily with his knife. The children watched him for a long time in silence, and they thought what a fine thing it must be to work like the old man for Saint Nicholas, in his little house of boughs under the forest trees. Then the old man said, 'You are

very small children; what are you seeking so far away from people?'
And Estelle answered, 'Our old grandmother is very sick, and we are
looking for meat to make broth to make her well.' The old man was
sorry he had no meat, for he lived on other food. He told them that some
distance farther along there was a butcher who always kept meat; but
the butcher, he said, was a very wicked fellow and sometimes little
children who entered his shop never came out again. The children
were very frightened when they heard what the old man said and they
wondered if they had better go back home. But the old man thought for
a long time in silence as he whittled his willow wands, and then he said,
'I will give you each a whistle, and when you blow it, Saint Nicholas
will always hear it; you must never blow it except when you are in great
trouble or distress, and when Saint Nicholas hears it he will know that
you are coming to grief or that harm is already upon you and he will
come himself or send someone to your assistance. But you must blow
only one blast. The whistle should be given only by Saint Nicholas
himself when he comes at holly-time into the land. But you are good
children and your old grandmother is sick, and you are trying to make
her well, and I know that Saint Nicholas will not say that I have done
wrong.' So he gave the children each a whistle, and then fear left them,
for they knew they could now come to no harm if they had the aid of
Saint Nicholas.

It was growing late in the afternoon and the children set out on their
way to find the wicked butcher. But they had many misgivings, and as
they went on they grew faint of heart, for they wondered if the old man
had told them the truth about the whistles or if he was in reality a
secret agent of the wicked butcher trying to lure them to their death.
They resolved to search for meat elsewhere and to keep away from the
butcher's shop.

For a long time they searched, but without success. There was no
meat to be had in all the land at any of the places they stopped to ask.
Soon they came in sight of the butcher's shop. They were very
frightened. But the sun had already gone down behind the trees, and
night was coming on, and they had still no meat. And they knew that if
their old grandmother was to get well she must have meat to make
broth. The shop, too, looked very pleasant and attractive in the cold
winter evening. Warm light was shining from a fire through the door,
and in the windows were sausages, and fat birds, and big yellow pumpkins and cakes with red berries on the top. The children were hungry

and wished for something to eat by the warm shop fire. They decided to enter the shop notwithstanding their fear, to buy some food, and to get meat for their grandmother's broth as quickly as they could. But before they entered the shop they thought it would be well, in order to be safe, to blow a blast on their whistle as the old man had told them so that Saint Nicholas would know that they were in dread of harm. They stood for a time in the shadow of the great trees before the door and made ready to blow together. Pierre gave the signal and blew a long soft blast. But Estelle could not get her whistle from her pocket and Pierre had finished his blast, all out of breath, before she was ready to blow. 'Don't blow now,' he said, 'you are just like a girl, always too late.' But blow she would, as the old man had told her, and before Pierre could stop her she blew a long soft blast on her whistle. Pierre was very cross, for he thought that now no good could come of it, as two blasts had sounded, but with his sister he entered the butcher's shop.

The wicked butcher was in his shop, but not another person was about the place. It was all very quiet. The man was very glad to see the children and he seated them by the warm fire, and gave them food, and although he shut the door tight behind them, their fear soon vanished. After they had eaten well and were warm again, they asked for meat to make broth for their old grandmother, and the butcher said he would give them plenty of good meat although it was very scarce in all the land. There was a barrel standing in one corner; in another corner was a large hogshead reaching almost to the ceiling, and the butcher said that both of these were full of meat.

Now the butcher was really the friend and partner of a wicked giant who lived in the forest. The giant's greatest delight was to eat little children. He liked no meal so well as a meal of little children, two at a time, pickled first in brine. He ate them always when he could get them, but he was not always successful in his search, for children were scarce in the land. He was a great hunter and he was able to kill many animals in the forest and to secure much meat, so great was his strength, and once a week regularly he brought a great load of meat to the butcher and traded it for any little children the butcher managed to entice into his shop. So the butcher got much meat at little cost. And the old man of the house of boughs was right when he said that many little children who entered the shop never came out again.

The butcher was very glad when he saw the two pretty little children. He was expecting the giant that evening on his weekly visit, and he thought gleefully of the great load of meat he would get from the giant in exchange for the children, for he would ask a big price, and he knew the giant would give all the meat he had for so good a meal. And he thought too of all the money he would get for the giant's load of meat. So he resolved to kill the children and pickle them in brine to await the giant's coming.

When the children had finished their meal and had warmed themselves by the fire they made ready to go home and they asked for their meat. The butcher said he would get it for them. They looked up at the shelves, laden with more food than they had ever seen before—hams and cabbages and strings of onions. And the little children said, 'There are good onions up there; we will buy some and take them home to our grandmother to put in her broth.' The butcher said, 'There are many kinds of onions in the box on the high shelf. You must pick out the kind you want. I will lift you up to the shelf so that you can see for yourselves.' So he caught them each by the coat between the shoulders, and because of his great strength he lifted them high until they could look into the box and pick out the onions they wanted. As he took them down he thrust them straight out from his body at arm's length and held them there and they laughed because of his great strength. Then he brought them together with terrible force so that their heads struck one against the other and they were stunned by the cruel blow. Then he threw them head first into the barrel in the corner which was filled with brine, not with meat as he had said, and he left them there to pickle well. He was greatly pleased with the fine load of meat he would get in exchange from the giant, who, he knew, would appear before many minutes had passed.

Soon the giant arrived. He carried on his back a great load of meat and he also drew a sled heavily laden with many dressed carcasses of animals he had killed. 'What cheer for me to-night and what fortune?' he said to the butcher as he entered the warm shop with his load. And the butcher said, 'Good cheer and fine fortune. I have a good fat pair for you to-night already pickling in the brine.' Then he uncovered the barrel in the corner and showed the giant the two little children sticking head first in the pickle. The giant smacked his fat lips and chuckled and rubbed his great hands, so pleased was he with the sight of so good a meal. And he said, 'We will let them steep well in the brine until to-morrow. I always like them very salt.' They covered up the barrel, and then they bargained about the purchase of the meat.

157

The giant agreed to give the butcher all his meat in exchange for the children. Then they sat by the fire drinking and eating until far on into the night. And the giant said that before they went to bed he would take another look at the children to see how they were pickling. So they went and uncovered the barrel.

Now it chanced that Saint Nicholas was in the land at that time, as the old man of the House-of-boughs had said. He had come into the land to bring his yearly gifts to little children. In the evening he was many miles away from the butcher's shop. But he heard the long soft blast of a whistle, borne on the still evening wind. He knew it to be one of his own whistles, and it told him that little children were in danger. But it was followed by another soft blast—the late blast of Estelle's whistle—and the two blasts meant that the danger was not yet very near to the children, that indeed it was far off, so he thought that there was no need to hurry to the children's aid. Moreover, Saint Nicholas was just then leaving tiny dolls for little babies in many little houses in the forest and he decided to take his time and finish the giving of all these gifts before he set out to the place from which the whistle-blasts had come.

At last he was able to go on his way. The snow lay deep in the forest, and travelling was hard, but the white winter moon was shining, and the path was bright and Saint Nicholas moved along quickly on his snow-shoes. Far on in the night he reached the butcher's shop from which he knew the children's note of fear had come. As he entered the shop, the giant and the butcher were just taking their last look before going to bed at the children sticking in the barrel of brine. They did not know Saint Nicholas, but when they saw him they quickly placed the cover on the barrel and were very much confused. Saint Nicholas was suspicious that they were about some wickedness, and he knew well that in some way or other the barrel was connected with the dreaded harm of which the children's whistle had told him, and he thought that perhaps the children were hidden in it. So he said, 'I have come for meat. I want meat that has been pickled in brine. I should like a piece from that barrel.' But the butcher said, 'It is not good meat. I have better meat in the inner room, and I will get it for you.' So the butcher and Saint Nicholas entered the inner room and closed the door behind them while the giant sat on the barrel in the corner, trying to hide it with his great fat legs.

In the inner room was a barrel filled with brine, but with only a small piece of meat at the bottom. Saint Nicholas said he would take that piece. The butcher bent far into the barrel to reach down in search of the meat. But as he did so, Saint Nicholas picked him up by the legs and pushed him head first into the barrel of brine. He spluttered and kicked, but he stuck fast in the barrel, and could not get out. Saint Nicholas placed the cover on the barrel, with a great weight on top of it, and that was the end of the wicked butcher.

Then Saint Nicholas returned to the shop where the giant was waiting, still sitting on the barrel. He told the giant that he wanted a piece of meat that lay in the bottom of the large hogshead of pickle in the other corner. He asked the giant to get it for him, as the hogshead was so high that neither he nor the butcher could reach down into it.

The giant bent far into the hogshead and began groping for the meat at the bottom. Saint Nicholas took a large bone that lay on the floor, and standing on a box beside the hogshead he struck the giant a powerful blow on the head. The giant was only slightly stunned, but in his surprise he lost his balance, and fell head first into the brine. He yelled and kicked for a time, but his huge shoulders stuck fast. Saint Nicholas covered the hogshead, leaving the giant sticking fast in the pickle, and that was the end of the giant.

Then Saint Nicholas uncovered the barrel in the corner into which he had seen the butcher and the giant looking when he had first entered the shop. There were the two children standing on their heads in the pickle with their feet sticking out at the top. He caught them by the legs and pulled them out and by his magic power he soon brought them back to life. He gave them food and warmed them by the fire and soon they were none the worse for their hour in the barrel of brine.

Then he gave them meat and brought them back to their grandmother. And they made broth for her and soon made her well, and they were all happy again. And the land was troubled no more by giants, for Saint Nicholas never again allowed great harm to come to little children if they always kept his whistle near them and blew softly upon it when they were in trouble or distress.

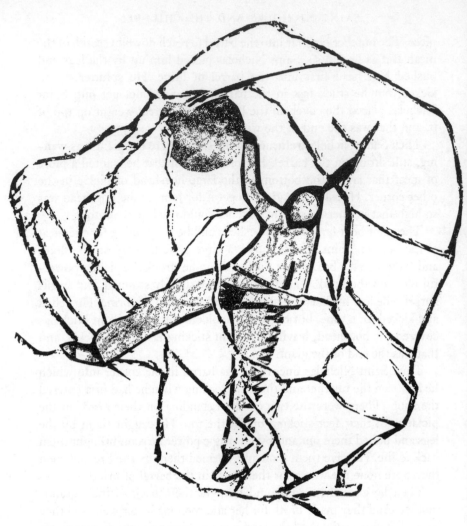

36. The Fall of the Spider Man

IN OLDEN times the Spider Man lived in the sky-country. He dwelt in a
bright little house all by himself, where he weaved webs and long
flimsy ladders by which people went back and forth from the sky to the
earth. The Star-people often went at night to earth where they roamed
about as fairies of light, doing good deeds for women and little children,
and they always went back and forth on the ladder of the Spider Man.
The Spider Man had to work very hard, weaving his webs, and spinning

the yarn from which his ladders were made. One day when he had a short breathing-time from his toil he looked down at the earth-country and there he saw many of the earth-people playing at games, or taking sweet sap from the maple trees, or gathering berries on the rolling hills; but most of the men were lazily idling and doing nothing. The women were all working, after the fashion of Indians in those days; the men were working but little. And Spider Man said to himself, 'I should like to go to the earth-country where men idle their time away. I would marry four wives who would work for me while I would take life easy, for I need a rest.'

He was very tired of his work for he was kept at it day and night always spinning and weaving his webs. But when he asked for a rest he was not allowed to stop; he was only kicked for his pains and called Sleepy Head, and Lazy-bones and other harsh names, and told to work harder. Then he grew angry and he resolved to punish the Star-people because they kept him so hard at work. He thought that if he punished them and made himself a nuisance, they would be glad to be rid of him. So he hit upon a crafty plan. Each night when a Star-fairy was climbing back to the sky-country, just as he came near the top of the ladder, the Spider Man would cut the strands and the fairy would fall to earth with a great crash. Night after night he did this, and he chuckled to himself as he saw the sky-fairies sprawling through the air and kicking their heels, while the earth-people looked up wonderingly at them and called them Shooting Stars. Many Star-people fell to earth in this way because of the Spider Man's tricks, and they could never get back to the sky-country because of their broken limbs or their disfigured faces, for in the sky-country the people all must have beautiful faces and forms. But Spider Man's tricks brought him no good; the people would not drive him away because they needed his webs and he was kept always at his tasks. At last he decided to run away of his own accord, and, one night when the Moon and the Stars had gone to work and the Sun was asleep, he said farewell to the sky-country and let himself down to earth by one of his own strands of yarn, spinning it as he dropped down.

In the earth-country he married four wives as he had planned, for he wanted them to work for him while he took his ease. He thought he had worked long enough. All went well for a time and the Spider Man was quite happy living his lazy and contented life. Not a strand did he spin, nor a web did he weave. No men on earth were working; only the women toiled. At last, Glooskap, who ruled upon the earth in that time, became very angry because the men in these parts were so lazy, and he sent Famine into their country to punish them for their sins. Famine came very stealthily into the land and gathered up all the corn and carried it off; then he called to him all the animals, and the birds, and the fish of the sea and river, and he took them away with him. In all the land there was nothing left to eat. Only water remained. The people were very hungry and they lived on water for many days. Sometimes they drank the water cold, sometimes hot, sometimes luke-warm, but at best it was but poor fare. The Spider Man soon grew tired of this strange diet, for it did not satisfy his hunger to live always on water. It filled his belly and swelled him to a great size, but it brought him little nourishment or strength. So he said, 'There must be good food somewhere in the world; I will go in search of it.'

That night when all the world was asleep he took a large bag, and crept softly away from his four wives and set out on his quest for food. He did not want anyone to know where he was going. For several days he travelled, living only on water; but he found no food, and the bag was still empty on his back. At last one day he saw birds in the trees and he knew that he was near the border of the Hunger-Land. That night in the forest when he stopped at a stream to drink, he saw a tiny gleam of light far ahead of him through the trees. He hurried towards the light and soon he came upon a man with a great hump on his shoulders and scars on his face, and a light hanging at his back, with a shade on it which he could close and open at his will. The Spider Man said, 'I am looking for food; tell me where I can find it.' And the humped man with the light said, 'Do you want it for your people?' But the Spider Man said, 'No, I want it for myself.' Then the humped man laughed and said, 'You are near to the border of the Land of Plenty; follow me and I will give you food.' Then he flashed the light at his back, opening and closing the shade so that the light flickered, and he set off quickly through the trees. The Spider Man followed the light flashing in the darkness, but he had to go so fast that he was almost out of breath when he reached the house where the humped man had stopped. But the humped man only laughed when he saw the Spider Man coming puffing wearily along with his fat and swollen belly. He gave him a good fat meal and the Spider Man soon felt better after his long fast. Then the humped man said, 'You are the Spider Man who once weaved webs in the sky. I, too, once dwelt in the star-country, and one dark night as I was climbing back from the earth-country on your ladder, carrying my lamp on my back to light the way, when I was near the sky you cut the strands of the web and I fell to the earth with a great crash. That is why I have a great hump on my back and scars on my face, and because of this I have never been allowed to go back to the sky-country of the stars. I roam the earth at nights as a forest fairy just as I did in the olden days, for I have my former power still with me, and I still carry my lamp at my back; it is the star-light from the sky-country. I shall never get back to the star-country while I have life. But some day when my work on earth is done I shall go back. But although you were cruel to me I will give you food.' The Spider Man remembered the nights he had cut the ladder strands, and he laughed to himself at the memory of the Star-fairies falling to earth with a great crash. But the man with the light knew that now he had his chance to take vengeance on the Spider Man. The latter did not suspect evil. He was glad to get food at last.

Then the humped man said, 'I will give you four pots. You must not open them until you get home. They will then be filled with food, and thereafter always when you open them they will be packed with good food. And the food will never grow less.' The Spider Man put the four pots in his bag and slinging it over his shoulder he set out for his home, well pleased with his success. After he had gone away, the humped man used his power to make him hungry. Yet for several days he travelled without opening the pots, for although he was almost starving he wished to do as the humped man had told him. At last he could wait no longer. He stopped near his home, took the pots out of the bag and opened them. They were filled with good food as he had been promised. In one was a fine meat stew; in another were many cooked vegetables; in another was bread made from Indian corn; and in another was luscious ripe fruit. He ate until he was full. He covered the pots, put them back in the bag, and hid the bag among the trees. Then he went home. He had meanwhile taken pity on his people and he decided to invite the Chief and all the tribe to a feast the next evening, for the pots would be full, and the food would never decrease, and there would be enough for all. He thought the people would regard him as a very wonderful man if he could supply them all with good food in their hunger.

When he reached his home his wives were very glad to see him back, and they at once brought him water, the only food they had. But he laughed them to scorn, and threw the water in their faces and said, 'Oh, foolish women, I do not want water; it is not food for a great man like me. I have had a good meal of meat stew and corn bread and cooked vegetables and luscious ripe fruit. I know where much food is to be found, but I alone know. I can find food when all others fail, for I am a great man. Go forth and invite the Chief and all the people to a feast which I shall provide for them to-morrow night—a feast for all the land, for my food never grows less.' They were all amazed when they heard his story, and the thought of his good meal greatly added to their hunger. But they went out and summoned all the tribe to a feast as he had told them.

The next night all the people gathered for the feast, for the news of it had spread through all the land. They had taken no water that day, for they wished to eat well, and they were very hungry. They were as hungry as wild beasts in search of food. The Spider Man was very glad because the people praised him, and he proudly brought in his bag of pots. The people all waited hungrily and eagerly. But when he un-covered the first pot there was no food there; he uncovered the second pot, but there was no food there; he uncovered all the pots, but not a bit of food was in any of them. They were all empty, and in the bottom of each was a great gaping hole. Now it had happened in this way. When the humped man, the Star-fairy, had given the pots to the Spider Man, he knew well that the Spider Man would disobey his orders and that he would open the pots before he reached his home. He chuckled to himself, for he knew that now he could take vengeance on the web-weaver who had injured him. So when the Spider Man had left the pots among the trees, the humped man used his magic power and made holes in the pots, and the charm of the food was broken and all the food disappeared. When the people saw the empty pots they thought they had been purposely deceived. The remains of the food and the smell of stew and of fruit still clung to the pots. They thought the Spider Man had eaten all the food himself. So in their great hunger and their rage and their disappointment they fell upon him and beat him and bore him to the ground, while the humped man with the lamp at his back hiding behind the trees looked on and laughed in his glee. Then the people split the Spider Man's arms to the shoulders, and his legs to the thighs, so that he had eight limbs instead of four. And the humped man—the Star-fairy named Fire-fly—came forth from behind the trees and standing over the fallen Spider Man he said, 'Henceforth because of your cruelty to the Star-people you will always crawl on eight legs, and you will have a fat round belly because of the water you have drunk;

and sometimes you will live on top of the water. But you shall always eat only flies and insects. And you will always spin downwards but never upwards, and you will often try to get back to the star-country, but you shall always slip down again on the strand of yarn you have spun.' Then Fire-fly flashed his light and went quickly away, opening and closing the shade of his lamp as he flitted among the trees. And to this day the Spider Man lives as the humped man of the lamp had spoken, because of the cruelty he practised on the Star-fairies in the olden days.

37. The Boy who was
Called Thick-head

THREE brothers lived with their old Indian mother in the forest near the sea. Their father had long been dead. At his death he had little of the world's goods to his credit and his widow and her sons were very poor. In the place where they dwelt, game was not plentiful, and to get food enough to keep them from want they had often to go far into the forest. The youngest boy was smaller and weaker than the others, and when the two older sons went far away to hunt, they always left him behind, for although he always wished to accompany them they would never allow him to go. He had to do all the work about the house, and all day long he gathered wood in the forest and carried water from the stream. And even when his brothers went out in the spring-time to draw sap from the maple trees he was never permitted to go with them. He was always making mistakes and doing foolish things. His brothers called him Thick-head, and all the people round about said he was a simpleton because of his slow and queer ways. His mother alone was kind to him and she always said, 'They may laugh at you and call you fool, but you will prove to be wiser than all of them yet, for so it was told me by a forest fairy at your birth.'

The Chief of the people had a beautiful daughter who had many suitors. But her father spurned them all from his door and said, 'My daughter is not yet of age to marry; and when her time of marriage comes, she will only marry the man who can make great profit from hunting.' The two older sons of the old woman decided that one of them must win the girl. So they prepared to set out on a great hunting expedition far away in the northern forest, for it was now autumn, and the hunter's moon had come. The youngest boy wanted to go with them, for he had never been away from home and he wished to see the world. And his mother said he might go. His brothers were very angry when they heard his request, and they said, 'Much good Thick-head can do us in the chase. He will only bring us bad luck. He is not a hunter but a scullion and a drudge fit only for the fireside.' But his mother commanded them to grant the boy's wish and they had to obey. So the three brothers set out for the north country, the two older brothers grumbling loudly because they were accompanied by the boy they thought a fool.

The two older brothers had good success in the chase and they killed many animals—deer and rabbits and otters and beavers. And they came home bearing a great quantity of dried meat and skins. They each thought, 'Now we have begun to prove our prowess to the Chief, and if we succeed as well next year when the hunter's moon comes again, one of us will surely win his daughter when she is old enough to marry.' But all the youngest boy brought home as a result of his journey into the game country was a large Earth-Worm as thick as his finger and as long as his arm. It was the biggest Earth-Worm he had ever seen. He thought it a great curiosity as well as a great discovery, and he was so busy watching it each day that he had no time to hunt. When he brought it home in a box, his brothers said to their mother, 'What did we tell you about Thick-head? He has now surely proved himself a fool. He has caught only a fat Earth-Worm in all these weeks.' And they noised it abroad in the village and all the people laughed loudly at the simpleton, until 'Thick-head's hunt' became a by-word in all the land. But the boy's mother only smiled and said, 'He will surprise them all yet.'

The boy kept the Earth-Worm in a tiny pen just outside the door of his home. One day a large Duck came waddling along, and sticking her bill over the little fence of the pen she quickly gobbled up the Worm. The boy was very angry and he went to the man who owned the Duck, and said, 'Your Duck ate up my pet Worm. I want my Worm.' The man offered to pay him whatever price he asked, but the boy said, 'I do not want your price. I want my Worm.' But the man said, 'How can I give you your Worm when my Duck has eaten it up? It is gone for ever.' And the boy said, 'It is not gone. It is in the Duck's belly. So I must have the Duck.' Then to avoid further trouble the man gave Thick-head the Duck, for he thought to himself, 'What is the use of arguing with a fool.'

The boy took the Duck home and kept it in a little pen near his home

167

with a low fence around it. And he tied a great weight to its foot so that it could not fly away. He was quite happy again, for he thought, 'Now I have both my Worm and the Duck.' But one day a Fox came prowling along looking for food. He saw the fat Duck tied by the foot in the little pen. And he said, 'What good fortune! There is a choice meal for me,' and in a twinkling he was over the fence. The Duck quacked and made a great noise, but she was soon silenced. The Fox had just finished eating up the Duck when the boy, who had heard the quacking, came running out of the house. The Fox was smacking his lips after his good meal, and he was too slow in getting away. The boy fell to beating him with a stout club and soon killed him and threw his body into the yard behind the house. And he thought, 'That is not so bad. Now I have my Worm and the Duck and the Fox.'

That night an old Wolf came through the forest in search of food. He was very hungry, and in the bright moonlight he saw the dead Fox lying in the yard. He pounced upon it greedily and devoured it until not a trace of it was left. But the boy saw him before he could get away, and he came stealthily upon him and killed him with a blow of his axe. 'I am surely in good luck,' he thought, 'for now I have the Worm and the Duck and the Fox and the Wolf.' But the next day when he told his brothers of his good fortune and his great skill, they laughed at him loudly and said, 'Much good a dead Wolf will do you. Before two days have passed it will be but an evil-smelling thing and we shall have to bury it deep. You are indeed a great fool.' The boy pondered for a long time over what they had said, and he thought, 'Perhaps they are right. The dead Wolf cannot last long. I will save the skin.'

So he skinned the Wolf and dried the skin and made a drum from it. For the drum was one of the few musical instruments of the Indians in those old times, and they beat it loudly at all their dances and festivals. The boy beat the drum each evening, and made a great noise, and he was very proud because he had the only drum in the whole village. One day the Chief sent for him and said to him, 'I want to borrow your drum for this evening. I am having a great gathering to announce to all the land that my daughter is now of age to marry and that suitors may now seek her hand in marriage. But we have no musical instruments and I want your drum, and I myself will beat it at the dance.' So Thick-head brought his drum to the Chief's house, but he was not very well pleased, because he was not invited to the feast, while his brothers were among the favoured guests. And he said to the Chief, 'Be very careful. Do

not tear the skin of my drum, for I can never get another like it. My Worm and my Duck and my Fox and my Wolf have all helped to make it.'

The next day he went for his drum. But the Chief had struck it too hard and had split it open so that it would now make no sound and it was ruined beyond repair. He offered to pay the boy a great price for it, but the boy said, 'I do not want your price. I want my drum. Give me back my drum, for my Worm and the Duck and the Fox and the Wolf are all in it.' The Chief said, 'How can I give you back your drum when it is broken? It is gone for ever. I will give you anything you desire in exchange for it. Since you do not like the price I offer, you may name your own price and you shall have it.' And the boy thought to himself, 'Here is a chance for good fortune. Now I shall surprise my brothers.' And he said, 'Since you cannot give me my drum, I will take your daughter in marriage in exchange.' The Chief was much perplexed, but he had to be true to his word. So he gave his daughter to Thick-head, and they were married, and the girl brought him much treasure and they lived very happily. And his brothers were much amazed and angered because they had failed. But his mother said, 'I told you he was wiser than you and that he would outwit you yet although you called him Thick-head and fool. For the forest fairy said it to me at his birth.'

38. Rabbit and the Indian Chief

LONG ago an Indian Chief was living with his people far in the Canadian forest. Life was good and food was plentiful and the people were all very happy. But one day a wicked giant and his old witch wife came crashing into the land from a far country beyond the prairies. They devoured all the food they could lay their hands on and soon there was little left to eat in all the country; and often they carried off little children to their hiding-place and ate them up until not a trace of them remained. Somewhere far in the forest they dwelt in a hidden cave; they slept all day long, but at night they always stalked forth in search of plunder. The Chief was much troubled, and with his warriors he tried in every way to discover their hiding-place, but no one ever succeeded in finding it. For by the use of their magic power the giant and his old witch wife could make themselves invisible when they walked abroad among men and they could not be caught. The Chief called all his warriors to a council, and he said, 'Who can rid me of this pest? Who can kill the giant?' But not a man replied. And when he saw his people's store of food rapidly growing smaller and the little children of his tribe slowly disappearing, he was greatly puzzled as to what he should do.

One night of bright moonlight Rabbit was prowling through the woods, as was his custom, in search of someone on whom he could play a prank, for he was a great joker. Suddenly he came upon the giant and his old witch wife standing by an opening in the side of a low mountain. He watched them for a long time from the shadow of a great tree, and at last he saw them enter a large hole in the side of the hill. He knew now that he had hit by accident upon the giant's cave and he was well pleased by his discovery. But he kept his secret to himself, for he thought, 'Here is a good chance for me to win fame. I will kill the giants by a crafty trick and I will then be looked upon as a great warrior, the foremost in all the land, for all the Chief's men have failed to find the giants.'

So he went to the Chief and said, 'Oh, Chief, I know where the giants live and I swear to you that I am going to kill them. It is I alone who can rid you of these pests.' 'You!' said the Chief in great surprise; 'little harm the like of you can do to giants; they will eat you up in one mouthful,' and he laughed loudly at Rabbit's boldness. And he called to his warriors saying, 'See what a stout fighter we have here! Little Rabbit says he can do what we have failed to do; he swears that he will kill the giants; he is better fitted to kill a mouse!' And they all laughed loud haw-haws at Rabbit's vanity.

Poor Rabbit's pride was deeply hurt by the Chief's scorn and the warriors' cruel laughter, but it all made him more determined than ever to slay the thieving giants. So he went to an old woman who lived near-by and said, 'Give me an old faded dress and a ragged old shawl and your coloured spectacles and a hat with a feather in it.' The old woman wondered what tricks he was up to now, but she gave him what he asked for. He put on the tattered old dress and the battered old hat with a red feather sticking from the top, and he wrapped the old shawl about his face, and he wore the woman's coloured spectacles and he carried a crooked stick. And dressed in this fashion he set out towards evening for the giants' home. When he reached the mouth of the cave, he stood still and waited, leaning on his crooked stick, for night was coming on and he knew that the giants would soon be going out on their plundering rounds.

After a time when it was quite dark except for the moonlight, the giant's old witch wife came out of the cave. When she saw Rabbit in the dim light she said gruffly, 'Who are you, standing there in the shadows?'

'Oh, my dear niece,' said Rabbit, 'I have found you at last. I am your poor old aunt. I thought I had lost my way. I have come to see you from your home in the far country. It was a long journey and my poor old legs and back are stiff and sore, and I am very hungry and tired'; and he moved slowly towards the woman, hobbling along with his crooked stick. The giant woman was deceived, and she threw her arms around Rabbit and kissed him, and she did not feel his whiskers or his split lip because of the old shawl that was wrapped around his face. 'I have a pain in my jaw from sleeping out of doors,' said Rabbit, 'and I must keep my face wrapped up.'

'Come in and rest, and you will soon feel better,' said the giant woman.

'You will have to lead me in,' said Rabbit, not wishing to take off the shawl, 'for my eyesight is very bad.'

So she led Rabbit into the warm cave, which was so dark that they could scarcely see each other, and she called her husband and said, 'Here is my dear old aunt who has come all the way from the far country beyond the prairies.' And the giant, believing Rabbit to be his wife's kindred, for he could not see him very clearly, treated him very kindly. And they showed him the bed where he was to sleep.

The woman then gave Rabbit a large piece of dried meat to eat. But Rabbit said, 'I cannot eat it, for I am old and I have lost all my teeth. Give me an axe to cut it up small.' So the woman brought him a sharp axe and he chopped the meat into small pieces and ate it all up. And he said, 'I will keep the axe by me, for I shall need it at all my meals,' and he placed it beside his bed. The giant said, 'We are going away to see some friends, but we shall be back before midnight.' But before they went away Rabbit said to the woman, 'I hope your husband sleeps soundly; I have a bad cough and I sometimes moan because of the pain in my face and head and I do not wish to disturb him.'

And the old giant woman answered, 'He slumbers too well. When we sleep we both snore loudly, and when you hear us snoring you may cough as much as you please, for then you will know that we are sound asleep.' Then the man and his witch wife went away.

When the giants came home, Rabbit pretended to be fast asleep. They brought back with them much food which they hid in a secret place at the side of the cave. Rabbit watched them through the holes in the old shawl around his head. Soon they went to bed, drowsy after their fat meal. When Rabbit heard them snoring loudly like a great waterfall, 'chr-r-r, chr-r-r,' he arose very quietly and crept softly to their bedside. With two blows of his axe he killed the giant and his wife, one after the other. Then he ran away as fast as he could, carrying with him his old dress and hat and shawl, for he thought he might need them again.

In the morning he went to the Chief's house and told the Chief what he had done. The Chief laughed scornfully and he would not believe it until Rabbit brought him to the cave and showed him the slain giants cold and stiff in their bed. The Chief's men then took back to the village the great store of food the giants had hidden in the secret place. But the Chief and his warriors, although they were glad to be rid of the thieves, were angry at heart because Rabbit whom they had laughed at had done what they had failed to do, for they were very jealous of Rabbit's power.

One day soon afterwards the Chief called all the birds and the animals to a council, and he said, 'Now that the giants who robbed us of our food are dead and gone, and that we shall never again want for nourishment in my country, I am going to let each animal and bird choose the kind of food he would most like to live on if he could get it. And they shall never want for that kind of food if it can be provided.' And he called on each to make the choice. And the birds said 'Grain and seeds and worms,' and the Squirrel said 'Nuts', and the Fox said 'Chickens,' and the cat said 'Milk,' and the dog said 'Meat and bones,' and the weasel said 'Eggs,' and the wolf said 'Lambs,' and the bear said 'Fish from the frozen sea,' and so on until each animal was called upon and declared his liking. And the Chief said, 'It shall be as you have chosen.' But the Chief had purposely neglected to summon poor Rabbit to the council, and Rabbit was absent on a long journey. When he came home, he was very angry when he heard what had happened, for only the left-over in the world's food remained for him to choose. So he went to the Chief and said in great wrath, 'This is a fine return for ridding your land of giants. But that is a way you have; you always reward good deeds with evil.'

The Chief was very angry because of Rabbit's insolence, and he said, 'You are telling lies again.' But Rabbit called as witnesses to the truth of what he said Sheep and Goat and Duck who chanced to be passing by and who stood listening to the quarrel. And old Sheep said, 'Rabbit has spoken truly. When I was young I gave the Chief much wool to make clothes for his back and he used me well. But now that I am old he is going to kill me and eat me up. That is *my* reward.' And old Goat said, 'Rabbit has spoken wisely and justly. I served the Chief well in my time and gave him milk, but now that I am old and have no more milk he is fattening me and getting me ready for slaughter. That is *my* reward.' And old Duck said, 'That is a true saying of Rabbit. Once upon a time I gave the Chief many eggs and young ducklings, but now that I have stopped laying he is soon going to roast me in a pot. That is *my* reward.' The Chief could make no answer to these charges, for he knew them to be true, and he offered to do what was in his power for Rabbit. But Rabbit refused to make choice of food, for he said the best was already gone. He sulked for many months and lived alone by his own efforts as best he could.

At last he decided to take vengeance on the Chief. And he hit, as was his custom, on a crafty trick. The Chief had an old Bear which he prized very highly, for the Bear did for him many wondrous tricks and brought laughter to him and his warriors when he danced at their feasts. In those olden times Bear had a long bushy tail of which he was very proud. One day as Rabbit sat on the ice fishing—for it was now winter— Bear came along. There was to be a feast that night and he was going to dance for the Chief, and he was in very good spirits. 'Where did you get all the fine fish?' he asked, for he was a great fish eater. 'I caught them through the hole in the ice,' said Rabbit. 'It is very easy. Just drop your tail down through the hole and it will soon be covered with fine big fish.'

Bear did as he was told, and he sat on the ice for a long time waiting for his prey. He sat so long that the hole froze up, for it was very cold, and in it was frozen poor Bear's long bushy tail. 'Now,' said Rabbit, 'jump quick, for many fish are hanging to you.' Bear jumped with all his might, but his tail was held fast in the ice and it broke off close to the root. Rabbit laughed in great glee and ran away. And poor Bear howled with pain and shame. He could not dance at the feast because his stub of a tail was sore, and the Chief and the warriors were very angry at Rabbit because he had harmed their dancing pet. And since that time Bear has had a short stubby tail which to this day he tries to wag feebly.

Rabbit then hid for some days far from the Chief and his warriors. Then he decided to try another trick. The Chief's wood-cutter was old Beaver, who lived in a little house of reeds on the bank of a stream. He was very busy now cutting down trees for the Chief, for it was near to spring-time and the people were in need of logs for building roads over the rivers. One day Rabbit went to Beaver and said, 'The Chief sent me to you to bring you to a great tree he wishes you to cut down at once.' So Beaver went along with him. But when Beaver was busy at his task cutting down the tree, Rabbit hit him a savage blow on the head with a big stick hoping to kill him and thus again to anger the Chief. Poor Beaver fell to the ground and Rabbit ran away. But Beaver was only stunned. He got up after a time and went home muttering to himself and rubbing his sore head. Soon Rabbit came back to the tree and found Beaver gone. He knew that his blow had failed. Then he put on again his tattered old dress and his ragged shawl and his coloured spectacles and the hat with the red feather sticking to the top, and he went to Beaver's house by the stream, hobbling along with a stick. 'The Chief sent me to you to bring you to a great tree he wishes you to cut down at once,' he called. And Beaver said, 'I have already tried to cut a great tree for him today and I should have finished it had I not been beaten with a stick until I was stunned by the blow.' 'Who struck you?' asked Rabbit, laughing to himself. 'Rabbit struck me,' answered Beaver. 'He is a great brigand and a liar and a thief,' said Rabbit. 'He is all that,' said Beaver, rubbing the lump on his head. So Beaver went along with Rabbit. And Rabbit asked as they went along, 'How is it that you are alive after that cruel blow?' And Beaver said, 'Rabbit hit me on the head. If he had hit me on the back of my neck he would have killed me, for there I keep the secret of my life.'

When Beaver was busy again at his task cutting down the tree, Rabbit hit him a powerful blow on the back of the neck and poor Beaver fell down dead. Then he cut off his tail that was made like a file, and went away happy, for he knew that the Chief would be very angry when he found what had happened to his wood-cutter.

When the Chief learned that Beaver had been killed, his wrath knew no bounds, for he could ill afford at this time to lose his best wood-chopper. He blamed Rabbit for the deed, but he could not be sure that his suspicions were well-founded. Rabbit kept out of the Chief's sight for some weeks. But one day in early summer he was very hungry. He saw all the other animals filling their bellies with their favourite food, and he decided to forget his sulks and to ask the Chief for help. So he went to the Chief and said haughtily, 'I want you to give me food for my own special use as you have done with the other animals. You must do it at once or I will do you much harm.' Then the Chief remembered what Rabbit had done to his dancing Bear, and he thought of the death of Beaver, for which he blamed Rabbit without proof, and he grew red with anger. He seized Rabbit by the heels and said, 'Henceforth the dogs will always chase you, and you will never have peace when they are near. And you will live for the most part on whatever food I throw you into now.' Then he whirled Rabbit around his head by the heels, and he threw him from him with great force, hoping to drop him in a great black swamp near-by. Poor Rabbit went flying through the air for a great distance, farther than the Chief had hoped, and he dropped with a thud into a field of clover on the edge of which cabbages and lettuce were growing. And since that time the dogs have always chased Rabbit and he has lived for the most part on cabbages and lettuce and clover which he steals on moonlight nights from farmers' fields.

39. Great Heart and the Three Tests

SOMEWHERE near the sea in olden times a boy was living with his father and mother. He had no brothers or sisters. His father was a great hunter and the boy inherited something of his power, for he was always very successful in the killing of game. And his mother said, 'Some day he will be a great man, for before his birth a vision came to me in the night and told me that my son would win wide fame. And fairy gifts were laid by the fairies in his cradle.' And his father, listening to her boasting, said, 'Time will tell; time will tell; but if he is to be a great man it is his own deeds and not your boasting that must prove it.' As the boy grew up he became strangely beautiful and he had great strength. And his father said, 'It is time he set out to seek his fortune. I was in the forest doing for myself when I was no older than he.' And his mother said, 'Wait a little and be not so impatient. He is yet young and there is yet much time.' So the boy remained at home a while longer.

Now it happened that far away in a distant village there lived a young girl of very great beauty and grace. Her father had been a great Chief, but he was now dead. Her mother too was dead, and she was all alone in the world. But her parents had left her vast lands and a great store of goods and many servants, and because of her treasures and her great beauty she had many suitors. But she was not easily pleased by men and on all who came to seek her hand she imposed severe feats of skill to test their sincerity and their worth. She was carefully guarded by an old woman and many servants who kept troublesome and meddlesome people away.

Soon the fame of the girl's wealth and beauty spread through all the land. It reached the sea coast village where the young man dwelt. His father thought to himself, 'Here is a good chance for my son to prove his worth.' So he called his boy to him and said, 'It is time you were setting out to seek your fortune in the world and to find a wife, for your spring-time is passing and your summer of life will soon be here, and before you know it your autumn will be upon you and your winter will be near. There is no time to lose. Seek out the beautiful girl of the rich treasures in the distant inland village and try to win her as your wife.' And his mother gave him the fairy gifts which had been laid in his cradle at his birth, and he said goodbye to his parents and set out on his long journey. He had no misgivings, for he was very vain of his beauty and he was sure, too, of his strength.

As he travelled inland he came one day upon a man clad in scarlet sitting on the side of a rocky hill tying stones to his feet. 'Hello,' he said to the man, 'why are you tying these heavy rocks to your ankles?' 'I am a hunter,' replied the man, 'but when I follow the deer I run so fast that I am soon far in front of them instead of behind them, and I am putting heavy weights on my feet so that I will not run so rapidly.' 'You are indeed a wonderful man,' said the boy; 'but I am alone and I need a companion. Let us go along together.' 'Who are you?' said the man. 'I am Lad of the Great Heart,' said the boy, 'and I can do great deeds and I can win for you great treasure.' So the Scarlet Runner went along with him.

Towards evening when they were now far inland, they came to a large lake. Among the trees on the fringe of the lake a large fat man was lying flat on his stomach with his mouth in the water drinking as hard as he could. For some time they watched him, but still he drank and the lake grew smaller and smaller and still his thirst was not quenched. They laughed at such a strange sight, and as they approached him the boy said, 'Hello! Why do you lie there drinking so much water?' 'Oh,' answered the fat man, 'there are times when I cannot get enough water to drink. When I have drunk this lake dry I shall still be thirsty.' 'Who are you?' asked the boy. 'I am Man of the Great Thirst,' said the fat man. 'That is well,' said Great Heart, 'we two need a third companion. We can do great deeds and we can win for you great treasure.' So the three went along together.

They had not gone far when they came to a wide open plain where they saw a man walking along with his face raised upwards, peering at the sky. He moved along rapidly and seemed to find his way without his eyes, for he gazed steadily at the heavens. 'Hello,' said Great Heart as the sky-gazer rushed past him and almost knocked him over, 'what are you looking at so intently?' 'Oh,' said the man, 'I have shot an arrow into the sky and I am waiting for it to fall. It has gone so far that it will be some time before it drops.' 'Who are you?' asked the boy. 'I am the Far-Darter,' said the sky-gazer. 'We three need a fourth companion,' said the boy. 'We can do great deeds and win for you much treasure. Come along with us.' So the four went along together.

They had gone but a short distance across the plain to the edge of a forest when they came upon a man lying down at full length with his head upon his hand. The edge of his hand was on the ground and it was half closed around his ear, which rested upon it. As he saw the four men approaching him he placed a finger of his other hand upon his lips and signalled to them to keep quiet. 'Hello,' said Great Heart in a whisper, 'what are you doing there with your ear to the ground?' 'I am listening to the plants growing far away in the forest,' he answered. 'There is a beautiful flower I wish to find, and I am trying to hear it breathing so that I may go and get it. Aha! I hear it now.' So saying he rose from the ground. The boy said, 'Who are you?' 'I am Keen Ears,' said the listener. 'We four need another companion,' said Great Heart. 'We can do great deeds and win for you much treasure. Come along with us.' So the four men and the boy went along together, Keen Ears, and Scarlet Runner, and Far-Darter, and Man of the Great Thirst, and Lad of the Great Heart. Then Great Heart unfolded to the others his plan to win the beautiful girl who lived with her treasures in the distant village. And they gladly agreed to help him in his dangerous undertaking.

When they reached the village, the people were all very curious when they saw the five strangers. They marvelled at Great Heart's beauty. But when they heard that he wished to marry the daughter of the former Chief they shook their heads gravely and said, 'It will never be. She places hard conditions on all who seek her hand. He who fails in the tests is doomed to death. Many suitors have tried and failed and died.' But Great Heart was not alarmed, and with his four companions he went to the girl's home. The old woman who guarded her met him at the door and he made known his wishes. She laughed scornfully when she saw his great beauty, and she said, 'You look more like a girl than like a warrior. You cannot endure the tests.' But the young man insisted on making the trials.

The old woman said, 'If you fail in the tests you will die,' and Great Heart said, 'It is so agreed.' Then the woman said, 'If you wish to win the maiden you must first push away this great rock from before her window. It keeps the sunlight from her in the mornings.' Then Great Heart, calling to his aid the fairy gifts of his cradle, placed his shoulder against the huge stone which rose higher than the house, and he pushed with all his strength. With a mighty crash it rolled down the hill and broke into millions of pieces. The bits of rock flew all over the earth so great was the fall, and the little pebbles and stones that came from it are seen throughout the world to this day. The sunlight streamed in at the window, and the maiden knew that the first test had been successfully passed by a suitor.

Then came the second test. The old woman and her servants brought great quantities of food and drink and bade the strangers consume it all at one meal. They were very hungry, for they had eaten nothing all day and they easily ate up the food. But when Great Heart saw the great barrels of water, his spirits sank, and he said, 'I fear I am beaten.' But Man of the Great Thirst said, 'Not so fast, my friend. The spell of great stomach-burning is again upon me. I am very dry as if there was a fire in my belly. Give me a chance to drink.' He went from barrel to barrel and in a twinkling he had drained them all of every drop. And the people wondered greatly.

But there was still another test. 'You must have one of your party run a race,' said the old woman to Great Heart. And she brought out a man who had never been beaten in running. 'Who is your choice of runners?' she asked; 'he must race with this man, and if he wins you may have the maiden for your wife and all the treasure with her, for this is the final test. But if he loses the race you shall die.' Great Heart called Scarlet Runner to the mark and told the old woman that this was the man selected. Then he untied the rocks from the runner's feet, and when all was ready the race began. The course lay far across the plains for many miles until the runners should pass from sight, and back again to the starting point. The two runners kept together for some distance, talking together in a friendly way as they ran. When they had passed from sight of the village the maiden's runner said, 'Now we are out of sight of the village. Let us rest here a while on this grassy bank, for the day is hot.' The Scarlet Runner agreed to this and they both stretched out on the the grass. Now this was an old trick of the maiden's runner, who always won by craft rather than by speed. They had not lain down long on the grass when Scarlet Runner fell asleep under the hot sun, just as his rival had hoped. When the latter was sure that his rival was sound asleep, he set out for the village, running as fast as he could. The people soon saw their runner approaching far off on the plains, but there was no sign of the stranger, and they thought that the new suitor for the girl's hand had at last failed like all the others before him.

Great Heart was much puzzled when Scarlet Runner did not appear, and as he saw the maiden's runner coming nearer, he said, 'What can have happened? I fear I am beaten.' But Keen Ears threw himself flat on the ground and listened. 'Scarlet Runner is asleep,' he called; 'I hear him snoring on the plains far away.' And with his keen sense of sound he located the exact spot where the runner was lying. 'I will soon wake him,' said Far-Darter, as he fitted an arrow to his bow-string. The people all thought him mad, for they had never seen an arrow shot so great a distance beyond their sight. But Far-Darter was not dismayed. He quickly shot an arrow from his bow to the spot which Keen Ears had indicated. His aim was so true that the arrow hit Scarlet Runner on the nose and aroused him from his sleep. But when he rose to his feet he found that his rival was gone and he knew that he had been deceived. So in a great rage because of the trick and the pain in his nose, he set out for the village running like the wind. His rival had almost reached the end of the race, but by putting all his strength into his effort, Scarlet Runner quickly overtook him and passed him near the winning-post and won the race. And the people wondered greatly at these great deeds of the strangers.

Then the old woman said to Great Heart, 'You have won the maiden as your wife, for you alone have succeeded in these tests.' So the two were married with great ceremony. Great Heart gave much treasure to his companions, and they promised to help him always in his need. Then with his wife and her servants and her great store of goods he went back to his native village by the sea. His father and mother were glad to see him again and to hear of his success, and his mother said, 'I told you he would win great fame because of the fairy gifts that were laid in his cradle at his birth.' And they all lived together and were henceforth very happy.

40. The Boy of the Red Twilight Sky

LONG ago there dwelt on the shores of the Great Water in the West a young man and his younger wife. They had no children and they lived all by themselves far from other people on an island not far from the coast. The man spent his time in catching the deep-sea fish far out on the ocean, or in spearing salmon in the distant rivers. Often he was gone for many days and his wife was very lonely in his absence. She was not afraid, for she had a stout spirit, but it was very dismal in the evenings to look only at the grey leaden sky and to hear only the sound of the surf as it beat upon the beach. So day after day she said to herself, 'I wish we had children. They would be good company for me when I am alone and my husband is far away.'

One evening at twilight when she was solitary because of her husband's absence on the ocean catching the deep-sea fish, she sat on the sand beach looking out across the water. The sky in the west was pale grey; it was always dull and grey in that country, and when the sun had gone down there was no soft light. In her loneliness the woman said to herself, 'I wish we had children to keep me company.' A King-fisher, with his children, was diving for minnows not far away. And the woman said, 'Oh, sea bird with the white collar, I wish we had children like you.' And the Kingfisher said, 'Look in the sea-shells; look in the sea-shells,' and flew away. The next evening the woman sat again upon the beach looking westward at the dull grey sky. Not far away a white Sea-gull was riding on the waves in the midst of her brood of little ones. And the woman said, 'Oh, white sea bird, I wish we had children like you to keep us company.' And the Sea-gull said, 'Look in the sea-shells; look in the sea-shells,' and flew away.

The woman wondered greatly at the words of the Kingfisher and the

Sea-gull. As she sat there in thought she heard a strange cry coming from the sand dunes behind her. She went closer to the sound and found that the cry came from a large sea-shell lying on the sand. She picked up the shell, and inside of it was a tiny boy, crying as hard as he could. She was well pleased with her discovery, and she carried the baby to her home and cared for him. When her husband came home from the sea, he, too, was very happy to find the baby there, for he knew that they would be lonely no more.

The baby grew very rapidly, and soon he was able to walk and move about where he pleased. One day the woman was wearing a copper bracelet on her arm and the child said to her, 'I must have a bow made from the copper on your arm.' So to please him she made him a tiny bow from the bracelet, and two tiny arrows. At once he set out to hunt game, and day after day he came home bearing the products of his chase. He brought home geese and ducks and brant and small sea birds, and gave them to his mother for food. As he grew older the man and his wife noticed that his face took on a golden hue brighter than the colour of his copper bow. Wherever he went there was a strange light. When he sat on the beach looking to the west the weather was always calm and there were strange bright gleams upon the water. And his foster-parents wondered greatly at this unusual power. But the boy would not talk about it; when they spoke of it he was always silent.

It happened once that the winds blew hard over the Great Water and the man could not go out to catch fish because of the turbulent sea. For many days he stayed on shore, for the ocean, which was usually at peace, was lashed into a great fury and the waves were dashing high on the beach. Soon the people were in need of fish for food. And the boy said, 'I will go out with you, for I can overcome the Storm Spirit.' The man did not want to go, but at last he listened to the boy's entreaties and together they set out for the fishing grounds far across the tossing sea. They had not gone far when they met the Spirit of the Storm coming madly from the south-west where the great winds dwelt. He tried hard to upset their boat, but over them he had no power, for the boy guided the frail craft across the water and all around them the sea was calm and still. Then the Storm Spirit called his nephew Black Cloud to help him, and away in the south-east they saw him hurrying to his uncle's aid. But the boy said to the man, 'Be not afraid, for I am more than a match for him.' So the two met, but when Black Cloud saw the boy he quickly disappeared. Then the Spirit of the Storm called

Mist of the Sea to come and cover the water, for he thought the boat would be lost if he hid the land from the man and the boy. When the man saw Mist of the Sea coming like a grey vapour across the water he was very frightened, for of all his enemies on the ocean he feared this one most. But the boy said, 'He cannot harm you when I am with you.' And sure enough, when Mist of the Sea saw the boy sitting smiling in the boat he disappeared as quickly as he had come. And the Storm Spirit in great anger hurried away to other parts, and that day there was no more danger on the sea near the fishing grounds.

The boy and the man soon reached the fishing grounds in safety. And the boy taught his foster-father a magic song with which he was able to lure fish to his nets. Before evening came the boat was filled with good fat fish and they set out for their home. The man said, 'Tell me the secret of your power.' But the boy said, 'It is not yet time.'

The next day the boy killed many birds. He skinned them all and dried their skins. Then he dressed himself in the skin of a plover and rose into the air and flew above the sea. And the sea under him was grey like his wings. Then he came down and dressed himself in the skin of a blue-jay and soared away again. And the sea over which he was flying was at once changed to blue like the blue of his wings. When he came back to the beach, he put on the skin of a robin with the breast of a golden hue like his face. Then he flew high and at once the waves under him reflected a colour as of fire and bright gleams of light appeared upon the ocean, and the sky in the west was golden red. The boy flew back to the beach and he said to his foster-parents, 'Now it is time for me to leave you. I am the offspring of the sun. Yesterday my power was tested and it was not found wanting, so now I must go away and I shall see you no more. But at evening I shall appear to you often in the twilight sky in the west. And when the sky and the sea look at evening like the colour of my face, you will know that there will be no wind nor storm and that on the morrow the weather will be fair. But although I go away, I shall leave you a strange power. And always when you need me, let me know your desires by making white offerings to me, so that I may see them from my home far in the west.'

Then he gave to his foster-mother a wonderful robe. He bade his parents good-bye, and soared away to the west, leaving them in sadness. But the woman still keeps a part of the power he gave her, and when she sits on the island in a crevice in the dunes and loosens her wonderful robe, the wind hurries down from the land, and the sea is ruffled with storm; and the more she loosens the garment the greater is the tempest. But in the late autumn when the cold mists come in from the sea, and the evenings are chill, and the sky is dull and grey, she remembers the promise of the boy. And she makes to him an offering of tiny white feathers plucked from the breasts of birds. She throws them into the air, and they appear as flakes of snow and rise thickly into the winds. And they hurry westward to tell the boy that the world is grey and dreary as it yearns for the sight of his golden face. Then he appears to the people of earth. He comes at evening and lingers after the sun has gone, until the twilight sky is red, and the ocean in the west has gleams of golden light. And the people then know that there will be no wind and that on the morrow the weather will be fair, as he promised them long ago.

41. How Raven Brought Fire
to the Indians

MANY ages ago when the world was still young, Raven and White Sea-gull lived near together in Canada, far in the north country on the shores of the Great Water in the West. They were very good friends and they always worked in harmony and they had much food and many servants in common. White Sea-gull knew no guile; he was always very open and frank and honest in his dealings with others. But Raven was a sly fellow, and at times he was not lacking in treachery and deceit. But Sea-gull did not suspect him, and the two lived always on very friendly terms. In these far-back times in the north country all the world was dark and there was no light but that of the stars. Sea-gull owned all the daylight, but he was very stingy and he kept it always locked up in a box. He would give none of it to anyone else, and he never let it out of the box except when he needed a little of it to help himself when he went far away on his journeys.

After a time Raven grew envious of Sea-gull's possession. And he said, 'It is not fair that Sea-gull should keep the daylight all to himself locked up in a box. It was meant for all the world and not for him alone, and it would be of great value to all of us if he would sometimes let a little of it out.' So he went to Sea-gull and said, 'Give me some of your daylight. You do not need it all and I can use some of it with advantage.' But Sea-gull said, 'No. I want it all for myself. What could you do with daylight, you with your coat as black as night?' and he would not give him any of it. So Raven made up his mind that he would have to get some daylight from Sea-gull by stealth.

Soon afterwards Raven gathered some prickly thorns and burdocks and scattered them on the ground between Sea-gull's house and the beach where the canoes were lying. Then he went to Sea-gull's window and cried loudly, 'Our canoes are going adrift in the surf. Come quickly and help me to save them.' Sea-gull sprang out of bed and ran half-asleep on his bare feet. But as he ran to the beach the thorns stuck in his bare flesh, and he howled with pain. He crawled back to his house, saying, 'My canoe may go adrift if it pleases; I cannot walk because of the splinters in my feet.' Raven chuckled to himself, and he moved away, pretending to go to the beach to draw up the canoes. Then he went into Sea-gull's house. Sea-gull was still howling with pain; he was sitting crying on the side of his bed and he was trying to pull the thorns from his feet as best he could. 'I will help you,' said Raven, 'for I have often done this before. I am a very good doctor.' So he took an awl made from whale-bone and he caught hold of Sea-gull's foot, with the pretence of removing the thorns. But instead of taking them out he only pushed them in farther until poor Sea-gull howled louder than ever. And Raven said, 'It is so dark I cannot see to pull these thorns from your feet. Give me some daylight and I will soon cure you. A doctor must always have a little light.' So Sea-gull unlocked the box and lifted the cover just a little bit so that a faint gleam of light came out. 'That is better,' said Raven. But instead of picking out the thorns he pushed them in as he had done before, until Sea-gull howled and kicked in pain. 'Why are you so stingy with your light?' snapped Raven. 'Do you think I am an owl and that I can see well enough in the darkness to heal your feet? Open the box wide and I will soon make you well.' So saying he purposely fell heavily against Sea-gull and knocked the box on the floor. The cover flew open and daylight escaped and spread quickly over all the world. Poor Sea-gull tried his best to lure it back again into the box, but his efforts proved fruitless, for it had gone for ever. Raven said he was very sorry for the accident, but after he had taken all the thorns from Sea-gull's feet he went home laughing to himself and well pleased because of the success of his trick.

Soon there was light in all the world. But Raven could not see very well, for the light was too bright and his eyes were not accustomed to it. He sat for a time looking towards the east, but he saw there nothing of interest. The next day he saw a bit farther, for he was now getting used to the new conditions. The third day he could see distinctly a line of hills far in the east, rising against the sky, and covered with a blue mist. He looked long at the strange sight. Then he saw far away towards the hill a thin column of smoke lifting heavenwards. He had never seen smoke before, but he had often heard of it from travellers in strange places. 'That must be the country of which I have been told,' he said. 'In that land dwell the people who alone possess Fire. We have searched for it for many ages and now I think we have found it.' Then he thought, 'We now have the daylight, and what a fine thing it would be if we could also have Fire,' and he determined to set out to find it.

On the following day he called his servants together and told them of his plans. He said, 'We shall set out at once, for the distance is far.' And he asked three of his best servants, Robin, Mole and Flea, to go with him. Flea brought out his little wagon and they all tried to get into it, but it was much too small to hold them. Then they tried Mole's carriage, but it was much too frail, and it had scarcely started to move when it broke down and they all fell out in a heap. Then they tried Robin's carriage, but it was much too high and it toppled over under its heavy load and threw them all to the ground. Then Raven stole Sea-gull's large strong carriage, for Sea-gull was asleep, and it did very well, and they started on their journey, taking turns pushing the carriage along with a pole over the flat plain.

After a strange journey in queer places they reached the land of the people who owned Fire, guided along by the thin column of smoke. The people were not people of earth. Some say they were the Fish people, but that, no man knows. They sat around in a large circle with Fire in their midst, for it was autumn and the days and nights were chill. And Fire was in many places. Raven looked on for a while from afar thinking of the best plan to obtain Fire. Then he said to Robin, 'You can move faster than any of us. You must steal Fire. You can fly in quickly, pick it up in your bill and take it back to us and the people will not see nor hear you.' So Robin picked out a spot where there were few people, and he darted in quickly and picked up fire in a twinkling and flew back unharmed towards his companions. But he had only taken a very little bit of it. When he got half-way back to his friends, Fire was so hot in his bill that it gave him a strange pain and he had to drop it on the ground. It fell to the earth with a crash and it was so small that it flickered faintly. Robin called to his companions to bring the carriage.

Then he stood over Fire and fanned it with his wings to keep it alive. It was very hot, but he stood bravely to his task until his breast was badly scorched and he had to move away. His efforts to save Fire were of no avail, and before his companions reached him Fire had died, and only a black coal remained. And poor Robin's breast was singed, and to this day the breasts of his descendants are a reddish-brown colour because he was scorched while trying to steal Fire ages ago.

Then Raven asked Flea to make the attempt to steal Fire. But Flea said, 'I am too little. The heat would roast me to death; and, further, I might miscalculate the distance and hop into the flame.' Then Raven asked Mole to try, but Mole said, 'Oh no, I am better fitted for other work. My fur would all be singed like Robin's breast.' Raven took good care that he would not go himself, for he was a great coward. So he said, 'There is a better and easier way. We will steal the baby of the Chief and hold him for ransom. Perhaps they will give us Fire in exchange for him,' and they all thought this was a very good idea. Raven asked, 'Who will volunteer to steal the baby?' for he always made the others do all the work. Flea said, 'I will go. In one jump I will be into the house, and in another jump I will be out again, for I can hop a great distance.' But the others laughed and said, 'You could not carry the baby; you are too small.' The Mole said, 'I will go. I can tunnel a passage very quietly under the house and right up to the baby's cradle. I can then steal the baby and no one will hear me or see me.' So it was agreed that Mole should go. In a few minutes Mole made his tunnel, and he was soon back with the baby. Then they got into their carriage and hurried home with their prize.

When the Chief of the Fire people discovered the loss of his child he was very angry. And in all the land there was great sorrow because the Chief's heir, the hope of the tribe, had gone. And the child's mother and her women wept so bitterly that their tears fell like rain on all the land. The Chief said he would give anything he possessed to find his child. But although his people searched far and near, they could not find the baby. After many days a wayfarer who had come far from the Great Water in the west brought them news that a strange child was living far to the westward in the village by the sea. He said, 'He is not of their tribe. He looks like the children of your village,' and he advised them to go to see him for themselves. So the Chief sent his men to search for them guided by the wayfarer. When they reached Raven's village they were told that a strange baby was indeed there; the child was described to them, but he was kept out of sight, and Raven would not tell how he had happened to come there. And Raven said, 'How do I know he is your Chief's child? People tell strange lies these days. If you want him you can pay for him, for he has caused us much trouble and expense.' So the messengers went back and reported to the Chief what they had heard. From the description, the Chief knew that the child was his, so he gave the messengers very valuable presents of pearls and rich robes and sent them back again to ransom his boy. But Raven, when he saw the presents, said, 'No, I do not want these gifts; they do not pay me for my trouble,' and he would not part with the baby. The messengers again reported to the Chief what had happened. Then the Chief gave them still richer gifts, the best he had in all his land, and sent them back. But again Raven said, 'No, your gifts are valueless, compared with my trouble and expense. Say this to your Chief.'

When the Chief heard this from his messengers he was sore perplexed, for he had offered the best he had, and he thought that he had reached the end of his resources. So he said, 'Go back and ask the people to demand what they wish in exchange for my boy and they will receive it if it can be provided.' So the messengers went back to Raven and spoke as they had been commanded. And Raven said, 'Only one thing can pay for the child, and that is Fire. Give me Fire and you can take the baby.' The messenger laughed and said, 'Why did you not say so at first and save us all this trouble and anxiety? Fire is the most plentiful thing in our kingdom, and we hold it in no value.' So they returned happy to the Chief. And he sent back much Fire and received his child unharmed from Raven in exchange. And he sent Raven two small stones which the messengers taught Raven how to use. And they said, 'If you ever lose Fire or if it dies for lack of food you can always call it back to life with these two little stones.' Then they showed him how to make Fire with the two little stones and withered grass, and birch-bark and dry pine, and Raven thought it was very easy. And he felt very proud because he had brought Fire and Light to the earth. He kept Fire for himself for a long time, and although the people clamoured loudly for it, he would not give any of it away. Soon, however, he decided to sell a quantity of it, for he now had the power of making it. So he said to himself, 'This is a good way to get many wives,' and he announced that he would only sell some of his fire in return for a wife. And many families bought his fire and in exchange he received many wives. And to this day he still has many wives and he still moves about from place to place with a flock of them always around him. But the Indians when they arrived took Fire away from him. Thus Fire came to the Indians in the olden days. And when it has died, as it often does, they still sometimes use Raven's flint stones to bring it back to life.

42. The Girl who Always Cried

ON THE bank of a stream far in the West, Owl-man lived long ago in a little house under the ground. He had very strange habits. He always kept away from the Great Water and he dwelt for the most part in the forest. He had very few friends, and he usually went hunting by himself. He lived on toads and frogs and flies. He would say but little, and when other people sat around him talking pleasantly, he was always silent, gazing into space with wide-open eyes, and trying to look wiser than he really was. Because of this, people thought he was very queer, and strange stories about him soon spread far and wide. It was said that he was very cruel, and that he was silent because he was always brooding over his past wickedness or thinking about some evil deed he was soon going to do. And when children were troublesome or disobedient, their mothers always frightened them into goodness by saying, 'The Owl-man from the stream will come and take you if you do not mend your ways.' And although the Owl-man was a solitary fellow he thus had great influence in all the land.

Not far away lived a man and a woman who had one adopted daughter. Because she was the only child in the house she was much petted, and she was never satisfied, and she cried and fretted all the time, and kept always asking for things she could not get. She disturbed all the neighbours round about so that they could not sleep because of her constant wailing and complaining. At last her foster-parents grew tired of her weeping and they said, 'The Owl-man will carry you off if you do not stop crying.' But still she pouted and fretted. And the old man of the house said, 'I wish the Owl-man would come and take her away.' Now the old man was a great magician, and as he wished, so it came to pass.

That evening it happened that the people were gathered at a feast of shell-fish on the beach by the bright moonlight, as was their weekly custom. But the sorrowful girl would not go with the others. She stayed at home and sulked. As she sat alone in the house, old Owl-man came along carrying his basket full of toads and frogs. The girl was still crying when he came in. 'I have come for you,' he said, 'as the old man wished.' And he put her in his basket with the toads and frogs and carried her off. She yelled and kicked and scratched, but the lid of the basket was tightly closed and Owl-man laughed to himself and said, 'Now I have a wife at last. I shall be alone no more, and the people will not now think I am so queer.' So he took her to his underground house by the stream. That night the people noticed that the girl's cries were no longer heard and they said, 'What can have cured Sour-face; what can have pleased Cry-baby into silence?' And the girl's foster-mother wondered where she had gone. But only the old man knew that it had happened as he had wished, because of his magic power, and that Owl-man had taken her away.

The girl was not happy in her new home, for she would not be happy in any place. She still kept up her caterwauling and there was no peace in the house. Owl-man was a great hunter. Every day he went out hunting with his big basket on his arm, but he always locked his wife in the house before he went away. He was always very successful in the chase, and each night he came back with his basket full of toads and frogs and field-mice and flies. But his wife would eat none of them and she threw them in his face when he offered them to her, and said in a bad temper, 'I will not eat your filthy food. It is not fit food for gentle-folk.' And Owl-man said, 'Gentle-folk indeed! You should find a more suitable name; you are not gentle; you are a wild evil thing, but I am going to tame you.' And the girl wept again and sulked and stamped her feet in her temper.

At last the girl became very hungry, for there was little to eat except the food that Owl-man brought home for himself. He gathered a few berries for her, but even these did not satisfy her hunger. So she thought out a plan of escape. One day when Owl-man was away, she took some oil she found in the house and rubbed it all over her face and hair. When Owl-man came home in the evening, he said, 'You are very pretty tonight. What have you done to make yourself look so sleek and shiny?' And she answered, 'I have put on my face and hair gum which I picked from the trees last night when I went walking with you.' And he said, 'I should like to put some on too, for perhaps it would make me beautiful.' The girl told him that if he would go out and gather some

195

gum she would put it on his face and hair for him. So he went out and gathered a great store of gum from the trees and brought it back to her. She melted it on a hot stove until it was balsam again and would pour easily out. Then she said, 'Shut your eyes so that it will not harm your sight, and I will make your face and hair beautiful and shining like mine.' Owl-man shut his eyes, and the girl soon covered his face and head with the soft gum. She put it on very thick, and she said, 'Keep your eyes shut until it dries or it may blind you.' Owl-man did as he was told, but when the gum dried he could not open his eyes, and while he was trying to rub it off, the girl slipped out the door and ran back to her parents, far away by the Great Water.

Owl-man scraped the gum from his face and head as best he could, and when he could open his eyes again and could see pretty well, he went out into the night in search of his wife. And as he went along he cried, 'Oh, oh, oh, where is my wife? Where is my girl? I have lost my wife. I have lost my girl. Oh, oh, oh.' And when the people heard him calling they thought they would play a trick on him. So they said, 'She is here, she is here.' But when he entered their houses, the woman they showed him was not his wife, and he went away sorrowful. And the people all laughed at his confusion, and said, 'Owl-man is getting queerer each day. He is far gone in his head.' Owl-man went from house to house, but he could not find his wife. Then he went to the trees and searched among the branches. He pulled the trees up by the roots, thinking she might be hiding underneath. And he looked into the salmon-traps in the rivers, and kicked them to pieces in his frenzy. But nowhere was his wife to be found.

Then he went to the girl's house, where she was hiding, and he yelled, 'Oh, oh, oh, give me my wife. Give me my girl. I know she is here. Oh, oh, oh.' But the girl's foster-mother would not give her up. Then he began to tear down the house over their heads, for the old man of the house was away and there was no one else strong enough to stop Owl-man in his rage. When the woman saw her house in danger of falling about her ears, she cried, 'Stop; your wife is here.' And she brought forth the girl from her hiding-place. When Owl-man saw her, his rage left him and he was happy again.

But just then the old man of magic power came home. He had heard the hub-bub from a distance. When he came in and saw the great holes in the roof and the side of his house where Owl-man had torn away the logs, he was very angry and he said to himself, 'I will punish both Owl-

man and the girl for this night's work.' And he hit upon a plan. He said to Owl-man, 'We must give you a hot bath to melt the gum and take it from your hair, for it will do you no good, and it will take all the hair off your head.' And Owl-man gladly agreed. So they filled a great bark tub with water and heated it by placing at the bottom of it many red-hot stones, after the fashion of Indians in those old days. But the old man put so many hot stones in the water that it was soon almost boiling with the heat, and when they put Owl-man into the tub he was almost scalded to death and he yelled loudly in pain. Then the old man said, 'Now I will take vengeance. You will trouble me no more. You have broken my house. Henceforth you will be not a man but an Owl, and you will dwell alone in the forest with few friends, and you will live always on frogs and toads and field-mice, and people will hear you at night crying for your wife all over the land, but you shall never find her.' Then with his magic power he changed him to an Owl and sent him on his way.

He said to the girl, 'You have done me much harm too, and you have brought all this trouble upon me. Henceforth you will be not a girl but a Fish-Hawk, and you will always cry and fret and scream as you have done before, and you will never be satisfied.' And with his magic power he changed her into a Fish-Hawk, and sent her out to the ocean. And there she screams always, and she is a great glutton, for she can never get enough to eat. And since that time, Owl and Fish-Hawk have not dwelt together and have not been on friendly terms. They live far apart, and Owl keeps to the forest and the mountains, while the other keeps to the sea. Thus was the old man avenged, and thus was the weeping maiden punished for her tears. And the cries of Owl and Fish-Hawk are still heard in many places, one calling for his wife, the other screaming unsatisfied for something she cannot get.

43. Ermine and the Hunter

FAR away in the Canadian North Country an old man lived with his wife and children. They lived far from other people, but they were never lonely, for they had much work to do. The old man was a great hunter, and in summer he and his wife and children lived on the fish and game he captured in the winter. In the spring-time he gathered sap from the maple trees, from which he made maple syrup and maple sugar with which to sweeten their food. One day in summer he found three small bears eating his stock of sugar. When he came upon them, his sugar was all gone, and he was very cross. With a stout club he killed the little bears and skinned them and dried their meat. But his wife said, 'No good can come of it. You should not have killed the three little bears, for they were too young for slaughter.'

The next day the old Bear came along, looking for his lost children. When he saw their skins hanging up to dry he knew that they had been killed by the hunter. He was very sad and angry, and he called to the hunter, 'You have killed my little motherless cubs, and in return for that wickedness, some night when you are off your guard I will kill your children, and then I will kill you and your wife, and I will devour all your food.' The old man shot at him with his arrows, but the arrows did not harm him, for he was Brown Bear of the Stony Heart, and he could not be killed by man. For many nights and days the old man tried to trap him, but he met with no success. And each day he saw his store of food growing smaller, for Bear of the Stony Heart stole it always in the night. And he thought, 'We shall all surely starve before the winter comes, and game is plentiful again.'

One day in despair he resolved to look about him for someone who would tell him how to kill the Bear. He went to the bank of the river and sat there in thought and smoked long at his pipe. And he called to the God of the River and said, 'Oh, River-God, help me to drown Bear

199

when he comes to fish.' The river came from the Limestone country far back among the rocks, and it was flowing rapidly to the sea. And the River-God said, 'My water cannot tarry. There are millions of oysters down on the ocean shore waiting for shells, and I am hurrying down there with the lime to make them,' and he rushed quickly past.

Then the old man called to the Spirit of the Wind, and he said, 'Oh, Spirit of the Wind, stay here with me to-night and help me to kill Bear of the Stony Heart. You can knock down great trees upon his back and crush him to the earth.' But the Wind Spirit said, 'I cannot linger. Many ships with rich cargoes lie silent on the ocean waiting to sail, and I must hurry along with the force to drive them.' And like the River-God he hastened on his way.

Then the old man called to Storm Cloud, which was just then passing over his head, and he said, 'Oh, Spirit of the Storm Cloud, stay here with me to-night and help me to kill Bear of the Stony Heart, for he seeks to destroy my children. You can send lightning and thunder to strike him dead.' But the Storm Cloud said, 'I cannot loiter on the way. Far from here there are millions of blades of corn and grass dying from thirst in the summer heat, for I see the heat waves rising on the earth, and I am hurrying there with rain to save them.' And like the River-God and the Wind Spirit he hurried along on his business. The poor old man was in great sorrow, for it seemed that no one would help him to rid the land of Bear of the Stony Heart.

As he sat wondering what he should do, an old woman came along. She said, 'I am very hungry and tired, for I have come far. Will you give me food and let me rest here a while?' And he said, 'We have very little food, for Bear of the Stony Heart steals it from us nightly, but you may share with us what little we have.' So he went away and brought back to her a good fat meal. While she was eating her dinner he told her of his troubles with Bear, and he said that no one would help him to get rid of the pest, and that Bear could not be killed by man. And the old woman said, 'There is a little animal who can kill Bear of the Stony Heart. He alone can save you. You have done well to me. Here is a wand which I will give you. Go to sleep here, soon, on the bank of the river. Wave this wand before you sleep and say what I shall teach you, and when you awake call to you the first animal you see when you open your eyes. He will be the animal of which I speak, and he will rid you of the Bear.' She taught him a little rhyme and gave him a wand which she took from the basket on her arm; then she hobbled away, and the old man knew that she was the weird woman of the Fairy Blue Mountain, of whom he had often heard. He marvelled greatly, but he resolved to do as she had told him.

After the old woman had gone, the man waved the little wand three times, and cried:

> 'Animal, animal, come from your lair,
> Help me to slaughter the old Brown Bear!
> Make with my magic a little white dart,
> To pierce in the centre old Bear's Stony Heart!'

He repeated the rhyme three times. Then he felt himself getting drowsy and sleep soon came upon him. He slept but a short time when the heat woke him up, for the hot sun beat down upon him. He rubbed his eyes and looked about him. Watching him from behind a tree was a little animal with a shaggy brown coat. The old man thought to himself, 'Surely the weird fairy woman of the Blue Mountain has played a trick on me. That scraggy little animal with the dirty coat cannot kill the Bear.' But he resolved to test her word. He repeated his rhyme again, and the little animal came quickly towards him. 'Who are you?' said the man. 'I am Ermine,' said the little animal. 'Are you the animal of which the fairy woman of the Blue Hills has told me?' asked the man. 'I am indeed the same,' said Ermine. 'I have been sent to you to kill the Bear, and here I have the little darts made powerful because of your magic wand.' He pointed to his mouth and showed the old man his sharp white teeth. 'So now to your task,' said the old man in high spirits. 'Oh, not so fast,' said Ermine, 'you must first pay me for my work.' 'What can I do for you?' asked the man. 'I am ashamed of my dirty brown coat, which I have worn for a long time,' said the animal; 'you have great magic from the wand you received from the fairy woman of the Blue Hills. I want a sleek and shining white coat that I can wear always, for I want to be clean.' The man waved his wand again and wished for what the animal had asked him, and at once the shaggy brown coat of Ermine was replaced by a sleek and shining white coat as spotless as the new snow in winter. Then the animal said, 'I have one more condition to impose on you. You must promise never to kill a bear's young cubs when they are still following their mother in the summer-time. You must give them a chance to grow strong, so that they may be able to fight for their own lives.' And the man promised, placing his hand upon the wand to bind his oath. Then, when he looked again, the wand had vanished from his hand. It had gone back through the air to the fairy woman of the Blue Hills.

Then Ermine set out on his search for Bear. The afternoon was very hot, and the forest was still, and not a leaf or a blade of grass was stirring, and there was not a ripple on the stream. The whole world was drowsy in the dry summer heat. But Ermine did not feel the heat, he was in such high spirits because of his new white coat. Soon he came upon Bear, stretched out at full length on the bank of the river, taking his afternoon nap, as was his custom after his fat midday meal. He was lying on his back, and his mouth was open wide, and he was snoring loudly like a waterfall. 'This is your last sleep,' said Ermine, creeping softly to his side, 'for you are a dangerous thief; you shall snore no more.' And with a bound he jumped down Bear's throat, and in an instant had pierced with his teeth his strong stony heart, which the arrows of the Indians could never reach. Then as quickly as he had entered the Bear's mouth Ermine jumped out again and ran from the place. Bear snored no more; he was quite dead, and the land was rid of his thefts and terrors. Then Ermine went back to the old man and told him that the deed was done; and that night was a great feast night in the old man's home. And since that time Ermine in the North Country has worn a sleek white coat as spotless as the new snow in winter. And to this day the hunters in the far north will not kill, if they can avoid it, the young Bear cubs while they are still following their mothers through the forest. They give them a chance to grow up and grow strong, so that they may be able to fight for their own lives, as the fairy woman of the Blue Hills had asked.

'Animal, animal, come from
your lair,
Help me to slaughter
the old Brown Bear!
Make with my magic
a little white dart,
To pierce in the centre
old Bear's Stony Heart!'

44. How Rabbit Deceived Fox

LONG ago in Indian days in Canada, when Rabbit worked for Glooskap as his forest guide, he was a great thief. He liked most of all to steal by moonlight, and he crept quietly into gardens and fields where Indian vegetables were growing, for he was very fond of cabbage and lettuce and beans. Not far from his home there lived alone an old widow woman who had no children. She could not hunt game because she was a woman, and she had never been trained to the chase, so she kept a little garden from which she made a good living. All day long from dawn until sunset she toiled hard, tilling her little garden, watering her vegetables and keeping them free from weeds. And she grew green cabbages and red carrots and yellow beans and big fat pumpkins and Indian corn, which she traded with Indian hunters in return for fish and meat. In this way she always had plenty of food, and she lived very well on good fare. But Rabbit, going his rounds one day, discovered her garden, although it was deep in the forest, and every night by moonlight or starlight he robbed it, and grew sleek and fat from the results of his thefts. And morning after morning the old widow woman found that many cabbages and carrots were missing and that much harm had been done to her plants. She had an idea that Rabbit was the pilferer, for she had heard that he was a great thief, but she was not very sure. She watched many nights, but she was never able to catch the robber, so stealthily did he come, and it was not easy to see him in the shadows. So she said to herself, 'I will set up a scarecrow, a figure in the shape of a little man, and I will place it at my garden gate, and it will frighten away the robber, whoever he may be, for I must save my vegetables or I shall starve when the cold winter comes.'

She picked from the spruce and the fir trees close by a great store of gum and balsam. This she formed into a figure in the shape of a little man. She made two eyes from glass beads that would shine like fire in the starlight, and a nose from a pine cone, and hair from the corn tassels and yellow moss. Then she placed the figure at the entrance to the garden where she knew the robber would come. 'Now,' she thought, 'I will scare away the thief.'

When night fell and the moon rose above the trees, Rabbit came along, as was his custom, to steal his nightly meal. As he came near the garden very softly, he saw in the moonlight what he thought was a man standing in the path by the garden gate. The moon hung low over the forest, and there was a thin grey mist on the earth, for it was near to autumn and the nights were already cool; and the figure of the little man looked larger than human in the misty light, and it cast a long black shadow like that of a giant on the grass. Rabbit was much afraid and he trembled like an aspen leaf, but he stood quiet behind a tree and watched the strange figure. For a long time he stood still and watched and listened. But the strange figure did not move, and not a sound did Rabbit hear but the chirp of a cricket. Then with great caution he came closer. But still the figure did not move. Then his fear left him and he grew bolder, for he was very hungry, and he could smell the vegetables and the wild honeysuckle in the still night air. So he walked bravely up to the little dummy man and said, 'Get out of my way and let me pass.' But the man did not move. Then Rabbit struck the man a sharp blow with his fist. But still the figure did not move. Rabbit's fist stuck fast in the gum and he could not pull it away. Then he struck out with his other fist, and it too, like the other, was held firm. 'I shall kick you,' said Rabbit in a rage. 'Take that,' and he struck out wildly with his foot. But his foot, like his fists, stuck fast. Then he kicked with the other foot, but that too was held in the gum. Rabbit was now very cross, and in his anger he said, 'Now I shall bite you,' but when he bit the little man, his teeth, like his feet and hands, stuck fast. Then he pushed with his body with all his might, hoping to knock the little man down, but his whole body stuck to the dummy figure.

He cried out loudly, for he was now beside himself with fear, and the old woman, when she heard his yells, came running out of her house. 'Aha!' she said, 'so you are the robber who has been stealing from my garden. I will rid the world of a pilfering pest, for I will kill you this very night.' Then she pulled him away from the gum figure and put him in a strong bag and tied the mouth of the bag with a stout string. She left the bag on the path by the garden gate and went to look for her axe to kill Rabbit. While Rabbit lay there wondering how he was going

to escape, Fox came prowling along. He stumbled over the bag, for he
did not see it in the shadows, and he plunged forward headlong to the
ground with a great thud. He got up and rained kicks upon the bag. He
was mad because he had been tripped. He kicked poor Rabbit's back
until Rabbit cried in pain. 'Who are you in the bag?' asked Fox when
he heard the cries. 'I am your friend Rabbit,' was the answer. 'What are
you doing, hiding in the bag?' asked Fox. Then Rabbit suddenly
thought of a way of escape. He knew that Fox had long been looking for
a wife, but that no one would have him as no one trusted him because
his fame for treachery and slyness was so great. 'I am not hiding,' he
said. 'The old woman who owns this garden wants me to marry her
grand-daughter, and when I refused to do it she caught me and shut me
up in this bag; she has just gone to bring the girl from her house, for
she is determined to make me marry her here in the moonlight this very
night. I don't want to marry her, for she is very big and fat, and I am

very small and lean.' Then he cried 'Boo-hoo-hoo' again, and Fox said, 'I have been looking for a wife for a long time, and I like fat people. Let me get into the bag in your place, and I will marry the grand-daughter instead, for the old woman will not know me in the shadows.' And Rabbit gladly agreed. Then Fox untied the bag and let Rabbit out and got into the bag himself, and Rabbit tied up the mouth of the bag and hurried away as quickly as he could.

Soon the old woman came back, carrying her axe. She sharpened it on a stone and said, 'Now I will kill you, and you will thieve no more in my garden. A poor woman must live untroubled by such pilfering rogues.' When Fox heard these words and the sound of the stone upon the axe, he knew that he had been deceived by Rabbit, and when the old woman opened the bag he sprang nimbly out with a sudden bound and was away before she could catch him. He swore by the starlight that he would have vengeance on Rabbit. All night long he searched for him and all the next day, but he could not find him. At last in the gathering twilight he came upon him in an open space in the forest, on the other side of a stream, eating his fill of wild vegetables. Fox tried to coax him across the stream to his side, for he himself was afraid of the water, but Rabbit would not go. 'Why don't you eat some cheese?' said Rabbit; 'there is a big round cheese in the stream.' Fox looked into the stream where Rabbit pointed, and there he saw the reflection of the big round yellow moon. He thought it was a round cheese, and he plunged in after it, for he was very fond of cheese. Rabbit hoped he would be drowned, but the stream was shallow and Fox climbed out with no cheese and with only a bad fright and a wet coat for his pains. He was very cross, for he knew that Rabbit wished to do him harm, but he kept his anger to himself. Rabbit was still eating contentedly.

'What are you eating?' said Fox, trying to hold him in talk until he could think of a plan to catch him. 'I am eating good ripe fruit,' said Rabbit. 'I am eating Indian melons.' 'Throw me one,' said Fox, for he was hungry. Rabbit threw him a large round wild cucumber all covered with green prickles. 'Swallow it whole at a mouthful,' said Rabbit; 'it is very good that way.' It was night and the moon shone dimly through the trees, and Fox could not see what he was eating. He swallowed the cucumber at one gulp, as Rabbit had told him, but the prickles stuck in his throat and he almost choked to death. And while he was choking and spluttering and trying to cough up the cucumber, Rabbit ran away as fast as he could, laughing heartily to himself. Fox knew that he had been tricked again, and this time he swore he would kill Rabbit as soon as he could find him; he resolved that when next he saw him he would not give him a moment to live.

Rabbit hid among the dry underbrush all the next day. But when the day went down and the sky was red in the west and the wind was very still, he sat on a log, as was his custom, and played softly on his flute, for he was a great player on the Indian pipe. While he was playing, Fox suddenly came upon him unawares. Rabbit saw him watching him through the trees close at hand, but although taken by surprise, he was not to be outdone. Fox was just about to spring upon him when Rabbit said, 'The Chief's daughter has just been married to a great warrior, and the wedding party will soon be along this way. They asked me to sit here and make music for them with my flute as they pass by. They have promised to pay me well, and they have invited me to the wedding feast. Come and join me and play too, and you will be well paid, and we will go to the wedding feast together and get good things to eat.' Fox thought he would let Rabbit get the pay he had been promised, for he was a very greedy fellow; then he would rob him and kill him, and he would take his flute and go to the wedding feast alone, and his vengeance would then be complete. So he decided to let his anger cool for a little time. And he said, 'I have no flute, and I cannot therefore make music; but I will sit with you to see the wedding guests go by.' But Rabbit said, 'Take my flute. I have another at home. I will go and get it, for there is yet time.'

So Fox took the flute and began to play loudly, and Rabbit slipped hurriedly out of sight, pretending to go for his Indian pipe. But he resolved to make an end of Fox, for he feared for his own life, and instead of going home, he set the underbrush on fire. He kindled the fire at many places all around the log on which Fox sat. Fox could not hear the fire crackling because of the loud music of his flute, and he thought the light was but the bright light of the moon. And the fire was almost upon him before he knew that he was in danger. Then he tried to get away, but on all sides his escape was stopped by the flames and he could not find an opening. At last, in despair, to save his life, he jumped through the ring of fire. He escaped with his life, but his eyelids were singed, and his sleek black coat with its silver spots was scorched to a red-brown colour. He was in great pain. He concluded that Rabbit was too clever for him to cope with, and he resolved to leave him alone and to forego his revenge, for he was glad to get away with his life. But he decided never again to live on friendly terms with Rabbit. And since that night Rabbit and Fox have never hunted together. And to the present day the descendants of this Fox have red eyes and a red-brown coat, because Rabbit scorched their ancestor in the olden times.

45. The Boy and the Dragon

ONCE, long ago, before the white man came to Canada, a boy was living with his parents in a village near the ocean. As he had no brothers or sisters, he was often lonely, and he longed for adventure and companionship. At last he decided to set out to seek his fortune elsewhere. He was just on the point of leaving his home when it was noised abroad one day that there had come into the land a great dragon, who was doing great havoc and damage wherever he went. The country was in great terror, for the dragon carried off women and children and devoured them one by one. And what was still more mystifying, he had power to take on human form, and often he changed himself into a man of pleasing shape and manner and came among the people to carry out his cruel designs before they knew that he was near. The Chief of the tribe called for volunteers to meet the dragon-man, but none of his warriors responded. They were strong and mighty in combat with men, but it was a different matter to encounter a dragon.

When the youth heard this dreadful story and saw the terror of his people, he said, 'Here is my chance to do a great deed,' for somehow he felt that he had more than human power. So he said good-bye to his parents and set out on his adventure. He travelled all day inland through the forest, until at evening he came to a high hill in the centre of an open space. He said, 'I will climb this hill, and perhaps I can see all the country round about me.' So he went slowly to the top. As he stood there, looking over the country which he could see for many miles around, a man suddenly appeared beside him. He was a very pleasant fellow, and they talked together for some time. The boy was on his guard, but he thought, 'Surely this man with the good looks cannot be the dragon,' and he laughed at his suspicions and put them from his mind.

The stranger said, 'Where are you going?' And the boy answered, 'I am going far away. I am seeking adventure in the forest for it is very lonely down by the sea.' But he did not tell him of his real errand. 'You may stay with me to-night,' said the newcomer. 'I have a very comfortable lodge not far from here, and I will give you food.' The boy was very hungry and tired, and he went along with the man to his lodge. When they reached the house the boy was surprised to see a great heap of bleached bones lying before the door. But he showed no fear nor did he comment on the horrible sight. Inside the lodge sat a very old and bent woman, tending a pot. She was stirring it with a big stick, and the boy saw that it contained meat stew. When she placed the stew before them, the boy said he would rather have corn, for he feared to taste the meat. The old woman fried some corn for him, and he had a good meal.

After they had eaten, the man went out to gather wood for the fire, and the boy sat talking to the old woman. And she said to him, 'You are very young and beautiful and innocent—the most handsome I have yet seen in this place. And because of that, I will take pity on you and warn you of your danger. The man whom you met in the forest and whom you supped with to-night is none other than the dragon-man of whom you have often heard. He cannot be killed in ordinary combat, and it would be folly for you to try. To-morrow he will kill you if you are still here. Take these moccasins that I will give you, and in the morning when you get up put them on your feet. With one step you will reach by their power the hill you see in the distance. Give this piece of birch bark with the picture on it to a man you will meet there, and he will tell you what next to do. But remember that no matter how far you go, the dragon-man will overtake you in the evening.' The youth took the moccasins and the birch bark bearing the mystic sign and hid them under his coat, and said, 'I will do as you advise.' But the woman said, 'There is one more condition. You must kill me in the morning before you go, and put this robe over my body. Then the dragon-man's spell over me will be broken, and when he leaves me, I will rouse myself with my power back to life.'

The youth went to sleep, and the dragon-man slept all night beside him so as not to let him escape. The next morning, when the dragon-man was out to get water from the stream some distance away, the boy at once carried out the old woman's orders of the night before. First of all he killed the old woman with a blow and covered her body with a bright cloak, for he knew that when the dragon-man would leave the place she would soon rise again. Then he put the magic moccasins on his feet and with one great step he reached the distant hill. Here, sure enough, he met an old man. He gave him the piece of birch bark bearing the mystic sign. The man looked at it closely and smiled and said, 'So it is you I was told to wait for. That is well, for you are indeed a comely youth.' The man gave him another pair of moccasins in exchange for those he was wearing, and another piece of birch bark bearing another inscription. He pointed to a hill that rose blue in the distance and said, 'With one step you will reach that hill. Give this bark to a man you will meet there, and all will be well.'

The boy put the moccasins on his feet, and with one step he reached the distant hill. There he met another old man, to whom he gave the birch bark. This man gave him another pair of moccasins and a large maple leaf bearing a strange symbol, and told him to go to another spot, where he would receive final instructions. He did as he was told, and here he met a very old man, who said, 'Down yonder there is a stream. Go towards it and walk straight into it, as if you were on dry ground. But do not look at the water. Take this piece of birch bark bearing these magic figures, and it will change you into whatever you wish, and it will keep you from harm.' The boy took the bark and did as he was told, and soon found himself on the opposite bank of the stream. He followed the stream for some distance, and at evening he came to a lake. As he was looking about for a warm place to pass the night, he suddenly came upon the dragon-man, now in the form of a monster dragon, hiding behind the trees. The old woman's words had come true, for his enemy had overtaken him before nightfall, as she had said. There was no time to lose, so the boy waved his magic bark, and at once he became a little fish with red fins, moving slowly in the lake.

When the dragon-man saw the little fish, he cried, 'Little fish of the red fins, have you seen the youth I am looking for?' 'No, sir,' said the little fish, 'I have seen no one; I have been asleep. But if he passes this way I will tell you,' and he moved rapidly out into the lake.

The dragon-man moved down along the bank of the lake, while the youth watched him from the water. He met a Toad in the path, and said, 'Little Toad, have you seen the youth I am looking for? If he passed this way you would surely have seen him.' 'I am minding my own business,' answered the Toad, and he hopped away into the moss. Then the dragon-man saw a very large fish with his head above water, looking for flies, and he said, 'Have you seen the boy I am looking for?' 'Yes,' said the fish, 'you have just been talking to him,' and he laughed to himself and disappeared. The dragon-man went back and searched everywhere for Toad, but he could not find him. As he looked he came upon a musk-rat running along by the stream, and he said angrily, 'Have you seen the person I am looking for?' 'No,' said the rat. 'I think you are he,' said the dragon-man. Then the musk-rat began to cry bitterly and said, 'No, no; the boy you are looking for passed by just now, and he stepped on the roof of my house and broke it in.' The dragon-man was deceived again. He went on and soon came upon old Turtle splashing around in the mud. 'You are very old and wise,' he said, hoping to flatter him, 'you have surely seen the person I am looking for.' 'Yes,' said Turtle, 'he is farther down the stream. Go across the river and you will find him. But beware, for if you do not know him when you see him, he will surely kill you.' Turtle knew well that the dragon-man would now meet his fate.

The dragon-man followed the lake till he came to the river. For greater caution, so that he might be less easily seen, he changed himself to a Snake. Then he attempted to cross the stream. But the youth, still in the form of a fish and still using the power of his magic bark with the mystic sign, was swimming round and round in a circle in the middle of the river. A rapid whirlpool arose where he swam, but it was not visible on the surface. As the Snake approached it, he saw nothing but clear water. He failed to recognize his enemy, and as Turtle had told him, he swam into the whirlpool before he was aware of it, and was quickly drawn to the bottom, where he was drowned.

The youth fished him up and cut off his head. Then he changed back to his own form. He went to the dragon-man's lodge to see how the old woman had fared, but she had gone with her bright robe, and the lodge was empty. Then the youth went back to his home and reported what he had done. And he received many rich gifts from the Chief for his brave deed, and the land was never troubled again by dragons. But from that time the snake family was hated because its shape had concealed the dragon-man, and to this day an Indian will not let a snake escape with his life if he meets one of them in his path. For they still are mindful of the adventure of their ancestor in the old days, and they are suspicious of the evil power the snake family secretly possesses.

46. Owl with the Great Head
and Eyes

LONG ago, when Glooskap was the ruler of the Indians in Eastern Canada, and when the animals all worked for him and talked like men, Wolf was one of Rabbit's enemies. On the surface they seemed to be friends, but each was afraid of the other and each suspected the other of treachery. Rabbit was very faithful to his work as the forest guide who showed people the way to far places. But he was also a great trickster, and he delighted to play pranks on everyone he met. He liked more than all to pester Wolf, for he had a hatred for his cruel ways, and he was always able to outwit him.

It happened that Rabbit and Wolf lived close together, deep in the Canadian forest. Some distance from them, in a little house, lived a poor widow woman who had only one daughter. She was a very beautiful girl, with hair as black as the raven's wing, and with eyes like the dark of the underwater. Rabbit and Wolf each fell in love with her, and each in his own way sought her as his wife. Rabbit tried hard to win her love. When he went to her house he always dressed himself in a soft brown coat, and he put a bangle around his neck and bells upon his feet. And often he played sweetly on his flute, hoping to charm her with his music, for he was a great player upon the Indian pipe. And he tried to grow a moustache to hide his split lip; but he had little success, for his whiskers would not grow thick, and he has the thin scraggy moustache of a few hairs to this day. But no matter what Rabbit did to adorn himself, the girl gave him cold looks, and old Wolf seemed to be deeper in her favour, for she liked his willowy form and his sleek and bashful ways. And poor Rabbit was sore distressed.

One fine day in the spring-time, Rabbit came upon the girl and her mother gathering May-flowers among the moss. He crept close to listen to their talk. He heard the mother say, 'I have no stomach for little Rabbit, but Wolf pleases me well. You must marry Wolf. They tell me he is a great hunter, and if you marry him we shall never want for food.'

When Rabbit heard this he was very sad; he determined that on no account should Wolf marry the widow's daughter, and that he must use all his power to prevent it. That night he went alone to the girl's house. He spoke sneeringly of Wolf, saying with a bitter frown, 'Wolf is no hunter; he never catches any game because he is lazy and has no brains; I always have to feed him to keep him from starving; he is but a beast of burden; I always ride upon his back when I go to a far country, for he is good for nothing else.' The girl's mother wondered greatly, and she was very startled by this news, for she did not want her daughter to marry a good-for-nothing; but she was not sure that Rabbit spoke the truth, for she had heard that sometimes he told great lies. So she said, 'If you will ride Wolf over here I will believe you, and he shall not marry my daughter, and you shall marry her yourself.' And Rabbit went home well pleased and sure of a happy ending to his trick.

The next day Rabbit purposely met Wolf in the forest, and he said, 'Let us go together to see the widow's daughter.' And Wolf was glad to go. They had not gone far when Rabbit began to cry. Then he lay down on the ground, and rolled and moaned and rubbed his belly as if in great distress. 'I have a sharp pain in my belly,' he sobbed, 'I cannot walk any farther. If I walk I shall surely die, and I cannot go on unless you carry me on your back.' Wolf willingly agreed, for he wanted to see the beautiful girl, and he was very sorry for poor Rabbit in his pain; and Rabbit, laughing to himself, climbed on Wolf's back. Wolf ran along, not feeling the load, for Rabbit was very light. They had not gone far when Rabbit cried again and said, 'I cannot ride without a saddle, for your bare back hurts me and gives me blisters.' So they borrowed a little saddle from a field by the way and put it on Wolf's back. Soon Rabbit said, 'This is fine fun; let us play that you are a horse and that I am a great rider. I should like to put a little bridle on you, and to wear spurs on my feet and to carry a whip.' And Wolf, wishing to please Rabbit to make him forget his pain, gladly agreed. So they borrowed a little bridle and spurs and a whip from another field near by, and did as Rabbit asked, and together they went to the girl's home, Wolf trotting along like a little horse, and Rabbit laughing to himself, sitting in the saddle, with his spurs and his whip, holding the bridle reins. When they drew near the house, Rabbit made a great noise so that the mother and her daughter might look out to see where the shouting came from. He called loudly, 'Whoa, Whoa.' And the girl and her mother opened the door and looked out at them in wonder. Then as they were looking on, Rabbit, chuckling to himself, struck Wolf a stinging blow with his whip, and stuck his spurs deep into Wolf's sides and called him loudly a lazy beast. Wolf jumped and plunged and kicked because of the prick of the spurs and the sting of the whip; he was very cross, but he said nothing.

Some distance away, Rabbit tied Wolf to a tree, saying, 'Stay here and I will send the girl to you.' Then he went to the house, and he said to the woman, 'Now you will believe that Wolf is a beast of burden, for I have ridden here on his back.' And the woman believed him. She told him to give Wolf some corn or grass. But Rabbit said, 'He doesn't eat corn or grass; he eats only fresh meat,' for he knew well that Wolf would be quite contented if he got a good meal of meat. Then she gave him some fresh meat, which he brought to Wolf. And Wolf was happy, and his anger disappeared, and he forgot the pain of the spurs and the whip, and he thought it was fine fun to get a good meal so easily. The woman promised that Rabbit should marry her daughter, and when night fell Rabbit went home well pleased, leaving Wolf still tied to the tree. It was so dark that Wolf did not see him leaving the house, and for a long time he thought he was still inside, and he waited long in the starlight. At last he grew tired waiting, for he was hungry and he was cold standing still in the chill night air of early spring. He cut with his teeth the bridle rein that tied him to the tree, and then he went to the woman's house. But the woman would not let him in. She told him to go away, that she never wished to see him again, and she called him a lazy beast of burden. He went home in great anger, for he knew now that he had been tricked, and he swore that he would have vengeance on Rabbit.

The next day Rabbit learned from the woman that she had spurned Wolf from her door, and he knew that Wolf realized he had been deceived. He was somewhat frightened, for he dreaded Wolf's vengeance, and for several days he hid among the trees. Then hunger drove him out and he went forth to look for food. One evening he entered a garden in search of cabbage, and he was busy robbing it, when the people who owned the garden spied him. And they said, 'Here is the thief who has been stealing our vegetables. We will catch him and teach him a lesson.' Before Rabbit knew it, they were upon him, for he was eating heartily, he was so hungry, and they caught him and bound him fast to a tree and went to get scalding water to pour upon his back to teach him not to rob their garden again. But while they were away Wolf came along. He, too, was very hungry, for he had eaten no meal for many days, but he was glad when he saw Rabbit, for now he thought he would have his revenge. Rabbit saw him at a distance, and he resolved to try another trick on him, and to hail him as if he thought he was still his friend. And he cried out to him, 'Help me, Wolf! Help me! The people here asked me to eat up a nice little lamb, and when I refused to do it, they tied me up to this tree, and they have gone to bring the lamb to me.'

Wolf was too hungry to be cautious, and he forgot all about Rabbit's tricks, for spring lamb was his favourite food. And he said, 'I will eat up the little lamb,' and he smacked his lips as he spoke, and thought of the nice tender meal he would have. Then Rabbit said, 'Untie me and take my place, for the people will soon be here with the lamb.' So Wolf untied him, and Rabbit in turn bound Wolf fast to the tree, and laughing to himself because he had again outwitted stupid Wolf, he ran rapidly away. Far off he hid behind the trees to see what would happen. Soon the people came back, carrying the pots of scalding water. Wolf saw them coming, and he was in high spirits, for he thought the lamb he was to eat was in one of the pots. It was moonlight, and in the shadow of the great tree the people could not see very clearly, and they thought Wolf was Rabbit, still bound fast where they had left him. So they poured the scalding water on his back and kicked him and knocked him on the head with a big stick, and they said, 'Now, thief, we have taught you how dangerous it is to rob gardens in the spring moonlight.' Wolf howled with pain, for his back was blistered and his head was sore, and Rabbit heard him, and he sat on a log and shook with laughter because of the success of his prank.

Then the people untied Wolf and let him go. He went away wearily among the trees. And he again swore vengeance on Rabbit, and he resolved to kill him as soon as he set eyes upon him, for he knew he had been tricked a second time. For several days he searched for his enemy. At last, one night of bright moonlight, he came upon Rabbit sitting in a patch of Indian tobacco plants, eating his fill and contentedly chewing the tobacco leaves. Rabbit's mouth was full of tobacco, but he laughed loudly when he saw Wolf's back bound in bandages because of the blisters, and his sore head tied up in a cloth. But when he saw Wolf's angry eyes he was frightened, and he ran away into the woods. The moon was shining in the forest, and Wolf could catch a glimpse now and then of his brown coat among the trees, and he chased him for a long time. Rabbit tried all his tricks to shake him from his tracks, but without avail. At last, when Rabbit was almost worn out, he took refuge in a hollow tree, into which he slipped through a small hole, where Wolf could not follow him. And Wolf said, 'Now I have him in my power. I will kill him; but first I must go home to get my axe to cut down the tree and to chop off his head.' Then he looked around for someone to keep watch over the tree while he was gone, so that Rabbit could not escape. At last he saw Owl sitting quietly on a branch near. He called to him and said, 'Watch by this hole until I get back, and do not let Rabbit get away.' So Owl came down and sat by the hole and promised to keep guard over the prisoner, and Wolf went away to look for his axe.

But Rabbit was not caught yet; he had another trick left. After Wolf had gone away, he called to Owl sitting by the hole, and said, 'Owl, come and see what a nice little room I have here in the tree.' But Owl replied, 'It is too dark, I cannot see.' Then Rabbit said, 'Open your eyes wide and put your face close to the hole, for I have a light here and you can see easily.' Owl did as he was told, for he was a curious fellow. Rabbit had a great mouthful of tobacco juice from the Indian tobacco leaves he had been chewing, and when Owl put his face close to the hole he squirted the juice into Owl's eyes. Owl screamed loudly, for his eyes were smarting and he was blinded by the juice; he ran around the tree and stamped and shrieked and rubbed his eyes, trying to relieve them of their pain. And while he was about it, Rabbit slipped out of the hole and ran away, and Owl did not know he was gone.

Soon Wolf came back, carrying his big sharp axe. And he said, 'Now I shall kill him at last.' And Owl was afraid to tell him about his sore eyes; they were still open wide, and he could not close them. At once

Wolf chopped down the hollow tree. Then he split it open from end to end. But there was no sign of Rabbit. Wolf then thought Owl had tricked him, and that he had helped Rabbit to escape. But Owl said he had not. He sat with his eyes wide open, staring stupidly and moaning and making strange noises because of his pain. Wolf thought he was laughing at him and taunting him, for he did not know the meaning of Owl's strange cries, and in his rage he fell to beating him over the head with his axe-handle until poor Owl's head was swollen to a great size. And Owl cried, 'Hoot, Hoot, Hoot,' and his eyes stared from his swollen head even larger than before. Then Wolf went on his way, resolved to keep away from Rabbit. And since that time Owl has cried 'Hoot, Hoot, Hoot' at night, for he still remembers his pain; and his head is still swollen and bigger than that of other birds because of the beating Wolf gave him with his axe-handle; and his eyes are still large and they stare stupidly, and he cannot look at light, and he is blind in the daylight because of the tobacco juice Rabbit squirted into his eyes. And since that night Rabbit and Wolf have avoided each other, and they have not lived in the same place, and they have never since been friends.

47. The Tobacco Fairy
from the Blue Hills

A MAN and his wife and two little children were living long ago on the shores of a lake surrounded by large trees, deep in the Canadian forest. They lived very happily together, and as game was plentiful, they wanted for nothing. As the children grew up they became each day more beautiful and gentle, until the old women of the tribe said, 'They are too good and lovely for this world; their home is surely elsewhere in the West.' Before they grew to maturity a cruel plague spread over the land and carried them off with its ravages. Their mother was the next to go, slowly growing weaker, and wasting away before the eyes of her husband, who was powerless to save her.

The man was now left all alone upon the earth. The joy of his life had gone with his wife and children, and he went about in great loneliness and sorrow. Life was long to him and dreary, and often he wished that he too was dead. But at last he roused himself and said, 'I will go about doing good. I will spend my life helping others, and perhaps in that way I can find peace.' So he worked hard and did all the good he could for the weaker and the poorer people of his tribe. He was held in high esteem by all the people of the village, and in their affection for him they all called him 'Grandfather.' He grew to be very old, and because of his good deeds he found great happiness. But he was still very solitary, and the days and evenings were long and lonely, and as he grew older and his work grew less, he found it hard to pass away the time, for he could only sit alone and dream of his vanished youth and of his absent friends.

One day he sat thinking by the lake. Many people of the village were around him, but as usual he sat alone. Suddenly a large flock of birds, looking like great black clouds, came flying from the blue hills in the

distance toward the shore of the lake. They wheeled and circled about, and hovered long over the trees, uttering strange cries. The people had never before seen such large birds, and they were much afraid and said, 'They are not ordinary creatures. They foreshadow some strange happening.' Suddenly one of the birds fluttered for an instant and fell slowly to the earth with an arrow in its breast. No one in the village had shot at the flock, and where the arrow had come from no man knew. The mystery frightened the people still more, and they looked to the old man for counsel, for they knew that he was very wise.

The fallen bird lay fluttering on the ground, seemingly in pain. The other birds circled about it for a short time, uttering loud cries. Then they screamed and called to each other and flew back to the distant blue hills, leaving the fallen bird behind them with the arrow sticking in its breast. The old man was not frightened by the sight. He said, 'I will go to the stricken bird; perhaps I can heal its wound.' But the people, in great fear, said, 'Do not go, Grandfather, the bird will do you harm.' But the old man answered, 'It can do no harm to me. My work is ended and my life is almost done. My sky is dark, for I am full of sorrow, and with me it is already the twilight of time. I am alone in the world, for my kindred have gone. I am not afraid of death, for to me it would be very welcome. What matters it if I should die?' And he went to the stricken bird to see if he could help it.

As he went along, his path suddenly grew dark, but as he drew nearer, a bright flame suddenly swept down from the sky to the place where the bird was lying. There was a flash of fire, and when the old man looked he saw that the bird had been completely burned up. When he came to where it had lain, nothing but black ashes remained. He stirred up the ashes with his stick, and lying in the centre he found a large living coal of fire. As he looked at it, in a twinkling it disappeared, and in its place was a strange little figure like a little man, no bigger than his thumb. 'Hello, Grandfather,' it called, 'do not strike me, for I have been sent to help you.'

'Who are you?' asked the old man.

'I am one of the Little People from the distant blue hills,' said the tiny boy. Then the old man knew that the little fellow was one of the strange fairy people of the mountains, of whom he had often heard. 'What do you want?' he asked.

'I have been sent to you with a precious gift,' answered the little man. The old man wondered greatly, but he said nothing.

Then the fairy from the blue hills said, 'You are old and lonely. You have done many noble deeds, and you have always gone about bringing good to others. In that way you have found peace. And because of your good life, I have been sent to bring you more contentment. Your work is done, but your life is not yet ended, and you have still a long time to dwell upon the earth. You must live out your mortal course. You are longing always for your dead wife and children, and you are often thinking of your youth, and with you the days are long and time hangs heavy. But I have been sent to you with a gift that will help you to pass the time more pleasantly.'

Then the little man gave him a number of small seeds and said, 'Plant these at once, here, in the ashes from which I have just risen.' The old man did as he was told. At once the seeds sprouted and great leaves grew from them, and soon the place where the bird had been burned up became a large field of Tobacco.

The fairy then gave him a large pipe and said, 'Dry these leaves and place them in this pipe and smoke them. You will have great contentment, and when you have nothing to do it will help you to pass the time away, and when no one is with you it will be a companion. And it will bring you many dreams of the future and of the past. And when the smoke curls upwards it will have for you many visions of those you loved, and you will see their faces in the smoke as you sit alone in the twilight.'

The old man was very thankful for the fairy's gift. But the little man said, 'Teach other old men how to use it, so that they, too, may possess it and enjoy it.'

Then the fairy quickly disappeared, going towards the distant blue hills, and he was never seen in the village again. And with his pipe and his tobacco the old man went back to his dreaming, with more contentment than before. In this way Tobacco was brought to the Indians in the old days.

48. Rainbow and the Autumn Leaves

IN OLDEN days, long before the Indians came to Canada, all the animals talked and worked like men. Every year after midsummer they held a Great Council at which they were all present. But it happened once in the summer before the council met, that they all wanted to go to the sky to see what the country up there was like. None of them could find a way to go. The oldest and wisest creature on all the earth was Turtle. One day he prayed to the Thunder God to take him to the sky, and his prayer was soon answered. There was a great noise, as if the earth had been split asunder, and when the people next looked for Turtle he was nowhere to be found. They searched everywhere without success. But that evening, when they looked upwards, they saw him in the sky, moving about like a black cloud. Turtle liked the sky so well that he decided to live there always and to send his descendants, later, to the earth. And the sky-people agreed to keep him. They asked him, 'Where do you want to dwell?' And he answered, 'I should like to dwell in the Black Cloud, in which are the ponds and streams and lakes and springs of water, for I always dwelt near these places when I was young.' So he was allowed to have his wish. But when the Great Council of the animals met on earth in the time of the harvest-moon, he was always present. He came in the Black Cloud, but he always went back to the sky after the Council was ended. And the other animals envied him his good fortune, and they wished that they could go with him.

After a time the animals were greatly distressed and angered by the rumour that a new race of creatures was coming from far over the ocean to inhabit their land. They talked it over very carefully, and they all thought how fortunate it would be if they could all go to the sky with old Turtle, and live like him, free from fear and trouble and care. But

they were puzzled to know how to get there, for Turtle had never told any of them the way.

One day Deer, wandering about alone in the forest, as was his custom, came across Rainbow, who often built a path of many colours to the sky. And he said to Rainbow, 'Carry me up to the sky, for I want to see Turtle.' But Rainbow was afraid to do it, for he wished first to ask the Thunder God for permission, and he put Deer off, and to gain time he said, 'Come to me in winter, when I stay for a time on the mountain near the lake. Then I will gladly carry you to the place where Turtle dwells.'

Throughout the long winter months Deer looked longingly for Rainbow, but Rainbow did not come. Life was growing harder on the earth, and the animals were in terror of the new race that was soon to come to their land, and Deer was very timid and impatient. At last, one day in the early summer, Rainbow came again, and Deer hastened to meet him. 'Why were you false to me?' he asked; 'I waited for you all winter long on the mountain by the lake, but you did not come as you promised. I want to go to the sky now, for I must see Turtle.' Rainbow answered, 'I cannot take you now. But some day, when there is a Fog over the lake, I shall come back to drive it away. Come to me then, and I shall take you to the sky and to the place where Turtle dwells. This time I will not deceive you.'

Rainbow consulted the Thunder God, and received permission to do as Deer wished. Soon afterwards the Fog one day rolled in a thick bank across the lake, and Deer hurried out to wait for Rainbow. Sure enough, Rainbow came down, as he had promised, to drive the Fog away. He threw his arch of many colours from the lake to the blue hills far away, and the Fog at once disappeared from the place. And he said to Deer, who stood watching him, 'Now I will keep my promise. Follow my many-coloured path over the hills and the forests and the streams, and be not afraid, and you will soon reach Turtle's home in the sky.' Deer did as he was told, and soon he reached the sky. Turtle was glad to see him, and Deer liked the country so well that he decided to stay for ever. And he roamed over the sky everywhere, moving like the wind from place to place.

When midsummer had passed and the harvest-moon had come and the Great Council again met together, Deer was absent for the first time in his life. The animals waited long for him to appear, for they needed his advice, but he did not come. They sent the Birds out to find him. Black Hawk and Woodpecker and Bluejay all sought him in the forest, but they could not find a trace of him. Then Wolf and Fox scoured the woods far and near, but they came back and reported that he could not be found anywhere. At last Turtle arrived at the meeting of the Great Council, as was his custom, coming in his Black Cloud, in which were the ponds and lakes and streams and springs of water. And Bear said, 'Deer is absent from the Council meeting. Where is Deer? We cannot meet without him, for we need his advice.' And Turtle replied, 'Deer is in the sky. Have you not heard? Rainbow made a wonderful pathway for him of many varied colours, and by that he came to the sky. There he is now,' and he pointed to a golden cloud scurrying across the sky overhead.

Turtle advised that the animals should all go to the sky to live until they could be sure that the new race of creatures would bring them no harm. And he showed them the pathway that Rainbow had made, stretching from the earth in wonderful colours. The animals all agreed at the Great Council to take Turtle's advice. But they were all very angry at Deer for leaving them without warning, for they thought that all the animals should either stay together faithfully on the earth or go all together to the sky. Bear showed the greatest anger and annoyance. Because of his great strength, he had no fear of the new race that was said soon to be coming, and he had always been inclined to look with scorn on Deer's timid and impatient ways. 'Deer has forsaken us,' he said; 'he deserted us in the hour of our danger, and that is contrary to forest laws and to our code of defence.' And he thought to himself, 'I shall punish him for this when the time comes.'

In the late autumn, the time agreed upon came for the animals to leave the earth, and Rainbow again made his bright path for them to the sky. Bear was the first to go up because he was the leader, and because with his great weight he wanted to test the strength of the bridge of burning colours over which they had to pass. When he had almost reached the sky, he met Deer on the path waiting to welcome the animals to their new home. And he said to him in anger, 'Why did you leave us behind, without warning, for the land of the Turtle? Why did you desert the Great Council? Why did you not wait until all could come together? You are a traitor to your comrades, and you have been false to our faith.' And Deer answered, also in anger, 'Who are you to doubt me or my faith? None but the Wolf may ask me why I came or question my fidelity. I will kill you for your insolence.' Deer had grown very proud since he had gone to live in the sky, and he was no longer timid as he had been on earth. His eyes flashed in his fury, and he arched his neck and lowered his antlered head, and rushed madly at Bear to push him from the path.

But Bear was not afraid, for he had often tested his strength with Deer upon the earth. His low, hoarse growls sounded all over the sky, and he prepared to fight. They came together with a shock. For a long time they battled, until the bridge of burning colours trembled and the heavens shook from the force of the conflict. The animals waiting by the lake at the end of the path looked up and saw the battle above them. They feared the results, for they wanted neither Bear nor Deer to die. So they sent Wolf up to the sky to put a stop to the contest. When Wolf reached the combatants, Bear was bleeding freely, for Deer with his antlers had pierced his neck and side. Deer, too, was bleeding where Bear's strong claws had torn a great wound in his head. Wolf soon stopped the battle, and Bear and Deer went away to dress their wounds. Then the other animals went up to the sky over Rainbow's flaming path. And they decided to live in the sky and to send their descendants back to earth when the new race of creatures should come. And they can still sometimes be seen, like clouds hurrying across the sky, in the shape they had on earth.

But the blood of Bear and of Deer dropped from them as they moved to the sky from the scene of their battle along the Rainbow road.

It fell freely upon the leaves of the trees beneath them, and changed them into varied colours. And every year when autumn comes in the north country, the leaves take on again the bright and wondrous colours given to them by the blood of Bear and Deer when they fought on the Rainbow path ages and ages ago. And Bear and Deer have never since been friends, and their descendants no longer dwell together in peace, as they did in the olden days.

49. Rabbit and the Moon-Man

ONCE, long ago, Rabbit lived with his old grandmother deep in the Canadian forest, far from all other people. He was a great hunter, and all around, far and near, he laid snares and set traps to catch game for food. It was winter, and he caught many little animals and birds. He brought them home daily to feed himself and his old grandmother, and he was well pleased with his success. But after some weeks had passed he was unable to catch any game. He always found his traps and snares empty, although many tracks were always around them, and there were many signs that animals were prowling about. He knew then that he was being robbed nightly, and that a thief was pilfering his traps. It was very cold and the snow lay deep in the forest, and Rabbit and his old grandmother were in dire need of food. Every morning Rabbit rose very early and hurried off to his traps, but always he found them empty, for the thief had been ahead of him. He was greatly puzzled, for he could not think who the thief was.

229

At last one morning, after a new fall of snow, he found the mark of a long foot near his traps, and he knew it was the foot of the game-robber. It was the longest footprint he had ever seen, long and narrow and very light, like a moonbeam. And Rabbit said, 'Now I shall rise earlier in the morning, and I shall go to my traps ahead of the thief and take my game, so that they will all be empty when he comes.' Each morning he rose earlier to catch the thief, but the man of the long foot was always there before him, and his game was always gone. No matter how early Rabbit got up, the thief was always ahead of him and his traps were always empty.

So Rabbit said to his old grandmother, 'The man of the long foot, who robs my traps, is always up ahead of me, no matter how early I rise. I will make a snare from a bow-string, and I will watch all this night, and I will surely catch him.' He made a trap from a stout bow-string and set it beside his snares, and took the end of the bow-string some distance away to a clump of trees, behind which he hid. He hoped that the thief would step into the trap; then he would pull the bow-string and tie him fast to a tree. He sat very quiet, waiting for the man of the long foot to appear. It was moonlight when he set out, but soon it grew very dark in the forest. The Moon suddenly disappeared. But the stars were all shining on the white snow and there were no clouds in the sky, and Rabbit wondered what had happened to the Moon. He waited very still and a little frightened in the starlight.

Soon he heard someone coming, sneaking stealthily through the trees. Then he saw a white light which dazzled his eyes. The light went towards the snares, until it stopped just at the trap Rabbit had set. Then Rabbit pulled the bow-string, closed the trap as he had hoped, and tied the string fast to a tree. He heard sounds of a struggle, and he saw the white light move from side to side, but he knew that he had his prisoner fast and that the man of the long foot was caught at last. He was much afraid of the white light, and he ran home as fast as he could and told his old grandmother that he had caught the game-robber in the trap, and that he did not know who he was, for he was too frightened to look. And his grandmother said, 'You must go back and see who it is, and tell him he must stop robbing your snares.' But Rabbit said, 'I do not want to go until daylight, for the Moon has gone down and the forest is very dark.' But his grandmother said, 'You must go.' So poor Rabbit, although he was very frightened by what he had seen, set out again for his traps.

When he drew near to his snares he saw that the white light was still shining. It was so bright that his eyes were dazzled and he had to stop far from it. Then he approached nearer, but his eyes soon became very sore. There was a stream flowing beside him, and he bathed his eyes in the cold water, but it brought him no relief, and his eyes felt hot and red, and tears fell from them because of the dazzling light. Then he took great handfuls of snow and threw snowballs at the light, hoping thereby to put it out. But when the snowballs came near to the light they melted and fell down like rain. Then, with his eyes still smarting, Rabbit in his rage scooped up great handfuls of soft black mud from the bottom of the stream, and forming it into balls, he threw them with all his force at the white light. He heard them strike something with a dull thud, and he heard loud yells from the prisoner—the man of the long foot—behind the shining light. Then a voice came from the light, saying, 'Why did you snare me? Come and untie me at once. I am the Man in the Moon. It is near to the morning, and before dawn I must be on my way home. You have already spotted my face with mud, and if you do not loose me at once I shall kill all your tribe.'

Poor Rabbit was more frightened than before, and he ran home and told his old grandmother what had happened. And his grandmother was also very frightened, for she thought that no good could come of it. And she told Rabbit to go back at once and untie the Man in the Moon, for the night was almost spent, and the dawn would soon be breaking. So poor Rabbit, trembling in his fear, went back to his traps. From a great distance he cried, 'I will untie you if you will never again rob my snares, and if you will never come back to earth.' And the prisoner in the trap promised, and said, 'I swear it by my white light.' Then Rabbit approached very carefully. He had to shut his eyes and grope his way because of the bright light, and his lip quivered because of the great heat. At last he rushed in and cut the bow-string snare with his teeth, and the Man in the Moon hurried on his way, for he could already see the dawn in the East. But Rabbit was almost blinded while he was about it, and his shoulders were badly scorched. And ever since that time Rabbit blinks and his eyelids are pink, and water runs from his eyes when he looks at a bright light; and his lip always quivers; and his shoulders are yellow, even when he wears his white winter coat, because of the great light and heat on the winter night long ago when he loosed the Man in the Moon from the snare. And since that night the Man in the Moon has never come back to earth. He stays at his task in the sky, lighting the forest by night; but he still bears on his face the marks of the black mud which Rabbit threw at him. And sometimes for several nights he goes away to a quiet place, where he tries to wash off the mud; and then the land is dark. But he never succeeds in cleaning himself, and when he comes back to his work the marks of Rabbit's mud-balls are still upon his shining face.

50. The Children with One Eye

Two little children, a boy and a girl, lived long ago with their widowed mother in the Canadian forest. The woman was very poor, for her husband had long been dead and she had to work very hard to provide food for herself and her children. Often she had to go far from home in search of fish and game, and at times she was absent for many days. When she went on these long journeys she left her children behind her, and thus they were allowed to grow up with very little oversight or discipline or care. They soon became very unruly because they were so often left to have their own way, and when their mother returned from her hunting trips, she frequently found that they would not obey her, and that they did pretty much as they pleased. As they grew older they became more headstrong and disobedient, and their mother could do very little to control them. And she said, 'Some day they will suffer for their waywardness.'

One day the woman went to visit a neighbour not far away. She left a large pot of bear-fat boiling on the fire. And she said to the children, 'Do not meddle with the pot while I am gone, for the fat may harm you if it catches fire.' But she was not gone long when the boy said to the girl as they played around the pot, 'Let us see if the fat will burn.' So they took a burning stick of wood and dropped it into the fat, and stood looking into the large pot to see what would happen. The fat sputtered for an instant; then there was a sudden flash, and a tongue of flame shot upwards from the pot into the faces of the children. Their hair was burned to a crisp and their faces were scorched, and they ran from the house crying with pain. But when they reached the outer air, they found that they could not see, for the fire had blinded their eyes. So they stumbled around in darkness, crying loudly for help. But no help came.

When their mother came home she tried every remedy she thought might restore their sight. But all her medicine was unavailing, and she said, 'You will always be blind. That is the punishment for your disobedience.'

So the children lived in darkness for a long time. But they were no longer headstrong and unruly, and although they could no longer see, they were less trouble to their mother than they were when they had their sight, for they did not now refuse to do her bidding.

One day, when their mother was far away hunting in the forest, an old woman came along and asked the children for food. And they brought good food to her as she sat before the door. After she had eaten, she said, 'You are blind, but I can help you, for I am from the Land of the Little People. I cannot give you four eyes, but I will give you one eye between you. You can each use it at different times, and it will be better than no sight at all. But handle it with great care and do not leave it lying on the ground.' Then she gave them an eye which she took from her pocket, and disappeared. So they used the one eye between them, and when the boy had the eye and the girl wished to see anything, she would say, 'Give me the eye,' and her brother would carefully pass it to her. When their mother came home she was very glad when she found that they had now some means of sight.

One day when their mother was away again, the boy went into the forest with his bow and arrows. He carried the eye with him. He had not gone far when he saw a fat young deer, which he killed. The deer was too heavy for him to carry home alone. So he said, 'I will go and get my sister, and we shall cut it up and put it in a basket and carry it home together.' He went home and told his sister of his good fortune, and he led her to where the deer lay, and they began to cut up the body. But they had forgotten to bring a basket or a bag. He called to his sister saying, 'You must weave a basket into which we can put the meat to carry it home.' And his sister said, 'How can I make a basket when I cannot see? If I am to weave a basket, I must have the eye.' The boy brought the eye to her and she made a large basket from green twigs.

When she had finished making the basket the boy said, 'I must finish cutting up the meat. Give me the eye.' So she brought him the eye, and he proceeded to chop up the meat and to put it in the basket. Then he said, 'Why can we not have a meal here? I am very hungry.' His sister agreed that this was a good idea, and he said, 'You cook the meal while I pack the meat.' The girl made a fire, but she was afraid she would burn the meat, so she said, 'I cannot see to cook. I must have the eye.' By this time her brother had finished packing the meat into the basket, and he brought her the eye and she went on with her cooking. The fire was low and she said, 'I must have some dry wood. Bring me some dry pine.' The boy wandered off into the forest in search of wood, but he had not gone far when he stumbled over a log and fell to the ground. He called to his sister in anger, saying, 'You always want the eye for yourself. How can I gather dry pine when I cannot see? Give me the eye at once.'

His sister ran to him and helped him up and gave him the eye. She found her way back to the fire, but as she reached it she smelled the meat burning on the spit. She shouted, 'The meat is burning and our dinner will be spoiled. Give me the eye at once, so that I may see if the meat is cooked.' The boy was some distance away, and in his anger he threw the eye to her, saying, 'Find it. I am not going to walk to you with it if you are too lazy to come and get it.' The eye fell to the ground between them, and neither of them knew where it lay. They groped for it among the dead leaves, but as they searched for it, a woodpecker, watching from a branch of a tree near by, swooped suddenly down and gobbled it up and flew away.

As they were still searching for it, the old woman who had given it to them came along. She had been hiding among the trees, and she had seen the woodpecker flying away with her gift. She said, 'Where is the eye I gave you?' 'It dropped from my head,' answered the boy, 'and I cannot find it in the grass.' 'Yes,' said the girl, 'it dropped from his head, and we cannot find it.' 'You have lied to me,' said the old woman, 'and you have disobeyed, and for that I shall punish you.' And with her magic power she changed the boy into a mole and the girl into a bat, and said, 'Now live blind upon the earth, with only your sense of sound to guide you.' At once the boy and the girl were changed. And so the Mole and the Bat appeared upon the earth.

51. The Giant with the Grey Feathers

ONCE, long ago, when the Blackfeet Indians dwelt on the Canadian plains, there was a great famine in all the land. For many months no buffaloes were killed, and there was no meat to be had at any price. One by one the old people dropped off because of a lack of food, and the young children died early because there was no nourishment, and there was great sorrow everywhere. Only the strong women and the stronger warriors remained alive, but even they gradually grew weaker because of the pinch of the hunger sent into the land by famine. At last the Chief of the tribe prayed that the Great Chieftain of the Indians might come into his territory to tell the people what to do to save themselves.

The Great Chief was at that time far away in the south country where the warm winds were blowing and the flowers were blooming. But one night he heard the Chief's prayer borne to him on the winds, and he hastened northward, for he knew that his people on the plains were somehow in dire distress. Soon he arrived at the village of the hungry tribe. 'Who has called me here?' he asked. 'It was I,' answered the Chief. 'My people are all starving because there are no buffaloes in the country, and if you had not come we should soon have all perished.' Then the Great Chief looked upon his people and he noticed that the old folks and the little children had disappeared; only a few children were left and they had pinched cheeks and sunken eyes. And he took pity on them and said, 'There is a great thief not far distant. He is probably a wicked giant, and he has driven all the buffaloes away. But I will find him and soon you shall have food.' And the people were all comforted, for they knew that the Great Chief would keep his word.

Then the Chief took with him the young Chief's son and set out on his quest. The people wanted to go with him, but he said, 'No! We shall go alone. It is a dangerous duty, and it is better that, if need be, two should die in the attempt, than that all should perish.' They journeyed westwards across the prairies towards the Great Water in the West, and as they went, the youth prayed to the Sun and the Moon and the Morning Star to send them success. Soon they came to the rolling foothills covered with sweet-grass and scrubby pine. But still they saw no signs of buffalo. At last they reached a narrow stream, on the bank of which they saw a house with smoke coming from the chimney. 'There is the cause of all our troubles,' said the Chief. 'In that house dwells the giant Buffalo-thief and his wife. They have driven all the animals from the prairies until not one is left. My magic power tells me it is so!' Then by his magic power he changed his companion into a sharp-pointed straight stick, while he himself took the shape of a dog, and they lay on the ground and waited.

Soon the giant and his wife and their little son came along. The boy patted the dog on the head, and said, 'See what a nice dog I have found. He must be lost. May I take him home?' His father said, 'No, I do not like his looks. Do not touch him.' The boy cried bitterly, for he had long hoped for a dog of his own, and his mother pleaded for him so hard that at last the giant father said, 'Oh, very well. Have your own way, but no good can come of it.' The woman picked up the stick and said, 'I will take this nice straight stick along with me. I can dig roots with it to make medicine.' So they all went to the giant's house, the giant frowning angrily, the woman carrying the stick, and the boy leading the dog.

The next morning the giant went out and soon came back with a fat young buffalo, all skinned and ready for cooking. They roasted it on a spit over the fire and had a good meal. The boy fed some meat to the dog, but his father, when he saw what the boy was doing, beat him soundly, and said, 'Have I not told you the dog is an evil thing? You must not disobey me.' But again the woman pleaded for her boy, and the dog was fed. That night when all the world was asleep, the dog and the stick changed back to their human form and had a good supper of what was left of the buffalo-meat. And the Chief said to the youth, 'The giant is the Buffalo-thief who keeps the herds from coming to the prairies. It is useless to kill him until we have found where he has hidden them.' So they changed back to the shapes of dog and stick and went to sleep.

The next morning the woman and her boy set off to the forest near the mountain, to gather berries and to dig up medicine roots. They took

the dog and the stick with them. At noon, after they had worked for some time, they sat down to have their luncheon. The woman threw the stick down on the ground, and the boy let the dog run away among the shrubs. The dog wandered to the side of the mountain. There he found an opening like the mouth of a cave. Peering into the place he saw many buffaloes within, and he knew that at last he had found the hiding place of the giant's plunder. He went back to the woman and the boy and began to bark. This was the signal agreed on with his companion. The woman and her son thought he was barking at a bird, and they laughed at his capers as he jumped about. But he was in reality calling to his comrade. The stick understood the call and wiggled like a snake through the underbrush to the dog's side, unseen by the boy and his mother. They then entered the large cave in the side of the mountain, and there they found a great herd of buffaloes—all the buffaloes that had been driven from the prairies. The dog barked at them and snapped at their heels, and the stick beat them, and they began to drive them quickly out of the cavern and eastward toward the plains. But they still kept the shape of dog and stick. When evening came, and it was time for the boy and his mother to go home, the boy searched for the dog and the woman looked for her stick, but they could not find them, and they had to go home without them.

Just as the woman and her son reached their house on the bank of the river, the giant-thief was coming home too. He chanced to look to the east, and there he saw, far away, many buffaloes running towards the foot-hills where the sweet-grass grew. He was very angry, and he cried loudly to his son, 'Where is the dog? Where is the dog?' 'I lost him in the underbrush,' said the boy; 'he chased a bird and did not come back.' 'It was not a bird he chased,' said the giant; 'it was one of my buffaloes. I told you he was an evil thing and not to touch him, but you and your mother would have your way. Now my buffaloes are all gone.' He gnashed his teeth in a great rage, and rushed off to the hidden cave to see if any buffaloes were left, crying as he went, 'I will kill the dog if I find him.' When he reached the cave the Chief and the youth, still in the form of a dog and a stick, were just rounding up the last of the buffaloes. The giant rushed at them to kill the dog and to break the stick, but they sprang upon an old buffalo and hid in his long hair and, clinging on tightly, the dog bit the buffalo until the old animal plunged and roared and rushed from the cave, bearing the Chief and the youth concealed on his back. He galloped eastward until he reached the herd far away on the prairie, leaving the giant far behind to make the best of his anger. Then the Chief and the brave youth took their old form of men, and in high spirits they drove the herd of buffaloes back to their hungry people waiting patiently on the plains.

The people were very pleased to see the Great Chief and the youth returning to the village with the great herd of fat buffaloes, for they knew now that the famine was ended. But as they drove the animals into a great fenced enclosure, a large grey bird flew over their heads and swooped down upon them and pecked at them with its bill, and tried to frighten them and drive them away. The Great Chief knew by his magic power that the grey bird was none other than the giant-thief who had stolen the buffaloes, and who had changed himself into a bird to fly across the prairies in pursuit of them. Then the Chief changed himself into an otter and lay down on the bank of the stream, pretending to be dead. The grey bird flew down upon him, for he thought he would have a good meal of fat otter. But the Chief seized him by the leg, and changing back to his own form, he bore him in triumph to his camp. He tied him up fast to the smoke-hole of his tent and made a great fire inside. The giant cried, 'Spare me, spare me, and I shall never do you more harm.' But the Chief left him on the tent pole all night long while the black smoke from the fire poured out around him. In the morning his feathers were all black. Then the Chief let him down. And he said, 'You may go now, but you will never be able to resume your former shape. You will henceforth be a raven, a bird of ill-omen upon the earth, an outlaw and a brigand among the birds, despised among men because of your thefts. And you will always have to steal and to hunt hard for your food.' And to this day the feathers of the raven are black, and he is a bird of ill-omen upon the earth because of his encounter with the Great Chieftain long ago.

52. The Cruel Stepmother

ONCE long ago, when the Blackfeet Indians dwelt on the Canadian prairies, a poor Indian and his two children, a boy and a girl, were living near the bank of a great river. The children's mother had long been dead and they had long been left to the care of their father. Their father did not think it was right that they should grow up without a woman's kindness, and he decided at last to take another wife. So he went far away to a distant village and there he married a queer woman of another tribe. Soon times grew hard in the North Country, and it was very difficult to get food. The family lived for many days on roots and berries, and often they were very hungry because there was no meat. Now it happened that the woman the man had married was a very wicked witch-woman, who was capable of doing many evil deeds. She had no love for her stepchildren, and she treated them very cruelly. She blamed them for the lack of food in the house, and beating them soundly, she said, 'You gluttonous brats; you always eat too much. It is little wonder that we cannot keep the house supplied with food.' The man saw his wife's cruelty to the children, but although it made him sad, and at times angry, he did not interfere, for he thought the woman should rule her home.

One night in the early spring, as the man slept, his first wife appeared to him in a dream, and said, 'Hang a large spider web across the trail in the forest where the animals pass and you will get plenty of food. But be good to my children. Their cruel stepmother is planning to kill them.' And she told him where to look for the magical spider web. The next day the man found the large spider web, and he went far away into the forest and hung it from the trees over the trail where the animals passed. That evening when he went back to the web he found many animals entangled in its meshes, for it had magical power. He killed the animals and brought them home, and that night they had a good fat supper of roast deer meat. Day after day the magical spider web gave him great numbers of rabbits and deer, as the vision of his dead wife had told him in the night, and from that time on the family did not want for food.

But the man's success in hunting only angered his witch-wife. She had now no cause for complaint against the little children, and she could no longer scold them and say that because of them there was no food in the house. Her hatred for them grew stronger each day, and at last she decided to kill them and to kill their father as soon as she could. Their father was going away on the morrow in search of wood to make arrows for his bows, and she thought she would have a good chance to kill them while he was gone. Then she would kill their father when he returned. So she laid her plans. But that night the vision of his first wife came again to the man as he slept, and it said, 'Your present wife is a witch-woman. She plans to kill the children to-morrow when you are away, and when you come home she will kill you, too. You must kill her while there is yet time. Remember my little children.'

When the man awoke in the morning he was much alarmed because of the story told him by the vision of the night. He no longer trusted his witch-wife and he decided to get rid of her. But he feared she would attack the children before he could prevent it. So when the witch-wife went out to get water from the stream to make breakfast, he gave each of the children a stick, a white stone, and a bunch of soft moss, and he said, 'You must run away from here and stay away until I can find you, for you are in great danger. You will find these three things I give you of great use. Throw them behind you if any evil thing pursues you, and they will keep you from harm.' The children in great fear at once ran away into the forest. Then the man hung his magical spider web over the door of the house, and sat quietly inside waiting for his wife to come back. In a little while she came home, carrying a pail of water, but she did not see the web with its fine strands hanging across the door, and when she walked into it she was at once entangled in its meshes. She struggled hard to get free, but her head was inside the door while her body was outside, and the web held her fast around the neck. Then the man said, 'I know now that you are a cruel witch-woman. You will beat my children no more.' With his stone axe he struck her a mighty blow which completely severed her head from her body. Then he ran from the house as fast as he could and went towards his children, who were watching him not far away.

But the man was not yet done with the cruel witch-woman. As he ran from the house her headless body, freed from the spider web, ran after him, while her severed head, with eyes staring and hair flying, followed the children, sometimes bumping along the ground and sometimes rising through the air. The father thought it would be well to go in a different direction from the children, and he went west, while they went east. The children were very frightened when they saw the horrible head behind them, slowly gaining upon them. Then they remembered their father's magic gifts. When the head was close upon them, they threw their sticks on the ground at their backs and at once a dense forest sprang up between them and their pursuer. The children said, 'Now we will rest here for a while, for we are nearly out of breath. The wicked head cannot get through that dense forest.' And they sat on the grass and rested.

Soon, however, the pursuing head emerged from the thick trees. The children got up and ran as hard as they could, but close behind them came the severed head, rolling its eyes and gnashing its teeth in a great frenzy, and uttering terrible yells. It was very near to them, when the children again remembered their father's gifts. They threw the white stones behind them, and at once a high mountain of white rock rose between them and their enemy. They sat on the ground and rested, and said, 'Oh dear, oh dear, what shall we do? We have only one means of safety left, these little bits of moss.' The wicked head hurled itself against the mountain, but it could not get through. A big buffalo bull was feeding on the grass near it, and the head called to him to break a road through the mountain. The bull rushed at the mountain with all his force, but the mountain was so hard that it broke his head and he fell down dead. Some moles were playing in the soft earth near by, and the head called to them to make a passage through the hill. So the moles searched and found a soft earthy place in the midst of the rock and soon they tunnelled a hole to the other side of the mountain, through which the head was able to pass. When the children saw their pursuer coming out of the moles' tunnel they cried loudly and ran away as fast as they could. At last, after a very long chase, the head was almost upon them, and they decided to use their last means of protection. They threw the wet moss behind them, and at once a long black swamp appeared where the moss had fallen, between them and their wicked follower. The head was going at such a great speed, bumping over the ground, that it could not stop. It rolled into the swamp and disappeared into the soft mud and was never seen again.

The children then went home to wait for their father. It was a long journey, for they had run far. But their father never came. Months and months they waited, but he did not come, and they grew up to be great magicians and very powerful among their tribe. At last, by their magic power, they learned what had happened to their father. Their stepmother's body continued to follow him as he ran towards the west. It followed him for many days. Then by his magic power, which the vision of his dead wife had brought to him, he changed himself into the Sun, and went to live with his wife in the sky-country. But the old witch-woman also had magic power, and she changed herself into the Moon and followed him to the land of the stars. And there she still pursues him. And while he keeps ahead of her and she cannot catch him, night follows day in all the world. But if she overtakes him she will kill him, and day will disappear and night shall reign for evermore upon the earth. And the Blackfeet of the plains pray that he will always keep in front in the race with his former witch-wife, so that there may be always Night and Day in succession in all the land.

53. The Boy who was Saved by Thoughts

A POOR widow woman once lived near the sea in Eastern Canada. Her husband had been drowned catching fish one stormy day far off the coast, and her little boy was now her only means of support. He had no brothers or sisters, and he and his mother, because they lived alone, were always good comrades. Although he was very young and small, he was very strong, and he could catch fish and game like a man. Every day he brought home food to his mother, and they were never in want.

Now it happened that the Great Eagle who made the winds in these parts became very angry because he was not given enough to eat. He went screaming through the land in search of food, but no food could he find. And he said, 'If the people will not give me food, I will take care that they get no food for themselves, and when I grow very hungry I shall eat up all the little children in the land. For my young ones must have nourishment too.' So he tossed the waters about with the wind of his great wings, and he bent the trees and flattened the corn, and for days he made such a hurly-burly on the earth that the people stayed indoors, and they were afraid to come out in search of food.

At last the boy and his mother became very hungry. And the boy said, 'I must go and find food, for there is not a crumb left in the house. We cannot wait longer.' And he said to his mother, 'I know where a fat young beaver lives in his house of reeds on the bank of the stream near the sea. I shall go and kill him, and his flesh will feed us for many days.' His mother did not want him to make this hazardous journey, for the Great Eagle was still in the land. But he said to her, 'You must think of me always when I am gone, and I will think of you, and while we keep each other in our memories I shall come to no harm.' So, taking his long hunting knife, he set out for the beaver's home in his house of reeds on the bank of the stream near the sea. He reached the place without mishap and there he found Beaver fast asleep. He soon killed him and slung him over his shoulder and started back to his mother's house. 'A good fat load I have here,' he said to himself, 'and we shall now have many a good dinner of roast beaver-meat.'

But as he went along with his load on his back the Great Eagle spied him from a distance and swooped down upon him without warning. Before he could strike with his knife, the Eagle caught him by the shoulders and soared away, holding him in a mighty grip with the beaver still on his back. The boy tried to plunge his knife into the Eagle's breast, but the feathers were too thick and tough, and he was not strong enough to drive the knife through them. He could do nothing but make the best of his sorry plight. 'Surely I can think of a way of escape,' he said to himself, 'and my mother's thoughts will be with me to help me.' Soon the Eagle arrived at his home. It was built on a high cliff overlooking the sea, hundreds of feet above the beach, where even the sound of the surf rolling in from afar could not reach it. There were many young birds in the nest, all clamouring for food. Great Eagle threw the boy to the side of the nest and told him to stay there. And he said, 'I shall first eat the beaver, and after he is all eaten up we shall have a good fat meal from you.' Then he picked the beaver to pieces and fed part of it to his young ones.

For some days the boy lay in terror in the nest, trying to think of a way of escape. Birds flew high over his head, and far out on the ocean he could see great ships going by. But no help came to him, and he thought that death would soon be upon him. And his mother sat at home waiting for him to return, but day after day passed and still he did not come. She thought he must surely be in great danger, or that perhaps he was already dead. One day, as she was weeping, thinking of her lost boy, an old woman came along. 'Why do you cry?' she asked. And the weeping woman said, 'My boy has been away for many days. I know that harm has come upon him. The men of my tribe have gone in search of him, and they will kill whatever holds him a prisoner, but I fear he will never come back alive.' And the old woman said, 'Little good the men of your tribe can do you! You must aid him with your thoughts, for material things are vain. I will help you, for I have been given great power by the Little People of the Hills.' So the woman used her thoughts and her wishes to bring back her boy.

That night the boy noticed that the beaver had all been eaten up and that not a morsel remained. He knew that unless he could save himself at once he would surely die on the morrow. The Great Eagle, he knew, would swoop down upon him and kill him with a blow of his powerful beak and claws. But when the boy slept, he saw his mother in his slumber. And she said to him, 'To-morrow when Great Eagle goes from the nest, brace your knife, point upwards, against the rock. When he swoops down to kill you his breast will strike the knife, and he will be pierced to death. You are not strong enough to cut through his feathers with your knife, but he is powerful enough to destroy himself.' The next morning when Great Eagle went out, the boy did as the vision of the night had told him. He braced his sharp hunting knife, point upwards, against the rock and sat still and waited. Then he heard the young eagles making a great noise and crying loudly for their breakfast. He knew that his hour had come. Soon the Great Eagle, hearing the screams of his young ones, came flying back to the nest to kill the boy. He circled around above him with loud cries and then with great force swooped down upon him, hoping to kill him with his beak and claws. But instead, he struck the blade braced upwards against the rock. The knife pierced far into his breast, and with a loud scream he rolled over dead into the nest. The boy then killed the young eagles, and he knew that now for a time he was safe.

But he did not know how to get down from the Eagle's nest, for it jutted out like a shelf far over the beach, and behind it was a wall of rock around which he could not climb. He had no means of making a ladder, and his cries would not be heard upon the beach because of the constant roaring of the surf. He thought he would surely starve to death, and that night he cried himself to sleep. But in the night he again saw his mother in his slumbers. And she said, 'You are a foolish boy. Why do you not use the thoughts I send you? To-morrow skin the Eagle and crawl inside the skin. If the wide wings can hold the Eagle in the air they can likewise hold you. Drop off from the cliff and you will land safely on the beach.' The next day the boy did as the vision of the night had told him. He carefully skinned the Great Eagle. Then he crawled inside the skin and thrust his arms through the skin just above the wings, so that his extended arms would hold the wings straight out beneath them. Then he prepared to drop down. But when he looked over the cliff, he was very frightened, for the sight made him dizzy. On the beach, men looked like flies, they were so far away. But he remembered the promise made to him in his slumbers. So he pushed himself from the cliff and dropped down. The wings of Great Eagle let him fall gently through the air and he landed safely and unhurt upon the beach. He crawled out of the skin and set out for his home. It was a long journey, for Great Eagle had carried him far away, but towards evening he reached his home safely, and his mother received him with great gladness.

The boy began to boast of his adventure, and he told how he had killed Great Eagle and how he had dropped down unscathed from the cliff. He spoke of himself with great pride and of his strength and his shrewdness. But the old woman from the Land of the Little People, the fairies of the hills, who was still present with his mother, said, 'Oh, vain boy, do not think so highly of yourself. Your strength is nothing; your shrewdness is nothing. It was not these things that saved you, but it was the strength of our thoughts. These alone endure and succeed when all else fails. I have taught you the uselessness of all material things, which in the end are but as ashes or as dust. Our thoughts alone can help us in the end, for they alone are eternal.' And the boy listened and wondered at what the old woman from the Land of Little People had said, but he boasted of his strength no more.

"Our thoughts alone can help us in the end, for they alone are eternal."

54. The Song-Bird and the Healing Waters

ONCE when the snow lay very deep on the ground and the days were grey with frost, there was great sorrow in an Indian village. A dreadful plague had come upon the place and had carried away many of the people. Neither old nor young were proof against its ravages, and the weak and the strong fell helpless before its power. The people tried every means to get rid of the plague, but they had no success. And they prayed to all their good spirits to help them, but no help came. In the tribe was a young warrior who had lost his parents and all his brothers and sisters because of the dreaded disease. Now his young wife fell sick, and he was in great sorrow, for he thought that she would soon follow his parents into the Land of the Shadows. And so he went about in great fear, not knowing when the end would come.

One day he met an old woman in the forest. 'Why do you look so sorrowful?' she asked him. 'I am sad because my young wife is going to die,' he answered; 'the plague will carry her off like the others.' But the old woman said, 'There is something that will save your wife from death. Far away in the East is a bird of sweet song which dwells close to the Healing Waters. Go until you find it. It will point you to the spring, the waters of which alone can heal.' And the young man said, 'I must find the Healing Waters. Wherever they may be upon the earth, I must find them.' So he went home and said good-bye to his friends, and set out eastward on his quest.

All the next day he searched eagerly for the Waters, listening always for the bird of the sweet song. But he found nothing. The snow lay deep in the forest and he moved along with difficulty. He met a rabbit in his path and he said, 'Tell me where I shall find the Healing Spring?' But the rabbit scurried away over the snow and made no answer. Then he asked a bear, but he met with the same rebuff. Thus for many days and nights he wandered on, crossing rivers and climbing steep hills, but always without success.

Then one day he emerged from the snow country and came to a land where the airs were warmer and where little streams were flowing. Suddenly he came upon the body of a dead man lying across his path. He stopped and buried the body, for he thought that it was not right to leave it lying bare upon the ground for the birds to peck at. That night as he went along in the moonlight he met a Fox in his path. 'Hello,' said the Fox. 'What are you looking for so late at night in the forest?' And he answered, 'I am looking for the bird of the sweet song, who will show me the way to the Healing Waters.' And the Fox said, 'I am the spirit of the man you buried yesterday by the forest path, and in return for your kindness to me I shall do a kindness to you. You have always been good to the animals and the birds, and you have never killed them needlessly, nor when you did not require them for clothing or for food. And you have always been careful of the flowers and the trees, and you have often protected them from harm. So now they want to be good to you, and I am going to guide you. But first you must rest, for you are tired from your long journey.'

Then the young man lay down to sleep and the Fox stood guard beside him. As he slept he dreamed. And in his dream he saw his wife pale and thin and worn, and as he looked he heard her singing a song of wonderful melody. Then he heard a waterfall rippling near him and it said, 'Seek me, O warrior, and when you find me your wife shall live, for I am the Healing Waters.' In the morning the Fox led him but a short distance through the forest and on the branch of a tree he heard a bird singing a song of wonderful melody, just as he had heard in his dream of the night before. He knew now that this was the bird of the

251

sweet song of which the old woman in the forest had spoken. Then, as he listened, he heard the sound of a waterfall rippling not far away. He searched for it, but he could not find it. And Fox said, 'You must seek it; you must not despair; it will not come to you unless you search.' So he searched again, and soon he thought he heard a voice speaking beneath his feet. 'Release us,' it called, 'set us free and your wife and your people shall be saved.' He seized a sharp stick and dug rapidly into the earth where he had heard the voice. He worked eagerly and quickly, and he had not dug far when the spring gushed forth and boiled upwards carrying to the world its healing power. And the young man knew that at last he had found the cure for his ills. He plunged into the spring and bathed himself in the water, and all his weariness left him and he was strong again.

Then the young man moulded from the soft earth a large pot. He baked it in the fire until it was quite hard. 'Now,' said the Fox spirit, 'I will leave you. Your kindness has been rewarded. You will need me no more, for you have found the Healing Waters.' And he disappeared as mysteriously as he had come. The young man filled his clay pot with the sparkling water and hastened back to his home, running through the forest with the speed of the wind, because of his renewed strength.

When he reached his native village, the people met him with sad faces, for the plague was still raging and they told him that his young wife was about to pass to the Land of the Shadows. But he hurried to his home, and he forced some of the Healing Waters between his wife's parched lips, and bathed her hands and her brow until she fell into a deep slumber. He watched by her side until she awoke, and when sleep left her she was well again. Then with his Healing Waters he cured all the people in the village, and the cruel plague left them and there was no more sickness in the land. And since that time no plague has spread among his tribe. In this way the Mineral Springs, the places of Healing Waters, came upon the earth, bearing health and happiness wherever they rise, and accompanied always by the songs of birds.

55. The Boy who Overcame the Giants

ONCE long ago, before the white man came to Canada, an orphan boy was living alone with his uncle. He was not very happy, for he had to work very hard, and tasks more fitted for a man's shoulders than for a boy's were often placed upon him. When his parents died and left him without brother or sister, his uncle took him to his own home because there was no one else to take care of him. But he treated him very cruelly and often he wished to get rid of him. It mattered not how well the boy did his work or how many fish and animals he caught, his uncle was never satisfied, and often he beat the boy harshly and with little cause. The boy would have run away but he did not know where to go, and he feared to wander alone in the dark forest. So he decided to endure his hardships as best he could.

Now it happened that in a distant village near the sea there lived a Chief who was noted far and wide for his cruelty. He had a wicked temper, and he was known to have put many people to death for no reason whatsoever. More than all else, he hated boastfulness and he had scanty patience with anyone who was vain of his own strength. He pledged himself always to humble the proud and to debase the haughty.

The boy's uncle had heard of this wicked ruler, and he said, 'Here is a chance for me to get rid of the boy. I will tell lies about him to the Chief.'

It chanced just at this time that three giants came into the Chief's territory. Where they came from, no man knew, but they dwelt in a large cave near the sea, and they caused great havoc and destruction in all the land. They ate up great stores of food, and all the little children they could lay their hands on. The Chief used every means to get rid of the giants, but without success. Night after night his best warriors went to the cave by the ocean to seek out the giants, but not a man returned. A piece of birch bark bearing a picture of a warrior with an arrow in his heart, found the next day at the Chief's door, always told him of the warrior's fate. And the giants continued their cruel work, for no one could stop them.

Soon all the country was in great terror. The Chief wondered greatly what was to be done. At last he thought, 'I will give my daughter to the man who can rid me of these pests.' His daughter was his only child and she was very beautiful, and he knew that many suitors would now appear to seek her hand, for although the task was dangerous, the prize was worth while. When the wicked uncle in the distant village heard of it, he thought, 'Now I can get rid of the boy, for I will tell the Chief that the boy says he can kill the giants.' So taking his nephew with him he went to the Chief's house and begged to see him. 'Oh, Chief,' he said, 'I have a boy who boasts that before many days have passed he can free your land from the giants.' And the Chief said, 'Bring him to me.' The man said, 'Here he is.' The Chief was surprised when he saw the small boy, and he said, 'You have promised that you can rid my land of giants. Now we shall see if you can do it. If you succeed you may have my daughter. If you fail, you will die. If you escape from the giants, I will kill you myself. I hate vain boasters, and they shall not live in my land.'

The boy went and sat by the ocean, and cried as hard as he could. He thought that he would surely die, for he was very small and he had no means of killing the giants. But as he sat there an old woman came along. She came quietly and quickly out of the grey mist of the sea. And she said, 'Why are you crying?' And the boy said, 'I am crying because I am forced to attack the giants in the cave, and if I cannot kill them I shall surely die,' and he cried louder than before. But the old woman, who was the good fairy of the sea, said, 'Take this bag and this knife and these three little stones that I will give you, and when you go to-night to the giants' cave, use them as I tell you and all will be well.' She gave him three small white stones and a small knife, and a bag like the bladder of a bear, and she taught him their use. Then she disappeared into the grey mist that hung low on the ocean and the boy never saw her again.

The boy lay down on the sand and went to sleep. When he awoke, the moon was shining, and far along the coast in the bright light he could see an opening in the rocks which he knew was the entrance to the giants' cave. Taking his bag and his knife and the three little stones, he approached it cautiously with a trembling heart. When he reached the mouth of the cave he could hear the giants snoring inside, all making different noises, louder than the roar of the sea. Then he remembered the old woman's instructions. He tied the bag inside his coat so that the mouth of it was close to his chin. Then he took one of the stones from his pocket. At once it grew to immense size, so heavy that the boy could scarcely hold it. He threw it at the biggest giant with great force, and it hit him squarely on the head. The giant sat up staring wildly and rubbing his brow. He kicked his younger brother, who was lying beside him, and said in great anger, 'Why did you strike me?' 'I did not strike you,' said his brother. 'You struck me on the head while I slept,' said the giant, 'and if you do it again I will kill you.' Then they went to sleep again.

When the boy heard them snoring loudly again, he took a second stone from his pocket. At once it grew great in size and the boy hurled it with great force at the biggest giant. Again the giant sat up staring wildly and rubbing his head. But this time he did not speak. He grasped his axe, which was lying beside him, and killed his brother with a blow. Then he went to sleep again. When the boy heard him snoring, he took the third stone from his pocket. At once it grew to great size and weight, and he hurled it with all his force at the giant. Again the giant sat up with great staring eyes, rubbing the lump on his head. He was now in a great rage. 'My brothers have plotted to kill me,' he yelled, and seizing his axe he killed his remaining brother with a blow. Then he went to sleep, and the boy slipped from the cave, first gathering up the three stones, which were now of their usual small size.

The next morning when the giant went to get water from the stream, the boy hid in the trees and began to cry loudly. The giant soon discovered him and asked, 'Why are you crying?' 'I have lost my way,' said

255

the boy, 'my parents have gone and left me. Please take me into your service, for I would like to work for such a kind handsome man, and I can do many things.' The giant was flattered by what the boy said, and although he liked to eat little children, he thought, 'Now that I am alone, I ought to have a companion, so I will spare the boy's life and make him my servant.' And he took the boy back to his cave, and said, 'Cook my dinner before I come home. Make some good stew, for I shall be very hungry.'

When the giant went into the forest the boy prepared the evening meal. He cut up a great store of deer meat and put it in a large pot bigger than a hogshead, and made a good meat stew. When the giant came home in the evening he was very hungry, and he was well pleased to see the big pot filled with his favourite food. He seated himself on one side of the pot, and the boy seated himself on the other side, and they dipped their spoons into the big dish. And the boy said, 'We must eat it all up so that I can clean the pot well and ready for the corn mush we will have for breakfast.' The stew was very hot, and to cool it before he ate it the giant blew his breath on what he dipped out. But the boy poured his own share into the bag under his coat, and said, 'Why can't you eat hot food—a big man like you? In my country men never stop to cool their stew with their breath.' Now the giant could not see very well, for his eyesight was not very good, and the cave was dark, and he did not notice the boy putting the stew in the bag so quickly. He thought the boy was eating it. And he was shamed by the boy's taunts because he was so much larger than the boy, so he ate up the hot stew at once in great gulps and burned his throat badly. But he was too proud to stop or to complain.

When they had eaten half the potful, the giant said, 'I am full. I think I have had enough.' 'No, indeed,' said the boy, 'you must show that you like my cooking. In my country men eat much more than that,' and he kept on eating. The giant was not to be outdone by a boy, so he fell to eating again, and they did not stop until they had consumed the whole potful of stew. But the boy had poured his share into the bag and when they had finished he was swelled out to an immense size. The giant could scarcely move, he had eaten so much, and he said, 'I have eaten too much; I feel very full, and I have a great pain in my belly.' And the boy said, 'I do not feel very comfortable myself, but I have a way to cure pains.' So saying he took his little knife and thrust it gently into the side of the bag and the stew oozed out and he was soon back to his normal size. The giant wondered greatly at the sight, but the boy said, 'It is a way they have in my country after they have had a great feast.' 'Does the knife not hurt?' asked the giant. 'No, indeed,' said the boy, 'it brings great relief.' 'My throat is very sore,' said the giant, for the hot stew had burned him. 'You will soon feel better,' said the boy, 'if you will do as I have done.' The giant hesitated to do this, but soon he felt so uncomfortable that he could bear it no longer. He saw that the boy was feeling quite well. So he took his long knife and plunged it into his stomach. 'Strike hard,' said the boy, 'or it will do you no good.' The giant plunged the knife in to the hilt, and in an instant he fell dead.

Then the boy took the stones and the bag and the knife which the Woman of the Mist had given him and went and told the Chief what he had done. The Chief sent his messengers to the cave to make sure that the boy spoke the truth. Sure enough, they found the three giants lying dead. When they told the Chief what they had seen, he said to the boy, 'You may have my daughter as your wife.' But the boy said, 'I do not want your daughter. She is too old and fat. I want only traps to catch fish and game.' So the Chief gave the boy many good traps, and he went into a far country to hunt game, and there he lived happily by himself. And his wicked uncle never saw him again. But the land was troubled no more by giants, because of the boy's great deeds.

56. The Youth and the Dog-Dance

ONCE long ago, when the Indians dwelt in the country in the north-west, a youth went far away from his native village to catch birds. His people lived near a lake where only small birds nested, and as he wanted large and bright-coloured feathers for his arrows and his bonnet he had to go far into the forest, where larger birds of brilliant plumage lived. When he reached the Land of Many Feathers far in the north country, he dug a pit on the top of a high hill. Then he covered the pit with poles and over the poles he spread grass and leaves so that the place looked like the earth around it. He put meat and corn on the grass, and tied the food to the poles so that the birds could not carry it away. Then he climbed down into the pit and waited for the birds to come, when he could reach up and catch them by the feet and kill them.

All day long and far into the night the youth waited for birds, but no birds came. Towards morning he heard a distant sound like that of a partridge drumming. But the sound did not come nearer. The next night, as the youth watched and waited in the pit, he heard the same sound, and he said, 'I will see where the noise comes from and I will discover the cause, for it is not a partridge, and it is very strange.' So he climbed out of the pit and went in the direction of the sound. He walked along rapidly through the forest until he came at dawn to the shore of a large lake. The drumming came from somewhere in the lake, but as he stood listening to it, the sound suddenly stopped. The next night the youth heard the drumming louder than before. Again he went to the lake. The sound was again distinct as it rose from the water, and when he looked he saw great numbers of birds and animals swimming in the lake in the moonlight. But there was no explanation of the strange sound. As he sat watching the animals and birds, he prayed to his

258

guardian spirit to tell him the cause of the drumming. Soon an old man came along. He was old and bent and wrinkled, but his eyes were kind. The youth gave him some tobacco and they sat down together on the edge of the lake and watched the swimmers in the dim light, and smoked their pipes.

'What are you doing here?' asked the old man. 'I am trying to learn the cause of the strange drumming,' said the youth. 'You do well indeed to seek it,' said the old man, 'and to seek to know the cause of all things. Only in that way will you be great and wise. But remember there are some things the cause of which you can never find.' 'Where have you come from?' said the boy. 'Oh,' said the man, 'I lived once upon a time like you in the Country of Fancy where great Dreams dwell, and indeed I live there still, but your dreams are all of the future while mine are of the past. But some day you too will change and your thoughts will be like mine.' 'Tell me the cause of the drumming,' said the boy. And the old man said, 'Take this wand that I will give you and wave it before you go to sleep, and maybe you will see strange things.' Then he gave the boy a wand and disappeared into the forest and the boy never saw him again. The boy waved the wand and fell asleep on the sand as the old man had told him. When he awoke he found himself in a large room in the midst of many people. Some of them were dancing gracefully, and some sat around and talked. They wore wonderful robes of skins and feathers, of many different colours. The boy wished he could get such feathers for his own clothes and his bonnet. But as he looked at the people he was suddenly aware that they were none other than the animals and birds he had seen for two nights swimming in the lake in the moonlight. They were now changed into human form, through some strange and miraculous power. They were very kind to the youth and treated him with great courtesy.

At last the dancing ceased and the talking stopped, and one who seemed to be the Chief stood up at the end of the room and said, 'Oh, young stranger, the Great Spirit has heard your prayers, and because of your magic wand we have been sent to you in these shapes. The creatures you see here are the animals and birds of the world. I am the Dog, whom the Great Spirit loves well. I have much power, and my power I shall give to you, and I shall always protect you and guard you. And even if you should treat me with cruelty I shall never be unfaithful to you, nor shall I ever be unkind. But you must take this Dance home with you and teach it to your people and they must celebrate the

259

Dance once a year.' Then he taught the youth the secrets of their Dance.

When the youth had learned the Dance, the Chief turned to his companions and said, 'My comrades and brothers, I have taught the young stranger the secrets of the Dance. I have given him my own power. Will you not have pity on a creature from earth and give him some of the power of which you too are possessed?'

For a long time no one spoke, but at last Owl arose and said, 'I too will help him. I have power to see far in the darkness, and to hunt by night. When he goes out at night I will be near him and he shall see a great distance. I give him these feathers to fasten in his hair.' And the Owl gave him a bunch of feathers, which the youth tied to his head.

Then Buffalo came forward and said, 'I too will help him. I will give him my endurance and my strength, and my power to trample my enemies underfoot. And I give him this belt of tanned buffalo-hide to wear when he goes to war.' And he gave the youth a very wondrous belt to fasten around his waist.

The animals and birds, one after the other, gave him gladly of their power. Porcupine gave him quills with which to decorate his leather belt and his bonnet, and he said, 'I too will aid you, and when you make war I will be near you. I can make my enemies as weak as children, and they always flee when I approach, for they fear the shooting of my quills. When you meet your foes you will always overcome them, for I give you power as it was given to me.'

And Bear said, 'I will give you my toughness and my strength, and a strip of fur for your leather belt and your coat. And when you are in danger, I will not be far away.'

Then Deer said, 'I give you my swiftness so that you may be fleet of foot. And when you pursue your enemies you will always overtake them, and should you flee from them, you will always out-run them in the race.'

Then the birds spoke again, and Crane said, 'I give you a bone from my wing to make a war-whistle to frighten your enemies away or to summon your people to your assistance when you need them. And I give you my wings for your head-dress.'

The giant Eagle then spoke and said, 'Oh, youth, I will be with you wherever you go, and I will give you my strength and my power in war. And even as I do, you will always see your enemies from afar, and you can always escape them if you so desire.' And he gave him a large bunch of wonderful eagle feathers to tie in his hair as a token of his fidelity.

And finally, Wild-Cat said, 'I give you my power to crawl stealthily through the grass and the underbrush and to spring unexpectedly on your foes and take them unawares. And I give you too my power of hiding from my enemies.' And he gave him strips of his fur to decorate his clothing in token of his friendship.

From all the animals and the birds the youth received power and gifts. Then he waved his magic wand and lay down to sleep. When he awoke, he found himself on the shore of the lake, and far in the east the dawn was breaking. But he could see farther than he had ever seen before, and away in the distance he could make out blue hills and smoke rising from far-off villages. And he knew that strange power was upon him. But not a sound came from the lake, and the drumming had for ever ended.

The youth took his magic wand and his gifts and set out for his home. And he told his people what had happened and he taught them the secrets of the Dance which was to make them strong and victorious in war. And among his people it became a great ceremony and was practised for long ages, and was known as the Dog-Dance. And since that time, the animals and birds have been friends to the Indians, and the Indians have acquired much of their cunning and skill and power. And ever after the night of moonlight by the lake when the youth with the magic wand received the strange gifts, the Indians have decorated their war clothes with fur and quills and feathers from the animals and the birds. And in the far north country, the Dog-Dance is still held at intervals out of gratitude for the gifts, for the Indians do not forget the promise of long ago.

57. Sparrow's Search for the Rain

LONG ago, in a village near the sea, many Indian people were living. Among them was a very nice old warrior who had been given great power at his birth, and who, therefore, could do many wonderful deeds. There was nothing that was beyond his understanding, for he knew all things. His wife had long been dead, but he had one daughter. She was very beautiful and gentle, and she was as nearly perfect as any woman could be. She took no interest in frivolous things and she lived a very quiet life, but all the people liked her well, and she was always welcome wherever she went. Her old father was very proud of her, and he said boastfully, 'She has inherited much of my wisdom, and some day she will marry a great man.' But the girl on her part had little thought of marriage or of men, for she said they had small minds, and she would rather live alone than listen always to their boastfulness and their foolish chatter.

Soon the daughter's fame spread far and wide through the sea-coast villages, and many suitors came seeking for her hand. But her father said, 'I have nothing to say. She will make her own choice. She must please herself. For today children please themselves and not their parents.' And she said, 'I will marry only someone who can amuse me and interest me and keep me company. I have scant liking for dull people.' One day Loon came to see her. He was very good looking although he was somewhat tall and skinny, and his neck was a bit longer and more scrawny than ordinary, but he wore good clothes and he had great skill as a fisherman. He came because he thought he was very handsome, and he believed that his good looks would win the maiden. But she had no love for Loon, for he had not a word to say. When she talked to him he only stared, and at last he burst out into loud and foolish laughter. Then the maiden said, 'You have a small mind like the others,' and in disgust she withdrew from his presence.

Then Fox came in an effort to win the maiden as his wife. And for a whole day he cut capers, and chased his tail round and round in a circle, trying to amuse the serious girl. But he did not succeed very well, and like Loon he departed in despair. And many others came, but they met the same fate, and at last the girl decided to see no more of them, but to live alone with her father. The young men of the village were all very angry because the girl had spoken of them all so scornfully, and often they talked among themselves of her proud and haughty air. 'She calls us Scattered-Brains,' said one. 'She says we have small minds,' said another. 'She must pay for these insults,' said a third. So they vowed that they would somehow break her proud spirit and bring her sorrow because of her ideas and her decision to stay single all her life. One of the great men of the village was Whirlwind. He could make himself invisible, and he was often guilty of many wicked pranks. So the young men went to him and asked his aid in humbling the pride of the haughty maiden. As they were talking to him, they saw the girl approaching not far off. And quite unawares, Whirlwind rushed towards her and knocked her down in the mud and tore her hat from her head and swept it into the sea. The young men looked on at her plight and they all laughed loudly, and the girl was very much ashamed. She went back home and told her father what had happened, and showed him her soiled clothes and her blown hair falling about her face. Her father was very angry, and he said, 'Whirlwind must pay for this. He shall be banished at once.'

Then her father went to the Chief and made complaint against Whirlwind, and the Chief decreed that Whirlwind must leave the village forthwith. He did not consider very carefully what the result of this decree might be, and he acted hastily and without thought, for he feared to differ from the wise man. So Whirlwind prepared to leave the place. Now his best friend was Rain. Rain had been born without eyes. He was black blind, and Whirlwind always had to lead him along wherever he wished to go. So Rain said, 'If you are leaving the village, I want to leave it too, for I cannot live here without you. I will be helpless if I have no one to lead me.' So the two set out together, Whirlwind leading old Rain along by his side. Where they went no man knew, for they had told nobody of their destination. They were gone for many months before the people missed them very much. Then their absence began to be felt in all the land, for there was no wind and there was no rain.

At last the Chief summoned a council, and the decree of banishment against Whirlwind was revoked. The people decided to send messengers to the two wandering ones to tell them what had happened and to bring them back. So they first sent Fox out on the quest. Fox went through the land for many weeks, running as fast as he could over many roads, in and out among marshy lake shores and over high wooded mountains. He searched every cave and crevice, but he had no success. Not a leaf or a blade of grass was stirring, and the country was all parched and the grass was withered brown and the streams were all getting dry. At last, after a fruitless search, he came home and shamefully confessed that his quest had failed.

Then the people called on Bear to continue the search. And Bear went lumbering over the earth, sniffing the air, and turning over logs and great rocks with his powerful shoulders, and venturing into deep caverns. And he made many inquiries, and he asked the Mountain Ash, 'Where is Whirlwind?' But Mountain Ash said, 'I do not know. I have not seen him for many months.' And he asked the Red Fir, and the Pine, and the Aspen, which always sees Whirlwind first, but they were all ignorant of his whereabouts. So Bear came home and said, 'Not a trace of either of them have I found.'

The Chief was very angry because of the failure of Fox and Bear, but the wise man said, 'The animals are useless in a quest like this. Let us try the birds. They often succeed where the animals fail.' And the Chief agreed, for the land was in great distress. Many fishing-boats lay silent on the sea near the coast unable to move because Whirlwind was away, and the wells and streams were all dry because Rain was absent,

and the grass and the flowers were withering to decay. So they called
the birds to their aid. The great Crane searched in the shallows and
among the reeds, thrusting his long neck into deep places, and Crow
looked among the hills, and Kingfisher flew far out to sea, but they all
came back and said, 'We, too, have failed. The wandering ones are
nowhere on the land or upon the sea.' Then little Sparrow took up the
search. Before he set out, he plucked from his breast a small down-
feather and fastened it to a stick no bigger than a wisp of hay. He held
the stick in his bill and flew off. For many days he went towards the
South-land, all the time watching the feather hanging to the stick in his
bill. But it hung there motionless. One day, after he had travelled a great
distance, he saw the down-feather moving very gently, and he knew
that Whirlwind must be not far away. He went in the direction from
which the feather was blowing. Soon he saw beneath him soft green
grass and wonderful flowers of varied colours, and trees with green
leaves and many rippling streams of running water. And he said to
himself, 'At last I have found the wanderers.' He followed a little
stream for some distance until it ended in a cave in the hills. In front
of the cave many flowers were blooming and the grass was soft and
green, and the tall grasses were nodding their heads very gently. He
knew that those he was seeking were inside, and he entered the cave
very quietly. Just beyond the door a fire was smouldering and near it lay
Rain and Whirlwind both fast asleep. Sparrow tried to wake them with
his bill and his cries, but they were sleeping too soundly. Then he took a
coal from the fire and put it on Rain's back, but it spluttered and fizzled
and soon went out. He tried another, but the same thing happened.
Then he took a third coal, and this time Rain woke up. He was much
surprised to hear a stranger in the cave, but he could not see him
because he was blind. So he woke up Whirlwind to protect him.

Then Sparrow told them of the great trouble in the north country
and of the great hardship and sorrow their absence had brought to the
people, and of how sadly they had been missed and of the decision of
the council to call them back. And Whirlwind said, 'We shall return
to-morrow if we are so badly needed. You may go back and tell your
people that we are coming. We shall be there the day after you arrive.'
So Sparrow, feeling very proud of his success, flew back home. But
when he arrived after many days, he went first to his own people to tell
them the good news. And the Sparrow-people all gathered together and
held a feast of celebration, and they twittered and danced and made a

great hub-bub in their excitement because Rain was coming back on the morrow. Then Sparrow went to the Chief and said, 'Oh, Chief, I have found Rain and Whirlwind and to-morrow they will be here,' and he told the story of his flight to the south and of his discovery. And the Chief said, 'Because of your success, you will never be hunted for game or killed for food.'

The next morning the two travellers who had been so long away came back to the land. Whirlwind came first and great clouds of dust foretold his coming, and the sea dashed high against the rocks, and the trees shrieked and tossed their heads, all dancing gaily because of his return. When Whirlwind had passed by, Rain came along following close, because of his blindness. For several days Rain stayed with the people and the flowers bloomed and the grass was green again and the wells and streams were no longer dry. And since that time Wind and Rain have never long been absent from the Atlantic Coast. And to this day the Sparrow-people know when Rain is coming, and to signal his approach they gather together and twitter and hop along and make a great hub-bub, just as they did when their ancestor found him by means of his down-feather in the olden days. But the Indians have been true to the Chief's promise, and they will not hunt Sparrows for game nor kill them for food or for their feathers. For they remember that of all the birds it was old Sparrow who long ago searched successfully for the Rain.

58. The Boy in the Land of Shadows

Two orphan children, a boy and a girl, lived alone near the mountains. Their parents had long been dead and the children were left to look after themselves without any kindred upon the earth. The boy hunted all day long and provided much food, and the girl kept the house in order and did the cooking. They had a very deep love for each other and as they grew up they said, 'We shall never leave each other. We shall always stay here together.' But one year it happened that in the early spring-time it was very cold. The snow lingered on the plains and the ice moved slowly from the rivers and chill winds were always blowing and grey vapours hovered over all the land. And there was very little food to be had, for the animals hid in their warm winter dens and the wild-geese and ducks were still far south. And in this cruel period of bad weather the little girl sickened and died. Her brother worked hard to provide her with nourishing food and he gathered all the medicine roots he thought could bring her relief, but it was all to no purpose. And despite all his efforts, one evening in the twilight his sister went away to the West, leaving him alone behind upon the earth.

The boy was heart-broken because of his sister's death. And when the late spring came and the days grew warm and food was plentiful again, he said, 'She must be somewhere in the West, for they say that our people do not really die. I will go and search for her, and perhaps I can find her and bring her back.' So one morning he set out on his strange quest. He journeyed many days westward towards the Great Water, killing game for food as he went, and sleeping at night under the stars. He met many strange people, but he did not tell them the purpose of his travels. At last he came to the shore of the Great Water, and he sat looking towards the sunset wondering what next to do. In the evening an old man came along. 'What are you doing here?' asked the man. 'I am looking for my sister,' said the boy; 'some time ago she sickened and died and I am lonely without her, and I want to find her and bring her back.' And the man said, 'Some time ago she whom you seek passed this way. If you wish to find her you must undertake a dangerous journey.' The boy answered that he would gladly risk any dangers to find his sister, and the old man said, 'I will help you. Your sister has gone to the Land of Shadows far away in the Country of Silence which lies out yonder in the Island of the Blest. To reach the Island you must sail far into the West, but I warn you that it is a perilous journey, for the crossing is always rough and your boat will be tossed by tempests. But you will be well repaid for your trouble, for in that land nobody is ever hungry or tired; there is no death and no sorrow; there are no tears, and no one ever grows old.'

Then the old man gave the boy a large pipe and some tobacco and said, 'This will help you in your need.' And he brought him to where a small canoe lay dry upon the beach. It was a wonderful canoe, the most beautiful the boy had ever seen. It was cut from a single white stone and it sparkled in the red twilight like a polished jewel. And the old man said, 'This canoe will weather all storms. But see that you handle it carefully, and when you come back see that you leave it in the cove where you found it.'

Soon afterwards, the boy set out on his journey. The moon was full and the night was cold with stars. He sailed into the West over a rough and angry sea, but he was in no danger, for his canoe rode easily on the waters. All around him he saw in the moonlight many other canoes going in the same direction and all white and shining like his own. But no one seemed to be guiding them, and although he looked long at them not a person could he make out. He wondered if the canoes were drifting unoccupied, for when he called to them there was no answer. Sometimes a canoe upset in the tossing sea and the waves rose over it and it was seen no more, and the boy often thought he heard an anguished cry. For several days he sailed on to the West, and all the time other canoes were not far away, and all the time some of them were dropping from sight beneath the surging waters, but he saw no people in them.

At last, after a long journey, the sea grew calm and the air was sweet and warm. There was no trace of the storm, for the waves were quiet and the sky was as clear as crystal. He saw that he was near the Island of the Blest of which the old man had spoken, for it was now plain to his view, as it rose above the ocean, topped with green grass and trees, and a snow-white beach. Soon he reached the shore and drew up his canoe. As he turned away he came upon a skeleton lying flat upon the sand. He stopped to look at it, and as he did so, the skeleton sat up and said in great surprise, 'You should not be here. Why have you come?' And the boy said, 'I seek my sister. In the early spring-time she sickened and died, and I am going to the Land of Shadows in the Country of Silence in search of her.' 'You must go far inland,' said the skeleton, 'and the way is hard to find for such as you.' The boy asked for guidance and the skeleton said, 'Let me smoke and I will help you.' The boy gave him the pipe and tobacco he had received from the old man, and he laughed when he saw his strange companion with the pipe between his teeth. The skeleton smoked for some time and at last, as the smoke rose from his pipe, it changed to a flock of little white birds, which flew about like doves. The boy looked on in wonder, and the skeleton said, 'These birds will guide you. Follow them.' Then he gave back the pipe and stretched out again flat upon the sand, and the boy could not rouse him from his sleep.

The boy followed the little white birds as he had been told. He went along through a land of great beauty where flowers were blooming and countless birds were singing. Not a person did he meet on the way. The place was deserted except for the song-birds and the flowers. He passed through the Country of Silence, and came to a mysterious land where no one dwelt. But although he saw no one he heard many voices and he could not tell whence they came. They seemed to be all around him. At last the birds stopped at the entrance to a great garden, and flew around his head in a circle. They would go no further and they alighted on a tree close by, all except one, which perched on the boy's shoulder. The lad knew that here at last was the Land of Shadows.

When he entered the garden he heard again many low voices. But he saw no one. He saw only many shadows of people on the grass, but he could not see from what the shadows came. He wondered greatly at the strange and unusual sight, for back in his homeland in that time the sunlight made no shadows. He listened again to the voices and he knew now that the shadows were speaking. He wandered about for some time marvelling greatly at the strange place with its weird unearthly beauty. At last he heard a voice which he knew to be his sister's. It was soft and sweet, just as he had known it when they were together on the earth, and it had not changed since she left him. He went to the shadow from which the voice came, and throwing himself on the grass beside it, he said, 'I have long sought you, my sister. I have come to take you home. Let me see you as you were when we dwelt together.' But his sister said, 'You have done wisely to keep me in your memory, and to seek to find me. But here we cannot appear to the people of earth except as shadows. I cannot go back with you, for it is now too late. I have eaten of the food of this land; if you had come before I had eaten, perhaps you could have taken me away. Who knows? But my heart and my voice are unchanged, and I still remember my dear ones, and with unaltered love I still watch my old home. And although I cannot go to you, you can some day come to me. First you must finish your work on earth. Go back to your home in the Earth Country. You will become a great Chief among your people. Rule wisely and justly and well, and give freely of your food to the poor among the Indians who have not as much as you have. And when your work on earth is done you shall come to me in this Land of Shadows beyond the Country of Silence, and we shall be together again and our youth and strength and beauty will never leave us.'

And the boy, wondering greatly and in deep sorrow, said, 'Let me stay with you now.' But his sister said, 'That cannot be.' Then she said, 'I will give you a Shadow, which you must keep with you as your guardian spirit. And while you have it with you, no harm can come to you, for it will be present only in the Light, and where there is Light there can be no wickedness. But when it disappears you must be on

271

your guard against doing evil, for then there will be darkness, and darkness may lead you to wrong.'

So the boy took the Shadow, and said good-bye for a season and set out on his homeward journey. The little white birds, which had waited for him in the trees, guided him back to the beach. His canoe was still there, but the skeleton-man had gone and there was not a trace of him to be found upon the sand. And the Island of the Blest was silent except for the songs of the birds and the ripple of the little streams. The boy embarked in his canoe and sailed towards the east, and as he pushed off from the beach the little white birds left him and disappeared in the air. The sea was now calm and there was no storm, as there had been on his outward journey. Soon he reached the shore on the other side. He left his canoe in the cove as the old man had told him, and in a few days he arrived at his home, still bearing the Shadow from the Country of Silence.

He worked hard for many years but he did no evil, and in the end he became a great Chief and did much good for his people. He ruled wisely and justly and well, as his sister had commanded him. Then one day, when he was old and his work was done, he disappeared, and his people knew that he had gone to join his sister in the Land of Shadows in the Country of Silence far away somewhere in the West. But he left behind him the Shadow his sister had given him; and while there is Light the Indians still have their Shadow and no harm can come to them, for where there is Light there can be no evil.

But always in the late autumn the Shadows of the Indian brother and sister in the Country of Silence are lonely for their former life. And they think of their living friends and of the places of their youth, and they wish once more to follow the hunt, for they know that the hunter's moon is shining. And when their memory dwells with longing on their earlier days, their spirits are allowed to come back to earth for a brief season from the Land of Shadows. Then the winds are silent and the days are very still, and the smoke of their camp fires appears like haze upon the air. And men call this season Indian Summer, but it is really but a Shadow of the golden summer that has gone. And it always is a reminder to the Indians that in the Land of Shadows, far away in the Country of Silence in the West, there are no dead.

INDEX

Index of Stories

Bad Indian's Ashes, The 17
Baker's Magic Wand, The 1
Blackfoot and the Bear, The 130
Boy and the Dancing Fairy, The 24
Boy and the Dragon, The 209
Boy and His Three Helpers, The 79
Boy and the Robbers' Magical Booty, The 91
Boy in the Land of Shadows, The 268
Boy of Great Strength and the Giants, The 112
Boy of the Red Twilight Sky, The 184
Boy who Overcame the Giants, The 253
Boy who was Called Thick-head, The 166
Boy who was Saved by Thoughts, The 246`
Boys and the Giant, The 134

Children with One Eye, The 233
Coming of the Corn, The 97
Cruel Stepmother, The 242

Dance of Death, The 100
Duck with Red Feet, The 82

Ermine and the Hunter 199

Fall of the Spider Man, The 160
First Mosquito, The 59
First Pig and Porcupine, The 103

Giant with the Grey Feathers, The 237
Girl who Always Cried, The 194
Glooskap and the Fairy 67
Glooskap's Country 34
Great Heart and the Three Tests 178

How Glooskap Made the Birds 141
How Rabbit Deceived Fox 203
How Rabbit Lost His Tail 40
How Raven Brought Fire to the Indians 188
How Summer Came to Canada 50
How Turtle Came 55

Indian Cinderella, The 76

Jack and His Magic Aids 12
Jack and His Wonderful Hen 119

Mermaid of the Magdalenes, The 20
Moon and His Frog-Wife, The 64
Mouse and the Sun, The 30

Northern Lights, The 85

Owl with the Great Head and Eyes 214

Partridge and His Drum, The 44
Passing of Glooskap, The 69

Rabbit and the Grain Buyers 147
Rabbit and the Indian Chief 171
Rabbit and the Moon-Man 229
Rainbow and the Autumn Leaves 224

Sad Tale of Woodpecker and Bluejay, The 123
Saint Nicholas and the Children 153
Shrove Tuesday Visitor, The 108
Song-Bird and the Healing Waters, The 250
Sparrow's Search for the Rain 263
Star-Boy and the Sun Dance 7
Strange Tale of Caribou and Moose, The 115
Stupid Boy and the Wand, The 126

Tobacco Fairy from the Blue Hills, The 220

Youth and the Dog-Dance, The 258